Social Theories of Risk and Uncertainty

Social Theories of Risk and Uncertainty: An Introduction

Edited by

Jens O. Zinn

Blackwell
Publishing

BLACKWELL PUBLISHING
350 Main Street, Malden, MA 02148-5020, USA
9600 Garsington Road, Oxford OX4 2DQ, UK
550 Swanston Street, Carlton, Victoria 3053, Australia

The right of Jens O. Zinn to be identified as the author of the editorial material in this work
has been asserted in accordance with the UK Copyright, Designs, and Patents Act 1988.

Designations used by companies to distinguish their products are often claimed as trademarks. All brand names and product names used in this book are trade names, service marks,
trademarks, or registered trademarks of their respective owners. The publisher is not
associated with any product or vendor mentioned in this book.

This publication is designed to provide accurate and authoritative information in regard to
the subject matter covered. It is sold on the understanding that the publisher is not engaged
in rendering professional services. If professional advice or other expert assistance is
required, the services of a competent professional should be sought.

First published 2008 by Blackwell Publishing Ltd

1   2008

Library of Congress Cataloging-in-Publication Data

Social theories of risk and uncertainty: an introduction / edited by Jens O. Zinn.
       p. cm.
    Includes bibliographical references and index.
    ISBN 978-1-4051-5335-5 (hardcover : alk. paper)
    ISBN 978-1-4051-5336-2 (pbk. : alk. paper)
1. Risk–Sociological aspects. 2. Risk Perception. 3. Risk–Social aspects. 4. Uncertainty–
Social aspects. I. Zinn, Jens.

HM1101.S64 2008
302'.12–dc22

                                                                    2007040796

A catalogue record for this title is available from the British Library.

Set in Galliard 10.5/13
by Newgen Imaging Systems (P) Ltd, Chennai, India
Printed and bound in Singapore
by Utopia Press Pte Ltd

The publisher's policy is to use permanent paper from mills that operate a sustainable
forestry policy, and which has been manufactured from pulp processed using acid-free and
elementary chlorine-free practices. Furthermore, the publisher ensures that the text paper
and cover board used have met acceptable environmental accreditation standards.

For further information on
Blackwell Publishing, visit our website at
www.blackwellpublishing.com

Contents

302.12
S678
2008

Tables

Contributors

Klaus P. Japp is Professor of Political Communication and Risk at Bielefeld University, Germany. He has been a visiting scholar at Harvard University and the University of California in Berkeley. Apart from the sociology of risk his main research interests are political communication research and sociological systems theory. His publications include: Distinguishing non-knowledge, in: *Canadian Journal of Sociology* (2000) 25(2), 225–38; *Risk* (Bielefeld transcript 2000); Zur Soziologie des fundamentalistischen Terrorismus, *Soziale Systeme. Zeitschrift für soziologische Theorie* (2003) 9(2), 54–87.

Isabel Kusche studied sociology in Dresden and New York. She is currently completing a PhD at Bielefeld University, Germany. Her thesis deals with the relationship between policy advice and political consulting from a systems-theoretical point of view. Her research interests include political communication research and the sociology of risk. She has published with Klaus P. Japp, Die Kommunikation des politischen Systems: Zur Differenz von Herstellung und Darstellung im politischen System, *Zeitschrift für Soziologie* (2004) 33(6), 511–531.

Stephen Lyng is a Professor of Sociology at Carthage College. His major areas of interest are the sociology of risk, sociology of the body, and sociological theory. He is the author of three books: *Holistic Health and Biomedical Medicine: a countersystem analysis* (SUNY 1990); *Sociology and the Real World* (with David Franks, Rowman and Littlefield 2002) and *Edgework: the sociology of voluntary risk-taking* (Routledge 2005).

Pat O'Malley is University Professorial Research Fellow at the University of Sydney. Recent publications include *Risk, Uncertainty and Government* (Glasshouse 2004) and *Governing Risks* (Ashgate 2006) and with Kelly Hannah-Moffatt, Gendered Risks (Routledge-Cavendish 2007). His current research focuses on the early development of risk in practices in fire prevention, the operation of urban security networks, and the use of money sanctions as means of regulating flows of action in "control societies."

John Tulloch is Research Professor in Sociology and Communication, and Director, Centre for Media, Globalisation and Risk, School of Social Sciences, Brunel University. His main recent books are *Trevor Griffiths* (Manchester University Press 2006); *One Day in July: experiencing 7/7* (Little, Brown 2005); *Shakespeare and Chekhov in Production and Reception: theatrical events and their audiences* (University of Iowa 2003); with Lupton, D., *Risk and Everyday Life* (Sage 2003); *Watching Television Audiences: cultural theories and methods* (Arnold 2000); *Performing Culture: stories of expertise and the everyday* (Sage 1999); with Lupton, D., *Television, Risk and AIDS: new cultural approaches to health communication* (Allen & Unwin 1997).

Jens O. Zinn is Senior Research Fellow in the ESRC Social Contexts and Responses to Risk network at the University of Kent, Canterbury campus. His recent research focuses on individuals' responses to risk and interdisciplinary risk theorizing. Recent publications include: *Risk in Social Sciences* (Oxford University Press 2006) and Current directions in risk research, *Risk Analysis* (2006) 26(2), 397–411 (both with P. Taylor-Gooby); A biographical approach: a better way to understand behaviour in health and illness, *Health, Risk & Society* (2005) 7(1), 1–10; Health, risk and uncertainty in the life course: a typology of biographical certainty constructions, *Social Theory & Health* (2006) 2(3), 199–221.

Acknowledgments

This book grew out of my work within the Social Contexts and Responses to Risk network (SCARR) funded by the Economic and Social Research Council (ESRC) under grant 336 25 0001. I am most grateful for the support of the SCARR network and its Director Peter Taylor-Gooby as well as the support of the School of Social Policy, Sociology and Social Research (SSPSSR). In particular, I would like to thank Chris Pickvance and Jenny Billings as well as my other colleagues and my family for their constructive and valuable comments and thoughts.

Jens O. Zinn

1 | Introduction: The Contribution of Sociology to the Discourse on Risk and Uncertainty

Jens O. Zinn

Risk looms large in present-day society. This is most apparent in technical catastrophes (e.g. Chernobyl), environmental changes (e.g. climate change), international terrorism and epidemics (BSE, bird flu), but it is in everyday life as well. We are concerned about whether and whom to marry, what to study, which occupation to learn, how to be financially secure in retirement, and even what to eat or drink. Our desire to minimize risk is evidenced as well by the spread of auditing and risk evaluation techniques in public and private companies (Power 1997, 2004). To help us to avoid risk, we can seek help from the vast amount of advisory literature, take part in training, or engage with supportive organizations.

The implication is that we must be kept safe. "Better safe than sorry" is a well-known proverb of recent times. But is it possible or really desirable to live without risk? Wouldn't life "be pretty dull without risk"? (Lupton & Tulloch 2002) What is the price we have to pay for taking risks and for reducing risk in our striving for safety, security, and certainty?

Regularly, risks are contested. Is world terrorism a risk which we have to fight by a "war on terror"? How much is global warming an effect of our production of CO_2 and what should we do about it? Is nuclear power a risky business not worth taking or is it a necessary risk which secures our growing need for energy? Do we keep children misinformed about contraception in a misguided attempt to prevent them becoming promiscuous? What probability of becoming handicapped justifies the abortion of an unborn? Does the "precautionary principle" delay crucial scientific advancement and thereby produce new economic risks rather than securing our ecological future?

And how do we respond to risks? Is it reasonable no longer to go by airplane and instead choose to go by car after the terrorist suicide attacks on September 11, 2001? As Gigerenzer (2006) showed recently, the American change from air travel to highway travel after 9/11 caused a jump in fatal highway crashes which significantly exceeded the deaths of 9/11. Is it therefore a reasonable response to the London tube bombings to make a similar switch?

A discourse into social risk behavior is as much a discourse on defining a problem, about different values and lifestyles, power relations, and emotions as it is about "real" risks and their rational management. However, to interpret issues in terms of risk seems itself to be a particular way of viewing our world in terms of politics, science, or everyday life. Therefore we have to examine not just how risk is understood and discussed in society, but how we observe risk as social scientists.

Why Theorize Risk and Uncertainty?

Everyday theories as well as scientific theories are instruments to make sense of our world. They give orientation and enable us to act. This is true not just for laypeople or social scientists, but for organized actors and society at large. Theories structure the notion of whether issues are relevant or not, and what we notice and ignore. Initial assumptions and decisions influence the subsequent theorizing and lead to different research programs as well as different interpretations of the results. Indeed, it makes quite a difference whether we interpret risk phenomena as a result of new and recent types of risk we have to face, as a change in style of governance, as caused by an increasingly differentiated society, as a response to alienating conditions of living, or as a problem of diverse cultural interpretations. This book addresses the implications of such different perspectives in theorizing on risk and uncertainty. It examines advantages and disadvantages of mainstream approaches to risk and uncertainty, which have been developed in several contexts and applied to understanding specific phenomena.

Since risk theorizing is deeply embedded in specific sociocultural backgrounds, the approaches are acknowledged in different ways. In Anglophone countries the *risk society* and *governmentality* approaches are widely disseminated, while in Germany *risk society* competes with *systems theory* while *governmentality* has only recently attracted more attention. *Cultural theory* was originally developed in the USA and has spread to northern European countries; some newer developments are evident in Australia. Few independent theoretical approaches have been developed in other continental European countries.

Risk discourse and theorizing is linked to historical constellations. It is inevitably confounded by "Zeitgeist" (*spirit of the age*). On the one hand, one might interpret the *Risk and Culture* approach by Douglas and Wildavsky (1982) in the context of a science-friendly US society where the resistance of social movements caused irritation, perceived by some as unreasonable and irrational anxieties. On the other hand, Beck's work on the *risk society* seems more influenced by the development of a broad societal movement against nuclear power and for an ecological lifestyle in Germany (in the late 1970s), which led to the birth of the Green Party. Thus, it was viewed much more positively as new "bottom-up" political-ization. In Britain the governmentality approach became famous in the aftermath of conservative Thatcherism and New Labour's neoliberalism. Consequently, public risk awareness is understood primarily in a frame-work of power strategies applied in a liberal style to govern societies.

However, in contrast to these interpretations it might sometimes appear more appropriate to explain theoretical decisions by personal preferences of the respective authors. Instead of referring to historical constellations, one might like to explain Douglas's and Luhmann's theorizing by their conservative political attitude, which sees public resistance to established political institutions as a negative social trend, while Beck interprets resistance as a necessary and reasonable response in order to prevent dangerous societal developments.

The book aims to introduce sociological theorizing on risk and uncertainty by drawing attention to such a variety of dimensions and by enabling and encouraging the reader to theorize self-reflexively and critically.

The Conceptualization of Risk

The use of the term "risk" in the increasing volume of interdisciplinary literature is so heterogeneous that some authors even argue that there are hardly any connections at all (Garland 2003). However, the main concepts of and approaches to risk are dissected and ordered in this sec-tion to give a first orientation.

The most general assumption shared by all approaches on risk is the distinction between reality and possibility. As long as the future is interpreted as either predetermined or independent of human activities, the term "risk" makes no sense at all (Renn 1992: 56). The concept of risk is tied to the possibility that the future can be altered – or at least perceived as such – by human activities. It might be that we can directly control the occurrence of an event or that we can at least make provisions for the aftermaths of an event.

As Luhmann argued, risks have to do with *expectations*, which can be more or less (un-)certain (1995: 307f.). We cannot even leave our bed in the morning without any expectations of the world. Expectations refer to knowledge and experiences of the past, and they can be developed in a formalized, more or less conscious way, referring to statistical techniques, or in a less formalized manner, referring to everyday knowledge and personal experiences. But what one considers as risky depends not just on knowledge but on sociocultural and individual values as well.

Having said that, it might sometimes be confusing that the term "risk" in interdisciplinary risk discourse is used in at least three different, albeit connected ways. Often, risk is understood as similar to *hazard, loss, damage*, or *threat*. Then it is just an indication of unwanted events. At the same time, the term is used for *risk calculation*. In a technical perspective, risk is then about the probability and extent of an (undesired) event (figure 1.1). However, in a less formalized perspective of everyday life, risk is often calculated by intuitive or pre-rational techniques. Finally, risk is not restricted to negative aspects. The notion of *risk taking* refers to a positive and a negative side as a weighing up between gains and losses. Research on voluntary risk taking has shown that seeking risks can become a value itself (Lyng 1990, 2005b, 2005c), thus questioning the underlying normative assumption of mainstream risk research that risks have to be avoided and reduced (Renn 1992: 58).

The risk concepts used in a variety of different disciplines and approaches are usually explained against the background of their "epistemological foundation" (compare Renn 1992: 68; Lupton 1999a: 35; Strydom 2002: 47; Taylor-Gooby & Zinn 2006: 407).[1] This refers to whether risk is primarily conceptualized as an entity, which has an objective existence and is objectively accessible beyond the social, or whether risks are primarily seen as being socially mediated or even socially constructed independent of its objective existence (compare table 1.1 for an overview).

In a first *realist perspective*, risks are primarily understood as real events or dangers which can be approached objectively without being

$$\text{risk} = \text{probability}_{\text{event}} \times \text{damage}_{\text{event}}$$

Figure 1.1 Technical-Objectivistic Definition of Risk.

confounded by subjective and social factors. Such a realist position dominates in a range of domains: for example, in actuarial applications, toxicological and epidemiological research, engineering, and probabilistic risk assessment as well as economic approaches including risk–benefit comparisons (Renn 1992: 56–7). When limits of calculability occur, they are rather interpreted as a lack of knowledge which we can overcome in principle by further research and better scientific analysis. The superior way to manage respective uncertainties is seen in the production of more objective knowledge, even where it is accepted that knowledge will always be limited. In such a realist perspective, risks are calculated by the probability of its occurrence and the amount of damage (compare figure 1.1). Such calculations are reliable as long as they are based on a high number of different events and the future conditions are comparable with the past ("ceteris paribus"). However, models and scenarios are developed in order to find orientation on how to act rationally regarding an uncertain future even when the knowledge is limited. But such models depend on more untested assumptions.

In a second *realist* perspective, people's management of risks is interpreted as *subjectively biased*. This means that although we can objectively find out what the best response to a risk would be, the observable subjective judgments and perceptions deviate systematically. These deviations are interpreted as unreasonable while the ideal is seen as the superior rational option to strive for.

For example, in economics, risk is conceptualized not as physical harm or other objective effect but as an expected utility (Renn 1992: 61). Expected utilities which are regularly expressed in terms of money have the advantage that it is possible to compare directly several risks and costs. The underlying assumption is that individuals try to maximize their utility and that the necessary information and time is available for balancing pros and cons. This conventional approach in economics is relaxed by the acknowledgment of subjective preferences. Subjective utilities acknowledge that individuals' preferences interpret utility subjectively, referring to different relatively stable values or interests, while the concept of rationality is maintained. When it comes to research on individuals' decision making, economics and psychology come close in assuming that there are objectively best decisions while systematic deviations are seen as undesired (Tversky & Kahneman 1987).

The *psychometric approach* (Slovic 2000) has intensively examined which risks people worry about and how much they are concerned. Using standardized questionnaires, psychophysical scaling, and multivariate analysis, this approach constructs "cognitive maps" of risk perception to discover general patterns and causalities. Risk perception research has shown how the quality of risks (e.g. its scale, dreadfulness, or likelihood) influences responses to risks (Renn 1992: 65; Zinn & Taylor-Gooby 2006a: 29ff.). Further studies attempt to integrate cultural and emotional factors (Slovic 1999) while the sociocultural and historical *dynamics* of risk communication are less examined. The understanding of the dynamics of interactive processes on risk remains underdeveloped as long as risks are understood as being significantly identified by their objective characteristics, and their perception as determined by general context-independent laws, even though a greater acknowledgment of sociocultural construction of risk has taken place recently (Taylor-Gooby & Zinn 2006).

When it comes to *sociological approaches*, the perspective changes from objective risks and subjective biases to socioculturally mediated or constructed risks. We see later on (compare Tulloch and Zinn in this book) that in sociological theorizing the link between the sociocultural mediation and construction of risk and its "objective" existence is more complex and diverse than a one-dimensional scale with different degrees of realist or constructivist status could express.

In some approaches, objective *risks* are interpreted *as mediated* by social factors. For example, Douglas assumes that even though risks are necessarily real, for focus of debate, they are socially selected and transformed. The selection and perception of risk and the response to risks of a social group would be determined by the group's institutional organization. The reality of a danger is a prerequisite for persistent debates and activities on risk while their politicalization is culturally determined.

Other approaches explicitly understand risk as primarily *socially constructed*, as opposed to being mediated. This implies that risk debates might occur and take off without any substantial relation to a "real" world. Even though these theories do not deny the existence of a material world, they conceptualize risk as brought into being and managed as part of social processes. Therefore, increasing public concerns can only be explained by social factors. For example, the governmentality perspective focuses on the social processes which constitute risk. Risk is understood as a specific way to manage uncertainty by calculative techniques (mainly statistical-probabilistic analysis) which are provided with meaning within institutional and discursive processes. On a similar epistemological level, the systems theory approach interprets risk as constituted by decision making and the ascription of decisions to social actors. Risks are therefore part of every decision! Nevertheless a harm or risk can be attributed to us even though we might have nothing to do with it. Too often social minorities such as foreigners are made responsible for growing unemployment rates. These approaches do not deny a real world in principle but such a world influences how we make sense of risk and uncertainty as social beings. They assume that we can only understand the conflictual struggles about risk by referring to *social* dynamics. Reality claims about the objective character of such risks are seen as a part of these processes.

Some approaches are difficult to position. They interpret risks as real and socially constructed at the same time. Beck (1999) claims to **combine both** a realist and a constructivist perspective. He emphasizes on the one hand the reality of risk (as danger, harm, etc.) and its social mediation, and on the other hand the social construction of risks by social institutions. Beck would therefore follow a *critical realist* perspective, as Tulloch argues in chapter 6 of this book. In his approach on *edgework*, Lyng (1990, 2005b) interprets the deadly risks of high risk taking as well as the experience of the accompanying "adrenaline rush" as quite real. At the same time he derives the seductive character of high risk taking from social contexts such as an over-socializing and alienating social world. Therefore the experience of risks is understood on the one hand as immediate and pre-social and on the other hand as socially mediated.

The Historical Development of the Notion of "Risk"

The term "risk" first occurs sporadically and in a great variety of contexts. The *Oxford English Dictionary* (Murray 1933; Simpson & Weiner 1989) like many others traces risk back to French (*risque*) and Italian (*risco*) but there seems to be no clear etymological origin of the term.

Table 1.1 Risk Epistemology in Different Disciplines and Approaches

Risk as …	Perspective	Approaches
real and objective	Objective calculation of events	Technical risk assessment, insurance, epidemiology, toxicology
subjectively biased	Objective risks are subjectively perceived and calculated	Psychometric paradigm, rational choice: objective/subjective utility
socially mediated	The subjective experience of real risks is socially mediated	Edgework
real and socially constructed	Reality and talk about risks mutually influence and produce each other	Risk society
socially transformed	Real threats are transformed into risks for sociocultural boundaries	Cultural theory
socially constructed	Events are risks insofar as they are part of a calculative technology	Governmentality
	Risks are socially ascribed decisions	Systems theory

At the end of the seventeenth century, "risk" was used in many societal domains, and Grimm and Grimm (1854) stated that the German *Risiko* became part of the everyday language in the eighteenth century. Luhmann (1993: 8ff.) argues that the appearance and dissemination of the term "risk" has to do with a new kind of experience which gains ground in the transitional period between the late Middle Ages and the early modern era and would indicate an historical new experience which takes place in several social domains. "Since the existing language has words for danger, venture, chance, luck, courage, fear, adventure (aventuyre) etc. at its disposal, we may assume that a new term comes into use to indicate a problem situation that cannot be expressed precisely enough with the vocabulary available" (1993: 10). He supposes that the occurrence of the early notion of risk was supported by the insight "that certain advantages are to be gained only if something is at stake. It is not a matter of the cost, which can be calculated beforehand and traded off against the advantages. It is rather a matter of a decision that, as can be foreseen, will be subsequently regretted if a loss that one had hoped to avert occurs" (1993: 11).

An early institutionalized form to enable risk taking and protecting oneself against possible losses was developed in the late Middle Ages in maritime trading. Traders stuck together in order to manage the always acute risk of losing one or more of their ships. They developed an early form of insurance (Luhmann 1993: 9f.). The success of the risk concept went on with the application of techniques of probabilistic risk calculation in a range of societal domains. The idea of insurance against accidents in industrial production and the development of compulsory *social insurance* were milestones in the societal usage of risk calculation and the management of populations. Ewald (1986) even interprets the development of an *insurance society* as an index of the transition into modernity. Presently, risk techniques are applied all over society. There are insurances against a huge variety of risks (e.g. life-, car-, social-, and third-party insurances) while industry routinely uses assessment tools to minimize the costs caused by unnecessary accidents. In medicine, similar calculative techniques are applied to find out about new treatments and drugs. Crime control uses risk techniques to calculate the risk of subsequent offences and psychology refers to them in order to evaluate single cases. We use knowledge about risks in everyday decision making: for example, how to behave during pregnancy. In some leisure-time activities, we explicitly seek the risk while simultaneously relying on the safety of the bungee jumping line or the unfolding of our parachute.

The idea of risk taking and the increasing application of risk techniques are expressions of a general change in the understanding of an increasingly disenchanted world, as formulated by Max Weber in "Science as a vocation":

> The increasing intellectualization and rationalization ... means ... the knowledge or belief that if one but wished one could learn it at any time. Hence, it means that principally there are no mysterious incalculable forces that come into play, but rather that one can, in principle, master all things by calculation. This means that the world is disenchanted. One need no longer have recourse to magical means in order to master or implore the spirits, as did the savage, for whom such mysterious powers existed. Technical means and calculations perform the service. (Weber 1948: 139)

Even though this idea of a rationalized world was never fully realized, it became a central societal semantic and as part of it the concept of risk as well. Risk implies that an uncertain future can be made available to human action foremost with the help of positivist science and technique. Many researchers believe that this position of confidence has been supplanted by an emphasis on the negative side of risk, the damages, losses, and injuries (Douglas 1992; Lupton 1999a; Tulloch & Lupton 2003), and would even cause unreasonable risk aversion or a culture of fear (Furedi 1997, 2002).

But the quality of the change, its assessment and the possible causes are still contentious. While some interpret the increase in risk communication as a rather undesirable development, others emphasize that it is a reasonable response to dangerous societal changes. Some judge life to be safer than ever, while others stress the special quality of new risks which would threaten the existence of all human life. The reasons for the increase in risk communication could therefore be interpreted either as a new sensitivity regarding risks, as an artifact caused by media coverage or as a fundamental change in the quality of the dangers we have to face.

The Sociological Contribution to Interdisciplinary Risk Research

Technological progress in the 1970s and 1980s had a strong impact on the establishment and expansion of interdisciplinary risk research and the social science contribution to it, even though technical and environmental risks are only one domain of risk theorizing in sociology.

When in the 1970s and early 1980s public resistance to new technologies gained ground, risk techniques were already developed and successfully applied in many societal domains. Large-scale incidents such as the near disaster of Three Mile Island close to Harrisburg (1979) and later the technical accident in Bhopal (1984) and the nuclear power catastrophe in Chernobyl (1986) seem to indicate the systematic safety limits of such large-scale technologies and our ability to control them. These concerns are reflected in Perrow's study on "Normal Accidents" (1984). He concluded after examining a huge range of techniques and accidents that in complex technologies, such as nuclear power, accidents are unpreventable, and because of their catastrophic character it would be irresponsible to introduce such technologies.

The growing public resistance to technological innovations became a great concern of politicians and technicians. It eroded the unquestioned consensus of the priority of technical and economic progress. As a result, political decisions became even more uncertain. Because of the urgent need to secure the basis for decision making, research increasingly concentrated on the question of which new technologies would be acceptable to the public. First a technician, Chauncey Starr (1969), attempted to predict the public acceptability of new technologies by comparing the public acceptance of already established technologies to produce energy with the new nuclear power technology and their respective costs (calculated in deaths per produced energy). He concluded that the relation between cost and benefit was significantly better than with other already accepted technologies, and was therefore acceptable. But his prediction failed because public risk aversion was not yet properly understood.

Cognitive psychologists, who by then were examining people's decision making in laboratory experiments, developed a different approach. They no longer derived public acceptance (*revealed preferences*) by comparing the effectiveness of old and new technologies. Instead they started to ask people directly about their concerns and worries regarding new technologies (*expressed preferences*). This kind of risk perception research, conducted with the help of standardized questionnaires and large-scale surveys, has become the most influential approach in interdisciplinary risk research, the *psychometric paradigm* (Slovic 2000). It originally followed a widely disseminated *deficit-model* of public risk perception, which explained faulty perception by the cognitive limitations of human beings (Slovic et al. 1977a).

Important insights resulted from this research, even though the certain knowledge necessary for far-reaching decision making was not obtained. Risk perception research shows that the perceived seriousness of risks (expected numbers of fatalities) and the catastrophic potential influence the acceptance of a risk even when its probability of occurrence is very low. Risks with a low probability but high consequences are perceived as more threatening than more probable risks with low or medium consequences. Additionally, having personal control over a risk or familiarity with a risk decreases the perceived risk (compare Rohrmann & Renn 2000; Slovic 2000; Zinn & Taylor-Gooby 2006a: 29–31).

Taylor-Gooby and Zinn have summarized more recent developments in psychological and psychometric research as showing more awareness of the impact of culture on risk perception, and even biographical experiences are occasionally acknowledged (compare Taylor-Gooby & Zinn 2006; Zinn & Taylor-Gooby 2006b). There is still a lack of knowledge, however, regarding the conceptualization of the dynamic processes of risk perception and responses which would allow reliable prognoses of people's responses to new (technological) risks. Moreover, the ambitious approach to bring together a range of empirical insights into the *Social Amplification of Risk Framework* (SARF; Pidgeon et al. 2003) has proved unable to produce further additional knowledge regarding the dynamic processes of risk perception and responses (Zinn & Taylor-Gooby 2006a: 32–4).

The rapid development of sociological research on risk in the 1980s was mainly supported by public resistance and controversies regarding new technological risks,[2] and the limits of technical and psychological analyses in explaining the dynamics of risk discourse and responses. Instead, the significance of social and sociocultural factors became more acknowledged in explaining resistance to and controversies about risk.

Most important for the sociological contribution to the discourse on risk was the expert/lay-people controversy. Early risk research assumed the superiority of objective science-based knowledge, while the lay-person's understanding of technologies and risks was seen as inferior and biased as a result of a lack of objective information and a contamination with irrational beliefs and emotions. It was therefore assumed that the best solutions to risk problems could be reached by enlightening and educating the public with the right knowledge. However, this *educational approach* in risk communication failed for several reasons.

Research within the sociology of scientific knowledge showed that professional expertise often lacks local and practical knowledge (Wynne 1982a, 1982b, 1987, 1992, 1996). Gained in the controlled and stable contexts of the laboratory, scientific results and insights regularly fail because they cannot be transferred directly to real-life conditions. Wynne (1992) argues, for example, that experts' ideas about safety regarding the application of pesticides were often rather naïve; neither does herbicide always arrive at the point of use with full instructions intact and intelligible; and nor do the farmers and other users apply the pesticides with full protective gear and in correct solvents, with proper spray nozzles and other equipment, and the weather conditions are often less ideal than assumed. Furthermore, Wynne shows that lay-people do not in principle act irrationally but follow another social and/or subjective rationality which includes their own experiences and experience of scientific and professional expertise, and their failures. Lay-people do not uncritically accept scientific knowledge as true, but read the "various elements of institutional 'body-language'" (Wynne 1996: 65) which give information regarding the reliability of the alleged objective knowledge. Research has repeatedly shown how misinformation by official institutions rapidly decreases trust in the reliability of such institutions, and how difficult it is to rebuild trust once it is lost (Zinn & Taylor-Gooby 2006b: 61ff.).

A variety of public participation measures (consensus-conferences, public debates, etc.) were applied as a result of such problems with knowledge, legitimacy, and resistance. Even though such strategies are often successful, this is not necessarily the case, since risk conflicts are not only a question of objective knowledge. Instead a range of issues are involved, such as value conflicts, conflicts regarding the acknowledgment of different rationalities, conflicts regarding power and finally emotional aspects (Zinn & Taylor-Gooby 2006b). Sociological theorizing therefore contributes on at least five dimensions to the discourse on risk: values, knowledge, rationality, power, and emotion.

Central is the sociocultural dimension of *values*. Risk questions are never just a question of the rational application of objective, value-free problems. Even in the highest technical application, values concerning the acceptability of a specific level of risk or uncertainty are involved. The outstanding merit of Douglas's work on risk and culture was to introduce the cultural dimension into discourse. She showed that selection and responses to risk are influenced by the sociocultural organization of a social group.

The sociology of scientific knowledge (Wynne 1975, 1982a, 1987, 1996, 2002) and theorizing on the risk society (Beck 1992b) contribute a new understanding of knowledge. The idea of objectified laboratory knowledge directly applicable in practical contexts is complemented or even supplanted in sociological theorizing by notions of *social* and *subjective knowledge*. Such forms of localized knowledge and their public negotiation by several competing organized agents are much more in the focus now. Additionally, questions address the cognitive reflexivity of knowledge and how other forms of *intuitive* or *pre-rational knowledge* are involved in the perception and management of risk.

That goes along with the question of *rationality* and whether, in a highly differentiated and complex modern society, reasonable decision making can rely on an overall integrating rationality. This is about competing *social* and *subjective rationalities* which are concerned with questions of values and social differentiation rather than with instrumental rationality. Instead of finding consensus, it is often more reasonable to seek and accept "second best" solutions (Japp 2000a; Zinn 2004: 17).

Sociological research shows that the objectivist discourse on risk covers societal *power* relations. The conflicts regarding the right knowledge, rationality, and values are embedded in power games and the governance of modern societies, constituted by a wide range of (organized) actors. Patterns of power develop historically and are therefore hardly predictable (O'Malley in chapter 3 of this book; Rose 1999; Dean 1999a).

Finally, defining and negotiating risk has a lot more to do with *emotions*, as generally acknowledged in the interdisciplinary discourse. This is not concerned solely with worries, concerns, and fears, but also with the physical experience of risks. It might be embodied in excitement, as in edgework (Lyng 2005a), or in social suffering (Bourdieu et al. 1999). Moreover, emotions are often used as a kind of advisor, referring to complex experiences which cannot be transformed into formalized objective knowledge.

The various streams of theorizing refer to these dimensions differently. While in the next five chapters respective authors present the different ways of theorizing, in the last chapter I will compare them systematically in terms of their underlying ideas and epistemological differences, and how they refer to central dimensions such as values, knowledge, rationality, power, and emotions.

Sociological Streams of Theorizing Risk and Uncertainty

Five central sociological streams of risk theorizing are presented.

The *risk society* approach was introduced by Ulrich Beck (1986) in Germany and internationally with its translation into English in 1992. Several publications followed (e.g. Beck 1999). This approach interacts fruitfully with the British discourse (Beck et al. 1994) and the work of Anthony Giddens (1990, 1991, 1999). More recent work emphasizes the concept of *reflexive modernization* (Beck et al. 2003). Chapter 2 outlines the development of the approach from early work on the risk society to the more recent contributions on reflexive modernization developed in the context of the collaborative research center known as Reflexive Modernization in Munich.[3]

The *governmentality* perspective on risk draws on Michel Foucault's work on governmentality (1991a), which was further developed by the historical work of a circle of researchers close to Foucault in France: Françoise Ewald ([orig. 1986], 1991), Daniel Defert (1991), Jacques Donzelot (1980, 1988), Giovanna Procacci (1978, 1998), and Pasquale Pasquino (1978, 1980). First and foremost, the approach spread out to Britain (e.g. Rose 1996a, 1996b, 1999) and Australia (e.g. Dean 1999a) to form a governmentality approach with a strong contribution to risk. Pat O'Malley, who contributed substantially to this debate (e.g. 2004), describes the development of the approach in chapter 3. He outlines the Foucauldian approach on power as governmentality and shows how risk is part of a specific kind of liberal governance. Finally, he suggests a broader theoretical approach to the management of uncertainty beyond risk.

The *systems theory* on risk, in the tradition of Niklas Luhmann (1993 [orig. 1991], 1989 [orig. 1986]), is mainly acknowledged in Germany. One of the central proponents of this approach is Klaus P. Japp (1996, 2000a). In chapter 4, he and Isabel Kusche outline the systems theory thinking on risk. They introduce its central concepts (functional systems, communication, code, second-order observation) and show how risk is positioned in the core of systems theory as "the modern form for observing decisions." They discuss risk in relation to the three dimensions of meaning – the time dimension, the material dimension, and the social dimension – and conclude by illustrating the systems theory style of thinking with two detailed examples, the conflict between Israel and Palestinians and the "war on terror."

The *edgework* concept was introduced by Stephen Lyng (1990, 2005a) and added the often less understood question of voluntary risk taking, as observable in high-risk sport or crime (Katz 1988). In chapter 5, Lyng outlines the development of the edgework approach and its different attempts to make sense of the growth in high-risk activities in late modernity. He starts from the embodied experience of risk and goes on to discuss a range of theoretical approaches. This leads him to a more general explanation of edgework in a framework of historical social change which is provided by Marxism and the risk society respectively.

The *cultural approaches* to risk were originally influenced by the early anthropological work of Mary Douglas (1963, 1966, 1985, 1992) and with Aaron Wildavsky (1982). John Tulloch's and Deborah Lupton's work on "Risk in everyday life" (2003; see also Lupton 1999a) contributes to a qualitative stream of cultural risk research which overcame the functionalist perspective in favor of a more open approach. Consequently, Tulloch frames his discussion of the contribution of culture to risk research (chapter 6) in a wider context of a more general "cultural turn" in humanities and examines to what extent risk theorizing is involved. The cultural turn addresses a quite heterogeneous movement which developed as a critique on traditional research. It focuses on the ordinary, everyday culture which would link structure and action, and critiques the values and power relations involved in alleged objective research. Interpreting all sociological approaches as sociocultural, Tulloch focuses on the epistemological differences between them and points out what risk theorizing could still learn from the cultural turn.

Notes

1. The epistemological status of risk in sociological theorizing is discussed in more detail in the contribution on risk and culture (Tulloch in chapter 6 of this book) and the comparison in the last chapter (Zinn in chapter 7 of this book).

2. In contrast, the historical work on insurance by Ewald (1986) and other research in the tradition of Foucault were inspired by historical analysis of the social changes in governmental power and control. Finally, the investigation of edgework was triggered by increasingly high-risk leisure activities from the 1980s onward (Lyng 1990).
3. Compare the homepage: http://www.sfb536.mwn.de/index_e.html

2 | Risk Society and Reflexive Modernization

Jens O. Zinn

The term "risk society" was coined by Beck in his book *Risk Society: Towards a New Modernity* (1992b) first published in Germany in 1986. The book was almost finished when the Chernobyl disaster happened in April 1986 and led to the book having an extraordinary impact. Much of the reception of the risk society in Anglophone sociology has focused on new technological risks and nuclear power, emphasized in the first part of the *Risk Society*, while the second part is about the self-transformation of society by individualization. In the third part, both lines are linked by considerations regarding the modes of general social change within modernity. Proceeding from the example of Germany between the 1950s and the 1980s, Beck later claims to develop a theory which is able to describe the significant social changes on an international level which would lead to a *World Risk Society* (1999).

The broader scope of Beck's argument was already set within the *Risk Society* and has shaped the subsequent discussion and developments of his theorizing on risk and reflexive modernization. Beck attempts to get a grip on the overall impact of a range of social phenomena, such as feminism, the ecological movement, the growth in citizen groups, flexibilization of employment and mass unemployment, and how they contribute to general social changes.

In a situation where new social developments challenged common concepts on social class (Marx, Weber) and other approaches to social structure (Parsons, Luhmann), Beck argued that new and future social developments cannot be conceptualized properly with the categories of past and present society. We could not see the changes if we still tried to apply the old "zombie" or "living-dead" categories from traditional class and sociostructural analysis to new developments (Beck 1998: 17f., 2000a: 8f.; Beck & Beck-Gernsheim 2002: XX, XXIV). Instead new categories were needed. Consequently, he developed new concepts such as "subpolitics," "organized irresponsibility," and the change from an "either-or" logic to an "as-well-as" logic to get a grip on the new, and to express ambivalences and contradictions in modernization.

Beck positions his theorizing between Marxist class analysis, Luhmann's functionalism, and postmodern approaches. He criticizes the traditional structural analysis in the tradition of Marx, which derives class consciousness from the sociostructural contradiction between labor and capital, although in many respects his form of theorizing is close to Marx, and he often explicitly refers to Marx's concepts. However, Beck clearly distances himself from the functionalist theorizing of Luhmann, who as in postmodern thinking emphasizes the contingency of the future which would limit the possibility of positive prognoses. Finally, Beck rejects all (alleged) tendencies of postmodern theorizing to position current societies beyond modernity. Instead he emphasizes that we are part of a self-transformation within modernization where fundamental principles of modernization remain while many institutions transform. In opposition to postmodern critiques on the possibility of predicting future social developments, Beck explicitly wants to go beyond pure descriptions and reconstructions of the past or a critique of the present. Instead, he aims to imagine possible futures (e.g. 1992, 2000a, 2006). Therefore he accepts in advance that the attempt to work out the new might sometimes "turn out shrill, overly ironic or rash" (1992: 9). He self-critically admits that the *Risk Society*, for example, "contains some empirically oriented, projective social theory – without any methodological safeguards" (1992: 9).

The *Risk Society* outlined a research prospect which was complemented by further publications on technological risks (1995b), changes in politics (1997, 2000a), globalization (1999, 2000c, 2005b, 2006), labor (2000a), gender relations (with Beck-Gernsheim 1995), and individualization (with Beck-Gernsheim 2002), and which was enriched by empirical research and theoretical developments within the DFG-funded collaborative research center Reflexive Modernization in Munich.[1]

Already developed in the *Risk Society*, the concept of *reflexive modernization* has become a larger focus in Beck's later work. Starting from the idea of a modernity which changes itself by applying its principles to its own institutions, recent research in the context of the research center Reflexive Modernization focuses much more on manufactured uncertainties than risks, and is therefore mainly concerned with the problems of blurring boundaries and the management of ambiguities, contradictions, and ignorance (Beck et al. 2003).

Research is conducted, for example, on the shifting boundaries of nature and society, by case studies on aesthetic surgery and genetic diagnosis, and others which focus on shifting and blurring distinctions between health and illness or body and mind. Another project focuses on the acknowledgment of different forms of everyday knowledge (e.g. tacit knowledge) which erode the monopoly of techno-scientific knowledge in practical applications at the workplace. Further studies examine changes in the realm of labor: for example, blurring boundaries within the organizational structure of firms through decentralization, flexibilization of work, reduction of hierarchies, and new forms of work (group and project work). On the level of politics, the growing transnationalization of political regulation and the remaining importance of national politics are examined. Finally, at the micro level, shifts are analyzed in the relation of social and special mobility, which lead to new forms of "virtual" mobility.[2]

Although the political was an important aspect of Beck's early work on the *Risk Society* (1992b) and the *World Risk Society* (1999), it becomes central in his more recent work on *Power in the Global Age* (2005b) and the *Cosmopolitan Vision* (2006). Cosmopolitanism places the global at the center of political imagination, action, and organization.

In particular, in the 1990s Beck's work on reflexive modernization interacted with the work of Anthony Giddens on late modernity (e.g. Giddens 1991; Beck 1997) and led to a critical exchange of ideas (Beck et al. 1994). While Beck went on to develop a more general societal theory, Giddens focused on the political implications of his theoretical considerations in *Beyond Left and Right* (1994a) and *The Third Way* (1999).

From Risk Society and Individualization to Reflexive Modernization

The core thesis and the point of origin of the *Risk Society* is that "in advanced modernity the social production of wealth is systematically accompanied by the social production of *risks*. Accordingly, the problems and conflicts relating to distribution in a society of scarcity overlap with the problems and conflicts that arise from the production, definition and distribution of techno-scientifically produced risks" (1992b: 19).

This change would result from two general developments. First, "it occurs ... where and to the extent that genuine material need can be objectively reduced and socially isolated through the development of human and technological productivity, as well as through legal and welfare-state protections and regulations" (1992b: 19). That does not mean that poverty would disappear. Instead, Beck assumes that the kind of poverty assumed by Marx as being the precondition of the appearance of a revolutionary working class has been overcome at a national level by Western industrialized societies (Beck & Beck-Gernsheim 2002: 34). Other forms of relative or life-phase-specific poverty gain relative importance while impoverishment loses its political impact, is silenced and disappears from social-institutional awareness. Therefore it can intensify, socially "unobserved" (Beck & Beck-Gernsheim 2002: 52).[3]

Second, "this categorical change is likewise dependent upon the fact that in the course of the exponentially growing productive forces in the modernization process, hazards and potential threats have been unleashed to an extent previously unknown" (1992b: 19).[4]

Indeed, the risk society is not restricted to technological risks. Besides a strong line of argument which focuses on the production of techno-scientifically produced new risks (e.g. nuclear, chemical, ecological, and genetic engineering risks) and their impact on society, a second line concerns societal self-transformation from within by processes of *individualization* or *institutionalized individualism* respectively (Beck & Beck-Gernsheim 2002: XXI; Zinn 2002).[5] They are brought into being in several societal domains such as gender (feminism), work (flexibilization, mass unemployment, or underemployment), and life course/ biography (de-standardization), which produces uncertainties, risks, and chances. Both lines converge into the transformation of the political within modernity and the question of how to do politics in reflexive modernization. Central are the blurring boundaries of science and politics, a growing *self-culture* or *self-politics* (Beck & Beck-Gernsheim 2002: 42–6) and the concept of *subpolitics* (Beck 1992b: 183–223; 1999: 91–108). Finally, the risk society is understood as a *world risk society* increasingly influenced by the management of transnational risks (e.g. ecological crisis and the crash of global financial markets) and processes of societal globalization (1999: 2, 2007).

In the broader theoretical perspective on *reflexive modernization*, Beck develops an outline of the general historical logic beyond these social changes (compare also 1999: 2). Differing from many other sociological approaches which have recently rejected the assumption of generalized historical logics of social development, Beck interprets the production of new risks as being part and parcel of modernization itself. The "risk society is not an option which could be chosen or rejected in the course of political debate. It arises through the automatic operation of autonomous modernization processes which are blind and deaf to consequences and dangers. In total, and latently, these produce hazards which call into question – indeed abolish – the basis of industrial society" (1999: 73).[6]

Beck derives the self-transformation of modernity from the immanent contradictions of modernization and counter-modernization (1992b: 13). First modernity (or industrialized modernity, or simple modernity) transforms itself by the application of modern principles to the (semi-modern) institutions of first modernity. First modernity is understood as half modernity because categories of status and class still maintain. "Modern" principles of Enlightenment are not fully developed in all societal domains (e.g. the gender division of labor contradicts the equality principles of modernity). Or more accurately it can be said that the specific contradictions of early modern society were the prerequisites of its success but are now objects of critique and transformation (e.g. the separation of work and family and its gender-specific ascription to men and women). Thus the increasing attempts to achieve gender equality are seen as the application of modern principles to a semi-modern first modernity or as one example of radicalized modernization (1999: 2) which transforms this contradiction into something new. The results are risks and chances or, better, growing uncertainties in many societal domains where old distinctions become increasingly blurred (gender differences, work–life, precarious work, voluntary work).

We can say that, during ongoing modernization processes, a range of modern institutions are questioned by the process of modernization itself, which became reflexive. However, "reflexive" does not necessarily imply growing self-awareness. It is about the application of institutional logics or principles to its own institutional basis. For example, in modernity, ongoing scientization does not alone conquer more and more societal areas. The application of scientific principles to itself discovers the implicit normativity, uncertainties, and limits of knowledge production. The enlightened and critical task of science is directed to its own fundaments. In so doing *reflexive scientization* is self-critical and tries to overcome its own weaknesses. At the same time, it loses some of its old authority (Beck 1992b: 156).

Similarly, a range of changes is taking place in central social domains: the nation state is being challenged by globalization (from international to transnational globalization),[7] the traditional life course by individualization, the political by *subpolitics* from outside the formal political institutions, the normal work life by flexibility and mass un-/underemployment, the traditional division of labor by feminism, and so on.

The Power of New Risks: The Enforced Risk Society

One central thesis of the risk society is the impact of new risks, such as nuclear, chemical, ecological, and genetic engineering risks, which differ significantly and in many respects from the dominant risks in preindustrial and classical industrial society. Accentuating the differences with the help of ideal types, Beck assumes that in pre-industrial high cultures the social conceptualization of risks is that of hazards and natural disasters such as the plague. These are experienced as unpredictable because they are interpreted as caused by gods and demons and are often understood as preexisting external destiny. Such hazards would have been incalculable and therefore politically neutral, because they were ascribed to external forces.[8]

In early modernity, the dominant reception and experience of hazards changed to risks that were taken voluntarily, such as smoking and driving. These risks are perceived as calculable, and if not controllable in themselves, the outcomes are seen as manageable by financial compensation. They are mainly regionally and temporally but also socially circumscribed. While the shift from pre-industrial to industrial experience of hazards is characterized by the calculability of risks, which allows effective practical control of uncertainties (justified by their practical success), with the new risks another significant shift is taking place within modernity.

Unlike pre-industrial risks, the new risks are understood as man-made side-effects of modernization, even though unexpected or ignored. But they differ from modern risks as well since they can no longer be managed by the usual modern strategies such as scientific control by knowledge[10] or statistical-probabilistic calculation of costs by insurance.[11]

Table 2.1 Risks and Hazards in Pre-Industrial, Classical, and Industrial Risk Society

	Pre-industrial high cultures	Classical industrial society	Industrial risk society
Type and example	Hazards, natural disasters, plague	Risks, accidents (occupational, traffic)	Self-jeopardy, man-made disasters
Contingent upon decisions?	No: projectable (gods, demons)	Yes: industrial development (economy, technology, organization)	Yes: nuclear, chemical, genetic industries and political safety guarantees
Voluntary (individually avoidable)?	No: assigned, pre-existing external destiny[9]	Yes (e.g. smoking, driving, skiing, occupation): rule-governed attribution	No: collective decision, individually unavoidable hazards Yes and no: organized non-responsibility
Range: who affected	Countries, peoples, cultures	Regionally, temporally, socially circumscribed, events and destruction	Undelimitable, "accidents"
Calculability (cause–effect, insurance against risks)	Open insecurity; politically neutral, because destined	Calculable, insecurity (probability, compensation)	Politically explosive hazards, which render questionable the principles of calculation and precaution

Source: Beck 1995b: 78.

In this perspective, "the entry into risk society occurs at the moment when the hazards which are now decided and consequently produced by society undermine and/or cancel the established safety systems of the welfare state's existing risk calculations" (Beck 1999: 77). Consequently, new risks question and transform these fundaments of modernization itself.

Epistemological status of risk

These considerations on the impacts of new risks have been the soil on which the critique flowered, that the risk society would give rise to a sociologically inappropriate *risk objectivism* (compare Alexander 1996a; Elliott 2002; Mythen 2004; Mythen & Walklate 2005) or at least would "waver uncertainly between a realist and weak constructionist approach" (Lupton 1999a: 28; compare the discussion by Tulloch in chapter 6 of this book).

Instead of separating realist and constructivist perspectives, Beck tries to integrate both by a concept of "risk as knowledge." In response to critiques, Beck (e.g. 1999: 23–31, 146, 150) refers to Latour and Haraway to clarify his position. Latour argues that the common distinction between nature and culture – or here between realism and constructivism – is introduced by modernity itself and is therefore a cultural ideology or construction (1993). Instead, nature and culture cannot be separated. Nature is never just nature but always culture as well, and culture never just culture but nature as well. Latour and Haraway conclude that entities are something in between, neither nature nor culture, while Beck reverses the argument and emphasizes that issues are both real and socially constructed (1999).[12]

It is important to understand the status of risk as constituted within knowledge, which implies that the tension between risk and its perception cannot be resolved. Hazards will have impacts even though we do not receive them until it is too late, or they might be hypothetical and therefore mainly brought into being by our concerns (1992b: 77). Therefore it is never clear whether it is the risks or our view of them that have intensified (1993: 55). However, our acknowledgment and knowledge about them is the basis for our activities.

Consequently, it can be argued that during the transition to a risk society, the knowledge is spreading that the sources of wealth are "polluted" by growing "hazardous side effects" (1992b: 20). The risks are real in the sense that they have real impacts, but the knowledge socially constructed by science and other instances is more or less uncertain. In contrast to early industrial risks, "nuclear, chemical, ecological and genetic engineering risks (a) can be limited in terms of neither time nor place, (b) are not accountable according to the established rules of causality, blame and liability, and (c) cannot be compensated for or insured against (Beck 1994: 2)" (Beck 1999: 77).

Knowledge is not restricted to science but includes everyday knowledge of lay-people, citizen groups, organizations, and societal institutions, often mediated by the media. Beck insists that science is still significant to make socially accepted knowledge claims. Even the recent British hysterias on mobile phones (Burgess 2004) and vaccination were supported by their alleged scientific foundation, and when the lack of scientific evidence was revealed the concerns regarding vaccination collapsed.[13] But still, the social impact of risk definitions is not determined by scientific evidence and provability (Beck 1992b: 32). Instead it is constructed by a range of social agents and science. Risks are socially brought into being by *relations of definitions.*

The concept of "relations of definition" (Beck claims to introduce the concept, analogous to Marx's relations of production) essentially says that risks are produced by all the specific rules, institutions, and capacities that structure the identification and assessment of risk in a specific sociocultural context. They are brought into being within the legal, epistemological, and cultural power matrix in which risk politics is conducted (Beck 1999: 149). Therefore Beck understands risks or hazards as "man-made hybrids" (1999: 146) or "quasi-subjects, whose acting-active quality is produced by risk societies' institutional contradictions" (1999: 150). For example, it was not the risk of BSE itself which brought the political crisis to Britain, but the institutional and political understanding, construction, or denial of possible harm which caused the crisis of its institutions later on, when BSE spread and the possibility of a link to the Creutzfeldt-Jakob disease became known. This said, BSE was produced by a specific mode of industrialized production of beef, which enables the illness to spread uncontrolled in the first place. But BSE's explosive character for the institutions involved was caused precisely by the institutional framework which failed to manage BSE properly.

Modern scientization and organized irresponsibility

The risk society thesis states that, since the notion of risk comprises hazards and their perception (or better, an expected threat), the monopoly of rationality of science is undermined (1992: 57f.). Even in the most technical considerations, risk would involve a normative component. The scientific construction of risk refers to a generally assumed consensus about the amount of risks to be taken and the directions of societal developments to be aimed for. This consensus was for a long time the priority of scientific and economic progress and wealth. Since this consensus is questioned by new risks and uncertainties, cooperation is needed "across the trenches of disciplines, citizens' groups, factories, administration and politics." However, this seems difficult to achieve; rather, more disintegrated definitions and struggles about definitions are observable (1993: 29). There are at least two reasons why the processes of negotiating risk are conflictual and contradictory.

First, knowledge production is fragmented into disciplines and specific domains within disciplines, while the risks are complex. They interact, are uneven distributed within society or cumulate socially and regionally. Therefore it is often very difficult to establish certain knowledge on causes and effects. Beck argues, for example, that thresholds for the use and emission of toxins focus on average levels of single substances. Therefore, above average concentrations and the accumulation and interaction of different substances are underestimated. Moreover, negative lists of forbidden or restricted substances always systematically lag behind the invention of new substances, because unless the harmful quality of such substances is proven, they are allowed. Finally, the strategy of showing by experiments with animals that substances are harmless is no substitute for the knowledge of how substances affect humans.[14]

Second, as long as measures can only be taken when the harm of a substance is proven beyond doubt, science supports and covers ongoing production of harms and dangers and the poisoning of the environment. When we acknowledge acceptable levels of emission of harmful substances by single factories, the risks of cumulative and interactive effects are covered and polluters are not held responsible for such effects. The "polluter pays" principle thereby supports the non-responsibility of the perpetrators. Finally, the assumption that a specific level of final probability would imply safety legitimizes a high level of risk: for example, the assumption that accidents such as happened in Chernobyl could never happen in nuclear power stations in western Europe. Beck argues that all these institutional forms which define risks at the same time legitimize and produce risks. They follow logics of *organized irresponsibility* (1992b: 62–9; 1995b: 58–69; 1999: 6).[15]

As a result, science does not lose its significance in producing legitimate knowledge and truth, but its previously indisputable authority is questioned. Beck argues that this indicates a systematic change within science during modernization.

Reflexive scientization

Even though science is part of the systematic production of risks, it is still the medium and solution to manage new risks (Beck 1992: 155). As a consequence, science undergoes an internal transformation.

In early modernity, scientization is understood and proceeds as an application of science to a given nature, people, and society (1993: 154). Scientific critique is organized and managed within science, while to the outside the claim of truth production is relatively unquestioned (1993: 164). Science convinces societal critique by its success or applicability and its social or economic benefit.

Confronted with its products, defects, and latent side-effects and secondary problems, science would shift to a reflexive phase. In *reflexive scientization* the claim of truth production and the enlightening character of its project is systematically demystified. Scientization continues but the internal and external relationships of science change (1993: 154). "The target groups and users of scientific results – in politics and business, mass media and everyday life – become more dependent on scientific arguments in general," while they become at the same time more "independent of individual findings and the judgment of science regarding the truth and reality of its statements" (1993: 167). One can select for one's own interest from a range of scientific theories and empirically proven knowledge.

As a result of its contradictory transformation, science is still necessary to give arguments persuasiveness and can therefore still be used to emancipate from social practice. But science can also be used to immunize ideologies and interests against the enlightening power of science. Because science is no longer the only unquestionable instance of truth, it has become part of social conflicts itself: for example, regarding the question what kind of science is to be applied and which areas of research are to be supported (e.g. on nuclear power or alternative forms of energy production). It is no longer science alone which determines the validity of knowledge. Instead science is dependent on societal acceptance and ethical compatibility (Weingart 1984: 66, cited in Beck 1986: 272f.) or political considerations in general.

In the early 1980s a number of studies showed how laboratory science produces its own knowledge, captured in specific assumptions of real life which repeatedly fail in practice and contribute to a critical public attitude regarding expertise and scientifically produced knowledge (Wynne 1982a, 1987, 1989). When laboratory science is applied, it is confronted with the practices of everyday life and local specialties. Wynne repeatedly showed – for example, in the discussions on the ban of the herbicide 2,4,5-T "Agent Orange" – how scientific knowledge covered the dangerous and harmful effects of the herbicide. The assumption was that the use of the herbicide "offers no hazard to users, to the general public, to domestic animals and to wildlife or to the environment generally, provided that the product is used as directed" (1989: 36). Therefore, the arguments of forestry and farm workers regarding the negative side-effects were seen as anecdotal and an application to ban the pesticide by the National Union of Agricultural and Allied Workers was rejected. Indeed, the scientists who tested the harmfulness of Agent Orange in their laboratories were right that it does not cause harm under laboratory conditions, but in everyday life these proper conditions were rarely met. After many unsuccessful attempts, Agent Orange was finally banned when it was proven that the laboratory assumptions regarding how it should be used did not meet real-life circumstances. Instead the pesticide caused harm and illness to the people who applied it.

Moreover, research on nuclear power and other high-risk technologies shows that experts and lay-people refer to different risks. While the experts balance the gains (cheap energy production) against possible deaths (Starr 1969) in the normal production process, lay-people regularly refer to the impacts of possible accidents even though they are very unlikely. When catastrophes such as happened in Chernobyl or personal catastrophes such as immediate death or major injury are considered, people tend to reject weighing risks and gains or profits at all. As a result, the implicit normative assumption which favors profit or progress is confronted by another position which prioritizes personal or future generations' security and quality of life. It is not science as such but the involved value decisions which are the cause of conflict. The inherent assumed necessities become the object of discourse. That is not about the politicalization of science. The crucial question is rather which kind of science to apply. This problem can be illustrated by the international conflicts on climate change.

While a growing alliance on reducing greenhouse gas has been formed, the main polluters such as the USA, India, and China are still resistant to joining in, even though slow seem to take place more recently. They resist changing their production logic, as is implied in the reduction of greenhouse gas CO_2 and suggested by the Kyoto protocol. Instead the US government is supporting scientists in developing ways of directly reducing the temperature of the atmosphere using smoke and giant space mirrors.[16] The implication is obvious. If we could control climate warming in the future, there would be no need to change our behavior today. Instead of acting cautiously, the production of wealth at the expense of nature could continue in an unrestricted way. It is exactly this logic of science in believing that we will always have a chance to manage the outcomes of today's activities in the future which is questioned by Beck. Instead of focusing on the outcomes, causes and prevention gain importance, and how we could learn without producing irreversible outcomes (Beck 1992b: 174f.).

Beck suggests reintegrating specialized and fragmented knowledge and establishing a new "*pedagogy of scientific* rationality which would conceive of that rationality as changeable by discussion of self-produced threats." This is about the idea of new forms of " 'self-control' and 'self-limitation' " of science (1992b: 181). Consequently, science and scientific development become involved in political processes which are discussed later on as part of "subpolitics."

However, according to Beck scientific-technological risks are not the only driving force for modernization. As part of the self-transformation of society, they are complemented by the risks and uncertainties which accompany *institutional individualism.*

The Self-Transformation of the Social: Institutional Individualism

The dynamics which result from technological-environmental risks overlap with other social transformations in individuals' life-world which cause social, biographical, and cultural risks and insecurities (1992b: 87). This second stream of social developments which drive industrial society into reflexive modernity is captured by the notion of *individualization*. "Individualization" is understood as a *new contradictory mode of societalization*[17] (1992b: 90, 127) that reshapes the basic structures and reproduction modes of industrial society, such as social class, family, gender relations and status, marriage, parenthood, and occupations (1992b: 87).

While in 1986 Beck assumed that individualization would take place in most of the industrialized western societies (1992b: 91, except Britain or France, footnote 2, 101f.), Beck and Beck-Gernsheim much more carefully formulate in 2002 (p. 33f.) that the "trends toward individualization ... have been realized in very few countries [yet] and even then only during the most recent phase of development". Individualization is seen as a rather complex process which depends on a range of contingent developments such as "economic prosperity, the construction of a welfare state, the institutionalization of interests represented by trade unions, the legal underpinning of labor contrasts, the expansion of education, the growth of the service sector and associated opportunities for mobility and the shortening of the working week".

The notion of individualization must not be confused with individualism, growing egoism, market individualism, or atomization. Nor is it about personalization, uniqueness, or emancipation. That might be true, but the opposite is possible as well (Beck 1992b: 128). Therefore individualization is seen as a *contradictory* mode of societalization (1992b: 90, 127) which is positioned on the institutional level, as *institutional individualism*. Beck is at pains to emphasize that he is referring to individualization as a concept of objective life situation and its demands and expectations. It is less about subjective consciousness and identity (1992b: 128). Outlining an ahistorical model of individualization, he explicitly neglects to say anything about the right side of table 2.2 which is about consciousness and identity. Instead he claims to argue about the objective life situation shown on the left side. Both columns are also blank because individualization is not restricted to the twentieth century. Instead we can trace back individualization processes at least to the Renaissance (the primary thrust of individualization) and the late nineteenth century (the secondary thrust) and can distinguish these earlier phases of intensified individualization from most recent processes (the tertiary thrust; compare Junge 1996: 734).

Table 2.2 The Ahistorical Model of Individualization.[18]

	Life situation: Objective	*Consciousness/identity:* Subjective
Liberation:		
Loss of stability:		
Reintegration:		

Source: Beck 1992: 128.

Beck analytically distinguishes between three aspects of individualization (1992b: 128): *removal or liberation, loss of stability,* and *reintegration.*

The *liberation dimension* stands for people's "removal" or "liberation" from "historically prescribed social forms and commitments in the sense of traditional contexts of dominance and support" (ibid.). Applied to the more recent changes within modernization, this means that people are increasingly set free from the sociocultural forms and institutions of class milieus and the societal division of labor between men and women (1992b: 87). Many of these traditional forms are eroded and supplanted by decisions (compare in more detail the paragraphs below on "Beyond Social Class" and "Gender Relations").

Liberation goes along with a *loss of stability.* In the disenchantment dimension, traditional securities regarding "practical knowledge, faith and guiding norms" lose value in orienting individuals' activities (ibid.). There are no longer unquestioned traditions available, referring to the nature of men and women. Instead family relationships, gender roles, and the division of labor have to be negotiated and justified. We can no longer apply them unquestioned. Moreover, the idea of life-long full-time employment in the same occupation, which developed particularly in Germany after World War II, has been at least partly supplanted by more flexible working conditions and structural unemployment (Beck 2000a).

Finally, people are reintegrated by new social commitments of *secondary institutions* such as the welfare state and markets (Beck 1992b: 131). Secondary institutions establish a new immediacy of the individual and society, and thereby risks and uncertainties. Individuals are even more affected by

> fashions, social policy, economic cycles and markets, contrary to the image of individual control which establishes itself in consciousness. Thus it

is precisely individualized private existence which becomes more and more obviously and emphatically dependent on situations and conditions that completely escape its reach ... Individualization thus takes effect precisely under general social conditions which allow an individual autonomous private existence even less than before. (1992b: 131)

To make this point quite clear, individualization means dependency on the market and welfare state. It hands over people to an external control and standardization that was unknown before (1992b: 132). Consequently, the individualized biographies become influenced even more directly by politics and market dynamics (1992b: 132). This takes place in a world where the norms of autonomous decision making and shaping one's own life course and identities spread. Even where no decisions are made because of a lack of alternatives or resources, the individual has to pay for the decisions not taken. Instead the individual moves from situation to situation, which has to be managed and decided *reflexively*,[19] without enough material and immaterial resources available. Under such conditions, where the control of one's own biography is increasingly improbable, a model of a self which orients people's activities is even more important to maintain their ability to act (1992b: 136). As a result, a growing subjectivization and individualization of risks takes place. In addition to the increase in risks, one must manage and bear new risks, such as the chosen, changed, and ascribed personal identity (1992b: 136).

Sometimes the notion of individualization is misunderstood as pure positive liberation from traditional bonds or surmounting of social inequalities. But both are wrong. There is a strong tension between the sociocultural framing of individualization as self-fulfillment or "liberation" and the "new political economy of uncertainty and risk." The individual's situation in the individualized society is rather one of *precarious freedoms*. "All too swiftly, the 'elective', 'reflexive' or 'do-it-yourself' biography can become the breakdown biography" (Beck 1999b: 12; Beck & Beck-Gernsheim 2002: 2f.).

Beyond class milieus

The core arguments for the individualization of class milieus – in particular, the working class – are the following. During industrialization, the pauperization of the working class supported the development of self-organized safety systems such as the friendly societies in Britain, which contributed to the development of a working-class consciousness based on mutual help and strong behavioral rules (Thompson 1963). With the introduction of welfare state legislation, such forms of collectivization were desiccated. The advantages of the more comprehensive state social welfare system were accompanied by a formalized insurance technology which no longer depends on direct regional control and mutual solidarity.

The decline of laborers in favor of employees during the twentieth century is another indication of the change in working conditions, as is the loss of members and influence of the trade unions. Moreover, ongoing individualization is supported by new forms of production which go along with a relative independence of professions and firms, a flexibilization of working hours, and decentralization of the work site. Instead new forms of flexible, pluralized underemployment take place in traditional sectors as well as the growing service sector (Beck 1992b, 2000c).

However, the risk society argues that the relations of inequality remain relatively stable (1992b: 87) or even increase while the material standard of living improves, and social security systems in many western industrialized countries protect and support people to cope with hardships of life. As a result, the citizens who are now removed from class-specific culture, commitments, and support systems are urged to manage their labor market biographies individually (ibid.). Liberated from sociocultural structures, they even have to choose between social group affiliation, lifestyles, and identities, with all the side-effects, and have to take the responsibility for themselves.

As a result, inequalities in an individualized society can no longer be explained by class consciousness and antagonism. Unemployment and poverty become part of working life in all social strata and a temporary experience for a growing number of people. Even though some social groups are still more affected by unemployment than others, this does not produce a new class consciousness. Instead it is experienced as individual failure and private fate (Beck 1992b: 88; Beck & Beck-Gernsheim 2002: 34, 52).

Beck concludes that "under the conditions of a welfare state, class biographies, which are somehow ascribed, become transformed into reflexive biographies which depend on the decisions of the actor" (1992b: 88). People have notoriously to decide without having the time and knowledge for carefully weighing their decisions, and there is little certain knowledge available regarding the future of labor-market dynamics and welfare state policy to which people can refer to. The result is that the "dynamism of the labor market backed up by the welfare state has diluted or dissolved the social classes *within* capitalism. To put it in Marxist terms, we increasingly confront the phenomenon of a capitalism *without* classes, but with individualized social inequality and all the related social and political problems" (1992b: 88).

Gender relations

It is not only changing class culture which drives modernization. At the same time, the social division of labor between men and women is challenged. That again is most plausible as a change within rather than beyond modernization. Industrial society is and always was a semi-industrial and semi-feudal society. Early modernity transformed the gender relations of feudal society into the new industrialized status-like division of labor where women were pinned down to the reproduction sphere of the family in the private, while men were fully available to the production sphere. Thus, industrialized society was only possible on the basis of the new division of labor. Since it was often understood as following the nature of men and women, it was protected against critique (1992b: 89).

During ongoing modernization, feminism claims equal rights for women with increasing success. This leads to a significant reduction in gender inequalities, even though they nevertheless remain in many domains. The traditional housewife's existence, financially covered by marriage and systematic differences in educational attainment, has changed. Technical facilitation of housework, the social acceptance of double-earning families, and the equalizing of school-level attainment support women's claim to an own piece of life to be shaped by them-selves (Beck-Gernsheim 1983). No longer can the lack of education justify lower wages or unfavorable career prospects. The whole distri-bution of labor within society and the family is under question. As a result, the modern family model is supplanted by a *negotiated provi-sional family* where gender relations and shares of work have to be con-tinuously negotiated. Consequently, even to follow the traditional model becomes a decision, as given "natural" patterns no longer exist.

New life situations and biographical patterns appear, such as succes-sive marriages with children from different relationships, which would lead to complex family relations. A growing number of single parents occur, and bringing up children alone is no longer exclusively seen as "abnormal" but is another possibility. The "patchwork biography" supplants the traditional pattern as a normal biographical expectation. In a *culture of divorce* (Hackstaff 1999), some couples are rather surprised when they find themselves still together after many years of cohabitation.

Self-culture

Beck and Beck-Gernsheim (2002: 42) assume that all these changes in the labor force and family relations are accompanied by an increasing self-culture which will develop to the extent that proletarian culture and bourgeois culture fade away. Self-culture is not restricted to the middle class but rather affects all societal strata, even though the specific effects on different social milieus are not known and are difficult to predict. Demographic data reflect such a change in a growing number of single-person households and a correspondingly high value placed on an autonomous and individually shaped sphere of life.

Beck and Beck-Gernsheim (2002: 43) single out three characteristics of self-culture. In a self-culture one is searching for and creating a self by developing an "aesthetically satisfying life-style." This goes along with an emphasis on freedom and autonomy in everyday life and is accompanied by a focus on practice and concrete problems and outcomes. It leads to prioritizing activities and engagements which cause direct results and personal gains, instead of responding to externally given policies prescribed by and decided within formalized hierarchical organizations in the political system. However, the authors emphasize that such a culture is not the same as emancipation. It may quite easily appear together with xenophobia, violence, and all manner of panic movements as well.

The individualization thesis can be summarized as follows. People are "*set free* from the social forms of industrial society – class, stratification, family, gender status of men and women" (Beck 1992b: 87). "*The individual himself or herself becomes the reproduction unit of the social in the lifeworld*" (1992: 90). That must not be equated with successful emancipation. "The detraditionalized individuals become dependent on the labor market and *with* that, dependent on education, consumption, regulations and support from social laws, traffic planning, product offers, possibilities and fashions in medical, psychological and pedagogical counseling and care. All of this points to the special forms of control which are being established here" (ibid.). "Intensification and individualization of social inequalities interlock." As a consequence, problems of the system are lessened politically and transformed into personal failure. In the detraditionalized modes of living, a new immediacy for individual and society arises, the immediacy of crisis and sickness, in the sense that social crises appear to be of individual origin, and are perceived as social only indirectly and to a very limited extent" (1992b: 89).

The former two lines of argumentation on new risks and individualization mutually complement in contributing to the transformation of the political.

The Political within Risk Society and Reflexive Modernization

The change of the political is a central issue in Beck's theorizing. It originates in his thesis of a change from a society primarily driven by class conflicts to a society driven by risk conflicts (1992b: 154). Class solidarity and pauperization would no longer have revolutionary impact, but society would be driven by the (assumed) effect of new risks. Nuclear power, climate change, genetically modified food, and so forth would concern people relatively independent of social class affiliation, while traditional risks are still allocated by class indicators.

Beck argues that even though unequal possibilities to respond to new risks might remain, the individual's chances of escaping risks decline (1992b: 36). We can, for example, try not to eat food produced with genetically modified plants, but without sufficient knowledge and control, it is difficult to prevent it. We can try to eat only ecologically produced meat, but when an illness such as BSE spreads, we might not be able to control it better by more resources or social capital. Finally, when we do not yet have the knowledge about the harmful character of an ingredient of our food, we can take measures only afterward. The result might be permanent concern about the unknown harms of food production without the possibility of preventing them. As such risks cannot be escaped, to some degree they have an egalitarianizing (or one might say "democratizing") effect. They do not distinguish between the poor and the rich. Therefore new risks would support the development of political coalitions and solidarity beyond class. These coalitions are not only initiated by the assumed affectedness of risks, but depend on the individualized creation of self-identity as well.

A similar argument applies at the international level. While international inequalities in the relationships between industrialized and Third World nations remain ("pollution follows the poor") (Beck 1992b, 1999: 5), some risks which have been successfully externalized to developing countries, such as the use of pesticides like DDT in food production, come back to us. So-called "boomerang effects" (Beck 1992b: 37f.) demonstrate that in a far-reaching perspective we cannot escape the risks we have produced (also obvious for climate change, etc.) and support the argument for a world risk society.

Risk and wealth conflicts become interwoven in many respects. That is clearly demonstrated in the discussion regarding climate change. Third World countries try to take their chance to get more money from the wealthy. Nations which still rely heavily on wealth production at the expense of the environment, such as the USA, India, and China, continue to resist making any far-reaching commitments to reduce their carbon dioxide production significantly.[20] It is mainly the wealthy industrialized nation states in Europe which support stronger legislation on carbon dioxide emission.[21] According to the world risk society (Beck 1999), such conflicts in the public sphere would be dominated by all-embracing new risks; even though wealth issues are involved, they are subordinated.

The coalition of anxiety, self-culture, and the question of the political subject

In *Risk Society* (1992b) Beck argued that concerns about new risks would lead to the creation of a new political subject. Social resistance would no longer be established by social class, but by new interest coalitions, so-called *coalitions of anxiety*, between different class members, occupational groups, generations, and civic action groups (1992b: 62).[22] Coalitions of anxiety rely not on class knowledge but on risk knowledge, which regularly lacks direct personal experience (1992b: 53). Therefore all the competitions, conflicts, and negotiations of defining risks and risk knowledge become crucial, and all the institutions which provide us with knowledge, such as the media, non-governmental organizations (NGOs), and consumer organizations, gain importance.

As a result, the political potential of the *risk society* rests on the production, dissemination, and negotiation of knowledge about risks.

Beck originally emphasized the *ecological morality* which would force cohesion in the *coalition of anxiety*. It is based on the wish not to become affected by any harmful side-effects of technological and industrial developments (1992b: 49f.), and includes a more apocalyptic prospect, the threat to all human life on earth. Referring to Hobbes, Beck claimed that the ecological crisis would breach fundamental rights not to endanger the preconditions of survival of the human species (1995a: 8f.). But he doubted whether anxiety could help to constitute a basis for a new relatively stable political subject (1992b: 49f.) comparable with Marx's working class.

However, new social movements respond not only to increasing risks, risk consciousness, and risk conflicts (Beck & Beck-Gernsheim 2002: 44). In addition, they are linked to other social changes within social classes and class structure, family forms and parenthood, gender status, or occupations. Social groups experiment with personal life, relationships and one's own body in the numerous variants of the alternative and youth subcultures (Beck 1992: 90). They use the new institutional space for developing a *self-culture politics* (Beck & Beck-Gernsheim 2002: 44) which is close to Giddens' concept of "life politics" (1991). Thus, a new political field of decision making occurs in everyday life. Formerly nonpolitical decisions such as what to eat or drink become highly political. During the BSE crisis we had to decide whether to believe the politicians and still eat beef or not. We can also decide whether we would like to support farmers in developing countries by buying fair trade food, to support small-scale ecological food production by local farmers, or to support large-scale food production by the big corporations. Finally, Beck refers to the Brent Spar controversy (Beck 1999: 40ff.) to illustrate how deciding where to fill the petrol tank of one's car became a highly political act which finally persuaded Shell not to dump its oil rig in the Atlantic. Beck and Beck-Gernsheim (2002: 45) argue that such activities which indicate the emergence of a new *political consumer* are very different from the common forms of state-organized parliamentary politics.

Growing self-politics is a response to the failure of state politics. It is a response to a lack of direct influence in indirect representative democracy where the power of citizens is limited to electing the parliament without having effective means of influencing the political process later on. Self-politics and conventional politics do not replace each other. Rather, they compete to influencing decision making in all areas of society (Beck & Beck-Gernsheim 2002: 45f.).

Interest groups and grass-roots movements are important in triggering and constituting critique and resistance, even though they are not "the political subject" in the risk society. Instead, Beck argues, since new global risks potentially affect everyone in the world risk society, the political subject is at the same time everybody and nobody (1999: 150; 1992b: 49). The political subject of the risk society is constituted by relatively short-term coalitions between a range of different political actors which populate and form the domain of *subpolitics*.

Subpolitics

Self-politics is part of the more general concept of *subpolitics*, which Beck introduced in order to show the significant changes that took place in the form of the political during modernization. In short, the notion of *subpolitics* refers to a new domain of politics outside and beyond the representative institutions and democratically legitimized policies of the political system of nation states (1999: 39, 91).

Beck claims that within industrial society the idea of a political domain as constituted by the state's political institutions (parliament etc.) and the institutionally vested rights of the *citoyen* (to political participation) can be distinguished from a non-political domain consisting of private interests in the field of work and business of a *bourgeois* (competing economically and shaping its private family life; 1992b: 183). In the nonpolitical domain, techno-economic innovations and developments and their accompanying side-effects were legitimized by the expected and achieved increase in well-being or the commonly shared ideology of "social change through progress" (1992b: 184f.).

This distinction between political and nonpolitical might be too sharp, but it is this ideal model which forms the basis for the concept of the regulatory capacity of the state, which was questioned during the 1970s in most western industrial states. Indeed, growing concerns about the influence of stakeholders and interest groups on political decision making in the "gray area of corporatism" (1992b: 188) and concerns regarding increasingly ungovernable societies are expressions of the relative loss of power and autonomy of the political system or the blurring boundaries between the political and the nonpolitical.

The demarcation between the political and the non-political holds as long as the development of productive forces and of scientization neither exceeds the radius of possible political actions nor threatens the model of social change through progress (1992b: 184f.). The fundamental changes within modernity – most significantly, "the continuing destruction of external and internal nature; the systemic transformation of work; the fragility of status-based gender orders; the loss of class traditions and the intensification of social inequalities; new technologies balancing on the verge of catastrophe" – blurred the boundaries between the political and the nonpolitical (1992b: 185f.).

On the one hand, formerly political decisions have migrated into the nonpolitical sphere. For example, decisions regarding conditions of work are dictated by international firms and market competition, which decrease the scope of individual nations for political regulation, while the European Union increasingly restricts autonomous national decisions in a growing number of areas. On the other hand, techno-scientific developments promise economical success but are accompanied by incalculable risks which can no longer be managed nationally. The innovations and developments of the techno-scientific system become political without actually returning its power to the political system. Politics is rather compelled to legitimize or respond to decisions already made elsewhere (1992b: 186f.). But sometimes an alarmed public urges politicians to regulate, and firms to restrict, the production and dissemination of new risks, such as for example produced by genetically modified food. That indicates the growth of a sub-political domain where techno-economical developments are discussed openly in the public. In subpolitical domains,

> legally responsible, governmental monitoring agencies and a risk-sensitive media publicity sphere begin to talk their way into and govern the "intimate sphere" of plant management. The direction of development and the results of technological transformation become fit for discourse and subject to legitimation. Thus business and techno-scientific action acquire a new political and moral dimension that had previously seemed alien to techno-economic activity. If one wished, one might say that the devil of the economy must sprinkle himself with the holy water of public morality and put on a halo of concern for society and nature. (1992b: 186)

The concept of subpolitics is often understood as a "bottom-up model" of politics (Mythen 2004: 170), following Beck's formulation that "subpolitics means the shaping of society from below caught up in the storms of political debate" (1999: 39). But this is misleading.

Even though the public is an important part of subpolitics, the latter is not necessarily the idea of a resistance built up from the bottom to the top. Rather other political actors such as NGOs legitimize their political claims by public support (which is not very distinct from the idea of democracy, but the form is more direct). The regularly used example is that of Shell's attempt to dump the Brent Spar oil rig into the deep water of the North Atlantic (Beck 1999: 40ff.; Holzer & Sørensen 2003: 85f.; Mythen 2004: 37, 49, 67). It was not so much the public which started the discourse, but a public discourse and a boycott initiated by Greenpeace which mobilized a large number of consumers,[23] well beyond the numbers organized in grass-roots organizations, green parties, or citizen groups.

This kind of subpolitics covers only *active subpolitics*, while *passive subpolitics* follows a different logic (Holzer & Sørensen 2003). Beck cited examples in science and medicine where the internal decisions and technical developments exceeded the common rules and norms, and urged politics and law to find regulations for already developed and applied possibilities to act (subpolitics of medicine, 1992b: 204–12; subpolitics of industrial automation, ibid.: 215–23). For example, the invention of in vitro fertilization was already being applied in the late 1970s and 1980s while in most European countries the political and legal consequences were still being discussed. Medicine was already producing social facts while the political and legal system tried to catch up with the practical consequences. (E.g. should it only be available for married partners or for single mothers as well? What should be the rules for implanting the embryos after fertilization? And who is responsible in the case of faulty selection?)

Beck discusses possible developments of the political in a globalizing world in further publications on cosmopolitism (Beck 2005a, 2006). He builds onto the two core concepts of the risk society thesis, the crisis of global risks (which includes not only ecological risks but social crises such as in financial markets as well), and the tensions between old and new boundaries and cultural identities. Both lead to a "mélange principle" at the world level. This includes cosmopolitan empathy and perspective taking as well as attempts to redraw old boundaries (2006: 7). In a global perspective, Beck consequently distinguishes between *subpolitics from below*, within the logic of the nation state, and *subpolitics from above* (2007: 188), which refers to transnational decision-making coalitions beyond the nation states, and would express a growing cosmopolitism.

Risks and Uncertainties in Reflexive Modernity

In the work on risk society and reflexive modernization there is a shift in emphasis from technological-environmental risks and individualization to the general logic of change in potentially all social domains within modernization. The explosive powers of risks as well as processes of individualization remain important, accompanied by an increasing focus on the effects of globalization. But theorizing on reflexive modernization focuses more generally on the blurring and multiplying of boundaries and manufactured uncertainties in all areas of society, which take place as a result of a critical mass of unintended side-effects of modernization (Beck et al. 2003: 2; Beck & Lau 2005).

To show how modernity transforms itself, and indeed does not dissolve, reflexive modernization theorizing distinguishes between *basic principles* of modernization, which remain in reflexive modernity, and *fundamental institutions* which change (Beck & Lau 2005; Beck 2007).[24] For example, the basic principle of statehood remains while the basic institution of the nation state is subject to change (Beck & Lau 2005: 532), and the idea of marriage as an organized form of living together remains while the traditional institution of the family fundamentally changes.

The perspective is Eurocentric (Beck et al. 2003: 7), referring to a specific historical constellation where the institutions of first modernity are already well developed, as the nation state, a welfare state (at least rudimentary), highly developed institutions of science and technology, and the institutionalized expectation of full employment. Only then can the assumed transformations take place.

Accordingly, a significant insight has been gained in more recent theorizing on reflexive modernization (Beck et al. 2004). Research in Reflexive Modernization Research Center has shown that it is not the clear-cut change from early modern *either/or* logic to the *both/and* principle, but new and different mixtures of both principles that indicate reflexive modernization. The new complements rather than supplants the old in many respects.

Table 2.3 General Criteria for Reflexive Modernization

	Simple, or first modern society	*Reflexive, or second modern society*	*Postmodern society*
The nature of boundaries	• Unambiguous, institutionally guaranteed boundaries (between social spheres, between nature and culture, between scientific and unscientific)	• A multiplicity of boundaries and fundamental distinctions • Recognition of this multiplicity • The necessity of institutionalizing self-consciously fictive boundaries • New problems of institutionalized decision making (conflicts of responsibility and boundary conflicts)	• A multiplicity tending toward the dissolution of boundaries • Recognition of this multiplicity

Source: Beck et al. 2003: 22.

Beck et al. (2003: 22) have introduced the following criteria to identify a change from the unambiguous, institutionally guaranteed boundaries (between social spheres, between nature and society, between scientific and unscientific) of first modernity (see table 2.3): In a growing number of social domains, a multiplicity of boundaries and fundamental distinctions supplant clear-cut institutional boundaries. This multiplicity is increasingly recognized, as is the necessity of institutionalizing self-consciously fictive boundaries. As a result, new problems and solutions for institutionalized decision making take place (Beck et al. 2003: 22). Beck et al. are at pains to argue that this is different from the claims of postmodernism that the multiplicity of boundaries would tend toward the dissolution of boundaries.

They identify several forms of how the multiplicity of boundaries, their recognition and the need to decide lead to new forms of institutional (and individual) strategies in all social domains. (For a more detailed overview, see: Beck & Lau 2005: 540ff.; Beck et al. 2003: 13ff.) One classical example is the change in family structures, which leads to new mixing of boundaries and institutional changes. With a growing number of single parents, same-sex couples with and without children, children from egg or sperm donation who would like to meet their biological mother or father, etc. further legislation is necessary to manage the new forms of living and intimate relationships. It is exactly this acceptance of the old and the new which indicates reflexive modernization, while institutional arrangements are under pressure to catch up with the new realities of living. This is a conflict-ridden process where different groups negotiate or argue about preserving old institutions and acknowledging actual and new forms of living. This is very obvious in social conflicts about the status of the "classical" family as something original which must still be supported and distinguished from other forms of living, such as unmarried couples and same-sex partnerships with or without children. While fragmented families and remarriages etc. were well-known throughout the Middle Ages, from first modernity onwards they were seen as deviations from the ideal model. Today, the idea of accepting deviations as normal or just another option is gaining ground, even though they are considered less desirable or are contested by different milieus and interest groups.

Another central example, which has already been presented, concerns claims to knowledge of experts and lay-people. The boundaries between scientific expert knowledge and lay-people's knowledge has become blurred. Scientific knowledge can no longer conclude a dispute where different expertise or a lack of certain knowledge exists. If there is no firm ground on which we can decide, new rules have to be established as the precautionary principle. Beck et al.'s (2003) argument that such decisions cannot be justified on scientific grounds only shifts the decision from pure science to the democratic negotiation of what is socially desirable. Thus, growing public controversies regarding risky decisions are an indication of a shift to reflexive modernization.

The last instance aims at the notion of the subject. In reflexive modernization, formerly unquestioned routines are supplanted by decisions. A multiplicity of possibilities and contradictory alternatives make decisions more difficult or even impossible. It is not just our own decisions but the decisions of others which make the future under conditions of individualization even more uncertain and in the long term lead to a change in the notion of the individual. The individual as a *quasi-subject* is no longer understood as a stable and unchangeable subject, as in first modernity, but as "the result as well as the producer of its networks, situation, location and form" (Beck et al. 2003: 25). The argument is that individuals' control of the life course decreases, while we expect and present ourselves even more as authors of our own biography. The *de jure* idea of an autonomously deciding and acting subject is preserved, while *de facto* this idea is even more impossible and unreal. Precisely this paradoxical situation is acknowledged in a book title by a Munich author, *You Have No Chance, Take It!* (Achternbusch 1983).

Critique

The merit of Beck's work in introducing risk, uncertainty, and ignorance as central categories of sociological theorizing is accompanied by a range of critiques which have been repeatedly directed at his work. Constructivists criticize his (alleged) risk objectivism (Alexander 1996a, 1996b; Lupton 1999a; Elliott 2002; Mythen 2004), which might be most obvious in *Ecological Politics in an Age of Risk* (1995b). However, a radical constructivist position has itself been criticized recently (see Tulloch in chapter 6 of this book, as well as post-social approaches of Knorr Cetina, 2003, and the actor network theory, Latour 2005). Beck's perspective therefore seems to flow in a similar vein to recent approaches which reconcile the contradictory positions of realist and constructivist epistemologies.

There is a more serious weakness within risk society regarding culture. While intending to sort out the new against the old, the *risk society* focuses on the new individualized culture which indulges a society integrated by individuals. Sociocultural backgrounds are seen (as by Luhmann or by Foucault) as a societal source of sense making, but there is no systematic conceptualization of specific characteristics of available cultures, milieus, or individuals' lifestyles. The question of how a society of individuals could be integrated when overall values are not available is still unanswered from the perspective of Beck and Beck-Gernsheim (2002) because they have not yet taken into account the sociocultural forms between (Douglas 1992) and the "embodied" foundation of the individual (compare Lyng 2005c). Even though risk culture (Lash 2000) might tend to neglect institutional and structural aspects of the risk society (Beck 2000b: 213), the question remains whether significant aspects in understanding the dynamics of risk societies get lost when we neglect the specific commitments and structural power of sociocultural milieus and lifestyles and the different personal needs or wishes for security.

Furthermore, the dissolution of social class consciousness as a result of individualization processes might be convincing in many respects. But when social inequalities regarding health and illness, for instance, are still cumulating in specific social strata, the question of the reproductive mechanisms of these inequalities has to be clarified. However, Beck's theorizing does not explain the continuities of such inequalities, which is vital to gain a fuller picture of the social.

Beck claims that "in the individualized society the individual must therefore learn, on pain of permanent disadvantage, to conceive of himself or herself as the center of action, as the planning office with respect to his/her own biography, abilities, orientations, relationships and so on" (Beck 1992b: 135). In the risk society, the normatively demanded self-ascription of individuals' fate competes with the counter-factual experiences of a lack of controllability. But why shouldn't a new humility or belief in coincidences take place in order to cope with the uncertainties of reflexive modernity? It is not yet clear whether a rejection of societal normative demands of the morals of market individualism or self-culture will necessarily cause "permanent disadvantage." Instead, we might even be better off in a world of uncertainties when we have some certain ground to stand on.

A theoretical approach which attempts to conceptualize the central social change at the macro level is often criticized for a lack of detail in (historical) analysis which would be needed to understand social change correctly. Careful historical analyses are obviously necessary to develop sound historical theorizing. This said, research which focuses on descriptive historical analyses tends to neglect theoretical generalization and loses the fruitfulness of hypothesis regarding possible futures. But we need some generalizations and general hypotheses to direct research. In particular, the question needs to be addressed of what other futures can be imagined and how social developments could take another direction. Moreover, general theories are often fruitful in triggering further research initiatives.

Perspectives

Since the risk society thesis is directed to the future, there is an ongoing task of observing whether and how social developments differ from previous observations and whether and where readjustments are needed. Furthermore, the theory outlines several paths for further consideration of such fundamental concepts as side-effects, differences between risks, the link between inequality and risk reproduction, and so on.

For example, a better understanding is needed of the sociocultural processes which shape the social if it is not fully determined by secondary institutions of markets and welfare policy. Further research and theorizing on the different strategies, everyday theories, or biographical constructions (compare Zinn 2004, 2005) which are used to manage the uncertainties of the risk society can help. This includes a more elaborated notion of emotions beyond the "anxiety thesis" and its impacts on the everyday.

It is important to acknowledge that there is no clear transition from an either/or to a both/and society. Rather, both logics take place at the same time (Beck & Lau 2005). Therefore future research might focus on the different sociocultural forms that societies develop during transformation toward a risk society. This said, they might never reach a fully developed risk society or reflexive modernity, but might be different forms of modernity which always link some "feudal," "traditional," or other forms of certainty constructions to the risks and uncertainties socially produced and managed. Some societies might be driven by a *culture of fear*. Others might be better described with a concept of life-cycles of risk discourses. There are certainly huge differences in people's experiences of individualization within nation states, which depend on the degrees of social security delivered by a strong or weak welfare state. Whether people are mainly "liberated" into the incalculable insecurities of the market, where they have to bear all the uncertainties themselves, or whether a welfare state delivers an amount of safety which allows them to act successfully within an uncertain world makes a huge difference to personal well-being and the individual's appetite to take risks.

Finally, it is still not fully understood under what conditions nonpolitical decisions become political and enter the sphere of subpolitics while others remain nonpolitical. The spectacular case of Shell and Brent Spar does not seem to be the rule, but leans toward exemption of publicly organized discourse coalitions. Obviously a complex set of circumstances have to coincide to mobilize such a broad political coalition.

Further reading

Adam, B., Beck, U. & Loon, J. V. (2000) *The Risk Society and Beyond: Critical Issues for Social Theory*. Sage, London and Thousand Oaks, Calif.

Beck, U. (1992) *Risk Society: Towards a New Modernity*. Sage, London and Newbury Park, Calif.

Beck, U. (1999) *World Risk Society*. Polity, Malden, Mass.

Beck, U. (2002) The terrorist threat: world risk society revisited. *Theory, Culture & Society*, 19(4), 39–55.

On individualization

Beck, U. & Beck-Gernsheim, E. (2002) *Individualization: Institutionalized Individualism and its Social and Political Consequences*. Sage, London and Thousand Oaks, Calif.

On reflexive modernization

Beck, U. & Lau, C. (2005) Second modernity as a research agenda: theoretical and empirical explorations in the "meta-change" of modern society. *British Journal of Sociology*, 56(4), 525–57.

Beck, U., Bonss, W. & Lau, C. (2003) The theory of reflexive modernization: problematic, hypotheses and research programme. *Theory, Culture & Society*, 20(2), 1–33.

Notes

1. The collaborative research center Reflexive Modernization in Munich was founded in 1999 and is financed until 2009 by the German Research Foundation (DFG). It consists of three areas where a range of projects empirically analyze the changes within modernization regarding knowledge production, social situations and identities, and institutional restructuring and redefinition of boundaries (compare http://www.sfb536.mwn.de/).
2. Compare: http://www.sfb536.mwn.de/index_e.html
3. At an international level, Beck argues that inequalities between countries have increased (e.g. 1999: 6).
4. This argument is emphasized in Beck (1995b).
5. Beck's perspective on individualization, which emphasizes its ambivalent character, is very different from the mainly negative understanding in the US discourse on selfish individualism (Bellah 1986).
6. Beck (1998: 20f.) explicitly expresses his contradiction to postmodernist rejections of grand narratives, general theory, and humanity: "Where most post-modern theorists are critical of grand narratives, general theory and humanity, I remain committed to all of these, but in a new sense."
7. "Transnationalism" emphasizes activities which transcend the nation state's boundaries. For example, the individual's identity would refer less to a single home country than to two or more countries. Or, instead of international relationships taking place only between nation states, transnational organisations and movements can shape politics beyond the nation state.
8. Competing interpretations might have seen such hazards as visitations for the sins of a social group or society. But such interpretations are developed afterward to find somebody to be blamed and punished. Despite all the attempts to control the future, the church was finally unable to "influence God's will effectively."
9. This assumption might be open to discussion when we recognize that such catastrophes were regularly ascribed to moral failures of social groups or communities and therefore would still lie in the responsibility of the human being. But there is obviously a tension between attempts to live a good life (agreeable to God) and the destiny/tasks provided by God, which seem/s to be unforeseeable.
10. That means that you can develop the necessary knowledge to control the appearance of a risk or just prevent it. Instead it is about the management of the unknown or contradictory knowledge produced by science.
11. If you cannot control a risk, you can insure against the negative outcomes by spreading the costs (e.g. by taking out car or life insurance).

12. Objective risks are always socially constructed by specific techniques, and socially constructed risks regularly have a true kernel and sometimes, when this is not the case they still have real effects within society when they are acknowledged as being real.
13. *Guardian*, October 20, 2005, "At last – the end of the MMR myth."
14. Compare the case of a drug trial in Britain: "Drug trial leaves men critically ill," *Guardian Unlimited*, March 15, 2006.
15. Another form of organized irresponsibility is the global market, which "is an institutional form so impersonal as to have no responsibilities, even to itself" (Beck 1999: 6f.).
16. *Guardian*, January 27, 2007, 1.
17. This means the processes of social integration and reproduction.
18. Even though Beck and Beck-Gernsheim (2002) do not refer to this model, it is still a good schema to clarify what individualization is about.
19. Beck emphasizes that reflexive in this context has to do with reflex and not with a growing self-awareness, in the sense of more reasonable self-reflection.
20. *Guardian*, January 27, 2007, on the meeting of the United Nations Organization in Paris on climate change.
21. The example of Germany showed that these attempts are sometimes contradictory. The economic interests of the car production industry in Germany prevented tougher European legislation on carbon dioxide emission, while Germany is leading in other domains.
22. Extending his argument to a global level, Beck similarly argues in the *World Risk Society* (1999: 16f.) that "*socialization of risk*" or "*risk sharing*" could become a "powerful basis of community, one which has both territorial and non-territorial aspects" in the sense of a "*world party.*"
23. Compare regarding *political consumers*: Holzer (2006).
24. Beck et al. (2003) argued that fundamental principles as well as institutions are subject to change.

3 | Governmentality and Risk

Pat O'Malley

Governmentality may be regarded as a particular analytical technique that came to the fore during the period in which Marxist theory lost favor and many "critical" social theorists were seeking an alternative framework that provided a new way of grasping issues of politics and power. In one of the pioneering papers of the approach, Donzelot (1979) suggested that Foucault's work on power/knowledge, and particularly on the rise and development of disciplinary power, had become subject to a specific set of misinterpretations. In the shadow of Marxist grand theory, in which history was driven by the unfolding of contradictions in the productive or class order, changes in the "mode" of power appeared in many analyses as a new subject or motor of history, to replace class and production. Yet the intention of Foucault and his colleagues had been precisely to undo this kind of reductionist thinking, a kind that subordinated all manner of particular and contingent developments to mere epiphenomena or effects of some "real" underlying metahistoric logic. In place of "capitalism" and "class," for some new "Foucauldians," the new master categories had become "sovereignty" and "discipline." A multitude of social phenomena had come to be analyzed as if all that was necessary was to demonstrate their disciplinary character, at which point they were "explained" or subsumed as part of the rise of disciplinary society, or as examples of the exercise of sovereign power.

Accompanying this tendency, and again reflecting Marxist (and broader sociological) habits, history was to be divided into epochs. "Disciplinary society" was preceded by societies dominated by "sovereignty," and disciplinary society itself was now being displaced by a "governmental" order that deployed a wide variety of strategies, technologies, such as risk, to achieve its ends. The intention of Foucault and his colleagues, however, had been to dispense with such forms of epochal analysis. In the example of sovereignty-discipline-government, for example, Foucault had argued (1991a [1978]) that the rise and continuation of discipline *relied* on the continuation of sovereign power, and that both sovereignty and discipline (rather than disappearing) are essential to the "complex" form of "government" that has emerged more recently. Thus the disciplinary regime of the prison was founded on the sovereign command to obedience, the exercise of coercive sovereign power was an essential resource in order to bring the offender into the disciplinary gaze, and so on. In consequence it was better to think of the contemporary relationship between these three modes of governance as "triangular" and interactive rather than linear and successive. In good measure, this rejection of grand theory and epochal view of history was driven by an intention to restore contingency to a central role in social analysis. In place of ultimately determinist, causal, sociologies, the effort was to promote a sense that the present was not how things had to be, and that as a corollary, the future is open rather than set on a course by some logic of development. Although there was a very ambivalent attitude toward ideas of human agency, political inventiveness was to be given a much more central role than in conventional sociology. Rather than promoting grand and systematic theories of power, stress was to be placed on the *multiplicity* of power relations, and the diversity of their origins, workings, and effects.

But this was not merely an analytical approach – although that is the primary focus of this chapter. It also reflected a certain kind of politics that was a response to the student-led revolutions of 1968, and particularly that which occurred in Paris. The analytic was hostile to the kind of politics that suggested that all social ills could be transformed by one grand revolution. It cast doubt on the idea that power could be "broken," and liberty and egalitarianism could be installed by seizing the state or the means of production. Even the idea that liberty or freedom was the aim of politics and the end of history was rendered problematic. Both analytically and politically, power was to be regarded as fragmented; understood as dispersed among a multitude of agencies and exercised in diverse ways through many apparatuses, institutions, and architectures. Equally, power was not to be thought of merely as constraining, for power is equally creative. Consequently, freedom and liberty were not to be thought of as natural states to which we can be restored or achieved by the stripping away of "social control" or by smashing "class domination." Power does not emanate from one source, nor does it work to one end or take one form. In a sense, to be alive is to wield and be subjected to power, to subject ourselves and others to power: and thus we can only ever imagine *kinds* of "freedom" – never simply the absence of constraint. Instead, governmentality focuses attention on the diverse ways in which we may govern the conduct of others *and* ourselves.

In this view, therefore, the role of analysis is not to point the way to some new programmatic politics which will liberate us all. Paradoxically, that would only expose us to new forms of subjection and "subjectification" – prescribed forms of identity or self such as "proletarian" or even "feminist" – for such programs always tell us both how to be free, and what we must do to achieve this state. For Foucault and his colleagues this was the main lesson to be learned from the politics of Marxism. Instead, the focus was to be on destabilizing and questioning the present by revealing its contingent formation, its non-necessity. In governmentality, emphasis would be on how that which appears as necessary is to be understood as assembled together out of available materials, ideas, practices, and so on, in response to a specific understanding of the nature of the problems to be solved. In tandem with this, emphasis was placed on the understandings and constructions of the world that give rise to efforts to change it. In this view, that which appears natural is not to be taken for granted as something – like "population" or "the economy" – unproblematically real and just waiting to be discovered. Rather, it is to be regarded as invented, reflecting or embodying governmental *understandings* of the way things are. In the same moment, as the arbitrariness of many taken-for-granted categories in the present is made visible, possibilities for change emerge – the analytic gives rise to insights into how things might have been otherwise, and thus how they *could* be different in the future. Thus, while the response of many was to regard the Foucauldian project as pessimistic or nihilistic, its self-image was of an analytic that invited us not to look for simplistic formulae for freedom, but to examine the implications of all governance for how we should each live, for an ethic of the self rather than a programmatic politics for others – in terms of which all will be governed "for their own good."

Given the ready tendency to reinterpret Foucauldian analyses in terms of grand theoretical schemas, Donzelot emphasized that power itself had to be reconstituted in such a way that it could not be mobilized in grand theoretical fashion. The foundations of this analytic are generally recognized to have been laid in Foucault's 1978 essay "Governmentality," a term that fuses the ideas of government and mentality and that refers initially to a certain mentality of government that emerged in seventeenth-century Europe. This emerging way of governing centered the view that what is to be governed is itself self-governing, and thus any act of governance must take account of the self-regulating order of things. The aim of government shifted away from a focus simply on command and obedience, toward regarding the central issue as the optimal harnessing of these self-governing capacities – the "conduct of conduct," in Foucault's words. With the emergence of Governmentality, Foucault stressed, governments must always address the question of the "right" balance between governing too much or too little, governing but not disrupting the self-governing capacities of that which it rules.

"Population" and "economy" are two of the central "self-governing" categories characteristic of governmentality, whose more or less contingent emergence Foucault sketches out in his germinal paper. By the end of the eighteenth century, he suggests, "the economy" had come to be understood as a natural order governed by its own laws (such as the law of supply and demand), which governments could not avoid taking into account. "Populations" were understood to have their own characteristic rates of birth, death, increase, and decline – which were "discovered" through the use of statistical measures, and which came to be taken for granted "real" entities subject to the expertise of "economists," "sociologists," and "demographers." But so too, "individuals" emerged as self-governing entities, whose capacities and potentials likewise had to be taken into account and optimized. Governmentality thus had to take account not only of these and many other self-governing entities. It also had to consider the relations between regulation of organic collective entities and the "microphysics" of selves: the government of "each and all" was to be one of its trademarks. In this way, not only did government become more complex, as it had to govern at so many "levels," but in the process it had to recognize the limits to its own knowledge and capacities. The absolutist dream of knowing everything, and thus governing perfectly by command, was displaced by a more *tactical* approach – so that even the sovereign command became only one tactic among many. Likewise, the vision of government being exercised by one omniscient center was displaced by one in which there are many centers of knowledge and many centers of government and self-government.

In turn, to understand this new and complex form of government, new techniques of analysis need to be developed, which give rise to the second meaning of "governmentality" (lower-case "g") – as that analytical approach appropriate to understanding "Governmentality."

The focus on "mentality" in "governmentality" immediately raises the old Marxist specter of idealism, which for Marxists was a false mode of analysis focusing on the "superficial" level of ideas rather than the "real" determining material domain. Central to the Foucauldian idea of mentality is indeed analysis of the ways of *thinking* about government – how problems and people are thought about, what solutions to problems are dreamed up, what ends are imagined as ideal outcomes. It is in this aspect of government that inventiveness is made explicit, together with the "made-up" nature of things. This is not intended to suggest that life has no reality, or that problems don't "really" exist – only that we can only recognize or imagine them in certain ways, and can never have unmediated access to the certainty of what lies "behind." The analytic of governmentality in this sense is concerned with the surfaces – the words used to describe problems, the discourses in terms of which subjects are characterized, the categories that are used to explain policies – rather than with any assumed generative substrate such as the productive order or class interests. In turn, this does not mean that governmentality studies mere philosophies of rule. Governmental mentalities are governmental precisely in the sense that they seek to shape the conduct of those things, events, and subjects they seek to govern. They are in this sense intensely *practical* – they imagine the world as governable: problems are construed in ways that make them subject to practicable solutions. Accordingly, such mentalities, or "government rationalities" (more or less consistent sets of problematics, goals, categories, subjectivities, and so on) are always linked to *technologies* for doing things, answers to the question "what is to be done?" Thus welfare liberalism, the governmental rationality that dominated much of the twentieth century in Europe, was linked to all manner of practical technologies – such as the risk-based schemes and apparatuses of social insurance – that literally changed the world. In this process not only is a governmental rationality distinguished from mere philosophy, but it is intended by its adherents to make real that which was once only thought about.

Risk in the Development of Governmentality

These ideas are only sketchily present in Foucault's paper on "Governmentality," and are laid out only in a very basic fashion by Donzelot. During the 1980s, they were extended and developed by a number of Foucault's colleagues, such as Defert, Ewald, Castel, and Donzelot himself. What is significant about all this work is that risk was to be one of the central technologies of government in terms of which the analytical framework was developed. Donzelot's 1979 paper on risk is the first example in which a governmentality (or a "governmental analytic") was developed, at least in English. While Ewald's (1986) *L'Etat providence*, focusing on risk as a central technology in the welfare state, was never translated, the publication in 1991 of *The Foucault Effect: Studies in Governmentality* (Burchell et al. 1991) brought this body of work to the attention of Anglophone sociology. In particular, the papers by Ewald, Defert, and Castels explored risk in terms of this emerging analytical framework, the first two dealing with insurance, the latter with psychiatry. As landmark papers in the development of governmental approaches to risk, they are worth special attention.

For all three of these writers, risk is understood as a "technology of government." That is, risks are not regarded as intrinsically real, but as a particular way in which problems are viewed or "imagined" and dealt with. What is specific to risk, in their view, is that risk is a statistical and probabilistic technique, whereby large numbers of events are sorted into a distribution, and the distribution in turn is used as a means of making probabilistic predictions. In this process, the particular details of each individual case, which had been the focus of disciplinary technologies, are submerged or stripped way, and only certain recurring characteristics attended to. Insurance, for example, is not interested in building up a detailed, unique case record of each insured party or object. Instead it focuses on relevant "risk factors," such as age or occupation, that act as predictors of insured events. In this process, "risk pools" are created: that is, a group of cases that have a similar probability of experiencing some uncertain condition in the future, and which for insurance purposes will deal with in the same fashion. Insurance creates risk pools, for instance, in terms of the age of drivers, as this is one of the best predictors of involvement in accidents. Age is thus a "risk factor." The point in governmentality research is not to evaluate whether such risk-based procedures are accurate or fair, but rather to analyze what are the specific characteristics of this way of governing uncertain future events.

In pursuing this analysis, Ewald (1991) begins by stressing that risk is a very abstract probabilistic technology, and that one consequence is that no concrete application of it to any problem of government can ever be the only, correct, or pure application. Rather, probability is always part of a complex assemblage of elements brought together to achieve some end. In the case of young drivers, it can be seen that the abstract technology of risk is used to calculate the differential money premiums to be paid by different driver categories (or to refuse insurance altogether). As will be explored shortly, this evidently differentiates insurance from techniques in which risk is used to predict outcomes, say, with respect to pregnancy, or to whether or not a prisoner will reoffend after release. For Ewald, insurance is an application of risk that is coupled with practices that convert events into capital: all things, even life itself, are converted into a money equivalent. Insurance pays out monetary compensation in the event that a specified uncertain harm – say, loss of life, crippling injury, or property loss – befalls the insured party. This monetization of events in turn is the specific medium through which insurance "spreads risks." On the one hand, the payment of premiums by individuals spreads their monetized risk over time. On the other hand, the collective payment of monetary premiums by all members of the risk pool spreads risks across the whole of the membership. An outline begins to emerge of a particular application of risk – still fairly abstract – that Ewald refers to as "insurance technology." But Ewald moves further to suggest that the technology may be assembled together with other elements to make for specific *forms* of insurance. For example, while many insurances take the form of an indemnity against loss, life insurance does not – with the consequence that unlike property insurance it is not necessary for the beneficiary of a life insurance policy to prove any loss when claiming against it (Knights and Verdubakis 1997).

At this point Ewald stresses the *genealogical* analysis of insurance – that is, a history that reflects the contingent development of "insurance imaginaries" and/or the voices that have been hidden by history. These are inventive ways of applying the abstract insurance technology to some currently useful purpose. New forms of insurance appear as responses to emerging opportunities, as these are envisaged, defined, and acted upon by insurance entrepreneurs. For example, as Bougen (2003) and

Ericson and Doyle (2004a) have shown, the insurance industry invented new insurance techniques in response to the emergence of terrorism as a catastrophic threat to life and property. In Bougen's words,

> reinsurers, capital market participants, catastrophe information systems, catastrophe-modelling agencies, investment-rating agencies, financial underwriters and existing financial products have all become imaginatively assembled. From a liberal government perspective, the very emergence of such risk networks capable of supporting securitization as an alternative method of catastrophe financing can itself be considered illustrative of the moving and creative possibilities of government. (2003: 262–3)

From this point of view, characteristic of governmentality analyses, there can be no linear history in which insurance or risk unfolds along a course determined by its "logic." At the same time, neither can we deduce any constant effects from insurance *per se*, let alone the more abstract technology of risk, for we must always attend to its specific form and its environment. Thus Defert (1991) reports on the contrasts between diverse techniques for managing hazards in France during the latter half of the nineteenth century. Over much of the century, liberal emphasis on individual prudence and responsibility for managing life's vicissitudes meant that personal savings or small-scale workers' community chests were primary resources in the struggle against want. These schemes generated considerable social solidarity among the workers, as they managed their own funds, usually knew their fellow members personally, and faced risks together. The development of social insurance in the latter part of the century, in which employers, workers, and the state pay some proportion into large-scale schemes managed by actuaries, had a dramatic effect on this. As Defert stresses (1991: 213), while the actuarial nature of these national schemes meant that they were financially much more robust than the workers' schemes, the new form of insurance meant that the insured no longer "constitute a social community among themselves ... The framework of sociability in industrial societies is displaced." Insurance thus disaggregated the insured from other solidarities, and reconstituted them in new distributions which, in Defert's view, created a *passive* form of solidarity that was attractive to employers and governments alike who feared worker solidarity. As others have stressed (Doran 1994), often this meant that workers bitterly resisted the encroachment of actuarially driven insurance. It is not simply, as might be argued today, that insurance is a "superior" technology for delivering security. Rather, it delivers a very specific form of security – the acceptance of which was by no means simply assured once it was "discovered." The invention and promotion of insurance, these writers argue, renders it not merely technically neutral but highly charged politically and morally – and this in turn bears on the ways in which it develops, is shaped, and adopted.

It was noted above that insurance is a rather specific form of risk technology. In another foundational paper, Castel (1991) outlines the deployment of risk technologies in relation to psychiatry. Like Ewald, he focuses on some of the implications of this application of risk technology for how we are to be governed. In Ewald's account of insurance, capitalization and the spreading of risks are central. Neither of these features characterizes the psychiatric model, which stresses risk *reduction*. For Castel, risk as a psychiatric category of risk is to be contrasted with that of "dangerousness." The latter

> implies at once the affirmation of a quality immanent to the subject (he or she is dangerous), and a mere ... quantum of uncertainty, given that the proof of the danger can only be provided after the fact, should the threatened action actually occur. Strictly speaking there can only ever be *imputations of dangerousness*, postulating the hypothesis of a more or less probable relationship between certain present symptoms and a certain act to come. (1991: 283; emphasis in original)

The result, he suggests, is that under medical regimes of dangerousness it was not possible to have "a fully fledged policy of prevention," because only those already diagnosed as dangerous could be subject to such policy. Diagnosing dangerousness, in this sense, involves a disciplinary technology whereby the patient is individually diagnosed as having an existing condition, and is treated or restrained in order to govern the possibility of harm (see also Pratt 1998). But the diagnosis produced by this disciplinary process remains subjective, based on a personal estimation by the psychiatrist, and a "second opinion" may always be called for. For Castel, the emergence of risk in psychiatry resolved this problem by making the "diagnosis" appear objective, an effect achieved by representing the particular case as simply an instance of an aggregate with known "objective" statistical properties. As with insurance, rather than trying to know my unique case in great detail, a diagnosis of risk simply identifies the presence of a risk factor and thus consigns me to a risk pool. This first appears in the psychiatric domain with the work of mid-nineteenth-century scientists, such as Morel, concerned with abnormalities among the poor. As Castel argues,

> Morel was already arguing in terms of *objective risks*: that is to say, statistical correlations between series of phenomena. At the level of practices, he also suggested that the public authorities undertake a special surveillance of those population groups which might by this stage already have been termed populations at risk, those located at the bottom of the social ladder. (1991: 284; emphasis in original)

Because such aggregate "objective" characteristics could be represented with statistical precision – that is, as "risks" – they came to be regarded as "real," visible, and manifest, rather than merely the hypothetical diagnoses of individuals based on medical opinion. Castel suggested that preventative strategies aimed at whole categories of people henceforward became both justified and possible. In turn, as this process advances, Castel (1991: 281) saw the use of professional judgment and the case method becoming progressively more marginal. The "new strategies dissolve the notion of a *subject* or a concrete individual, and put in its place a combinatory of *factors*, the factors of risk." At the same time, "the essential component of intervention no longer takes the form of the direct face-to-face relationship between the carer and the cared, the helper and the helped, the professional and the client." Under the emerging regime of risk, he argues, psychiatric specialists become marginalized and subordinated, merely filling in pro forma scales and routines provided by a remote managerial expertise. All this is achieved not simply by aggregation, for the dangerous had often been aggregated before: for example, in the idea of the "dangerous classes." The unpredictable, dangerous classes could be governed only as unpredictable mobs or individuals. But as the nineteenth century drew to a close, new risk-based technologies emerged – ranging from eugenics to social insurance – for governing them as "actuarial" entities, statistically knowable and calculable risks.

As this indicates, risk-related changes impact especially upon professional practices and the subjects of their expertise. In some instances, perhaps, Castel's scenario of the displacement of expertise and the client–patient relationship is accurate, but this is questioned in several ways by more recent governmentality research. Rose's (1998: 186–7) work, seemingly corresponding closely to Castel's, points to a shift toward psychiatrists' assessing the risks posed by patients at the expense of the priority of personal therapeutic intervention. But unlike Castel, Rose found that the process did not complete the transition from dangerousness to (statistical) risk. "Psychiatric risk," Rose suggests, is rarely a comparison of patients' risk scores to statistical tables in order to generate probabilistic predictions.

> Rather it entails calculating the consequences of a concatenation of indicators or factors co-occurring in certain regular patterns. Even if clinical diagnosis has become probabilistic and factoral, however, it is seldom numerical ... mental health professionals tend to resist the use of numerical risk assessment schedules and classifications. They stress that assessment of risk is a clinical matter, and has to take place within a clinical assessment of mental disorder ... (Rose 1998: 196–7)

Psychiatrists, it would seem, have avoided displacing or reducing their diagnostic assessments to mere numerical scores. Instead, perhaps because of the autonomy or status of their profession, they appear to have negotiated a compromise through which to govern mental illness. Castel's trajectory has been disrupted by the development of a new configuration of technologies. If Castel unwittingly slips into a mapping of an inevitable future, Rose's observations on the unanticipated emergence of a new pattern of governance retains a genealogical sensibility. No outcome is inevitable, new possibilities are always opening up. This is not to deny that risk is becoming more central in contemporary government – a matter to which I will turn shortly. Rather, it is to challenge the idea that this expansion is inevitable, and is being driven by the grand forces of the contradictions of modern scientific and technological development.

Additionally, while Castel maps out a certain pattern of risk-reducing technology, many others are possible, even within the medical area. For example, Lorna Weir (1996) has stressed that the more common pattern is where risk factors are taken as only one element in a case record. That is, the unique individual is not fragmented into a bundle of risk factors, nor is the patient–doctor relationship subordinated to risk. Rather, risk itself is subordinated to the professional model. In turn, this may have quite different consequences for the patient–doctor relationship than Castel imagined to be *the* effect of risk. The governance of pregnancy, for example, has seen this in a move from treating it as something akin to an illness afflicting women, toward treating it as a condition where both mother and fetus are regarded as "at risk." In this process, a variety of risk-management duties are invented and their performance assigned primarily to the mother. These relate to many hitherto unidentified risks associated with smoking tobacco, imbibing alcohol, ingesting caffeine, and other forms of drug consumption. There is heightened attention given to the need for proper diet, physical exercise, regular medical tests, and so on. All of these render the mother increasingly responsible both to her medical practitioner and to her fetus (Weir 1996; Ruhl 1999). As Rapp (1995: 180) has indicated, while previous generations of women might have been aware of some of these risks, it is only the present generation of "statistically graded pregnant women" who have been given specific risk figures and thus been led to identify "generic pregnancy anxieties with their particular characteristics and behaviors." In this environment, pregnant women are governed by means of risk technologies, and thus their present lives are shaped in terms of a *probable* future – a future that may never happen but that must be guarded against. Of course, precautions characterize previous forms of government. But now, even though there are *no* signs of an *existing* pathology, specific interventions may be called for.

In such governmentality work, attention is therefore paid to the ways in which the increasingly prevalent adoption of risk as a framework of government creates new subjectivities and redefines relationships. There is a focus on how it invents new techniques for self-government (or "techniques of the self") and for the government of others, and creates and assigns responsibilities accordingly. These studies explore and dissect what are often "details" of government that fall beneath the grand gaze of universal theories of risk society and global catastrophe, yet which restructure our existence in many important ways. Nevertheless, one of the criticisms of governmentality has been that it tends to focus on the "blueprints" for government – the governmental plans, White Papers, legislative specifications, commercial texts on how to live – rather than descending to see what actually happens (O'Malley et al. 1997). It is also suggested that the approach emphasizes a "top-down" vision of government, and assumes that the subjects of government, whether individuals, populations, or organizations, automatically adopt the practices presented to them (Frankel 1997).

One defense against such criticism is to point out that governmentality is not intended as a total sociology. Its ambitions are relatively modest, taking on a fairly specific task, and never claiming to provide a framework for the empirical study of how government "actually" works and is taken up. While this is a reasonable point, since no approach does everything, it is not altogether clear that this is always a viable defense, nor that it is an accurate characterization of the approach. We have already seen that Rose's work investigates how psychiatrists have resisted change and modified the nature of the risk regime in their domain. Working with his colleague Carlos Novas (Novas and Rose 2000), he has also investigated how the development of the internet has created new opportunities for "bottom-up" governance in the health field. While some visions of the development of genetic medicine paint a scenario in which risk-based diagnostics consign people to passive victims of their fate, Novas and Rose have found that with diseases such as Huntington's Chorea, the medical profession encourages (even expects) its "at-risk" patients to use the web in order to make themselves familiar with their risky condition and the options open to them. In turn, at-risk subjects have formed internet connections and established chat rooms and websites in order to articulate their own insights and experiences, to share information from a range of (often conflicting sources), and to create a parallel domain of "lay" expertise. The importance of such risk-oriented work is not simply to show that governmentality work can study social relations rather than blueprints, a point to which I will return shortly. Nor is it just that bottom-up governance can be recognized. Equally important, it overcomes the criticism that it is prone to homeostasis. This criticism suggests that, by emphasizing the systematic properties of rationalities of government, its tendency is to represent government as stable and fixed – tending to mute attention to the openings for change and future contingencies that were such an important part of its original mission. However, Novas and Rose's work is only one example of an increasing body of governmentality that attends closely to such matters. Nowhere is this clearer than with respect to risk and criminal justice, to which I now turn.

From Risk to "the Risk Society"?

The 1991 publication of the essays on risk and governmentality in *The Foucault Effect* was closely followed by a considerable expansion in sociological analysis of risk, but only a relatively small part of this can be put down to their impact. Coincidentally, Ulrich Beck's *Risk Society* (1992b [1986]) was published in English the following year, and was immediately adopted by many mainstream sociologists – Anthony

Giddens included (e.g. Giddens 1994b). Probably this reflected the fact that Beck's thesis was aligned far more closely with mainstream and Marxist sociologies than was the case for the governmentality writers. In stark contrast to the Foucauldian refusal of totalizing grand theories and epochal accounts, Beck proposed an account in which the trajectory of modernist development impels us out of the world of a "first modernity" into that of "risk society." As scientific and technological development advance hand in hand with market capitalism, Beck detects a qualitative shift from a situation in which harmful by-products are a manageable price for progress, to the present era in which "modernization risks" such as global warming, ozone-layer depletion, and nuclear contamination are now threatening human existence itself. In this new environment, progress is questioned, and risk consciousness increasingly displaces other forms of consciousness and solidarity. As well, increasing demands for research into new risks, and demands for protection against these new risks, form a vicious circle creating massive insecurity. Ironically, however, the nature of the emergent "modernization risks" renders risk almost useless as a technology for governing vital aspects of our existence. These processes are too rare, invisible, or unique to be the subject of statistical prediction, and thus for Beck risk becomes little more than a sham, an ideology that masks the true nature of our predicament.

This is not the place to rehearse the many arguments against Beck, although it is vital to note the almost polar opposition of Beck's work to the kinds of analysis of risk generated by the governmentality literature. Beck gives little or no attention to risk's diversity in form and implications; his theory deploys the vision of a thoroughgoing epochal rupture into the "risk society"; the account creates a privileged access to "reality" and on its foundation mounts a programmatic politics which guides our way into a new form of existence. In practice, therefore, governmentality and the theory of the risk society have tended to follow different courses. There are few instances, such as Ericson and Haggerty's (1997) *Policing the Risk Society*, that have attempted to overcome this divide. Following Beck, they argue that the rise of the risk society has created an "information society": the demand for new knowledge about risks has created the need for unprecedented volumes of knowledge relating to issues of security and safety. Central to this development has been the insurance industry, which acts as the hub of a network of agencies that focus on these matters (Ericson 1994).

Of equal importance, they argue, a governmentality analysis indicates that the police have shifted from being primarily an enforcement agency to being a pivotal information broker. Because of the special place of police in the governance of security, they are unusually situated to gather information about crime, accidents, urban hazards, traffic incidents, and so on, and to investigate contexts that are otherwise hidden from view. As a result, suggest Ericson and Haggerty, police now spend more of their time dealing with data than enforcing law. More important still, police services have responded to outside demands for information by creating recording systems that are coded largely in terms of risk categories.

Whatever its many strengths, in attempting to marry Beck and governmentality, *Policing the Risk Society* is the exception rather than the rule (but see too Ewald 2002). Far more work in the areas of crime control and criminal justice has been concerned not so much to map out the ways in which risk is inevitably spreading, although its increasing use is well noted, as to attend to the ways in which it mutates, often in significant and unexpected fashion. Consider the fate of two influential governmentality studies on risk and crime control that came out in the immediate wake of *The Foucault Effect*. Feeley and Simon's (1992, 1994) work on "actuarial justice," and O'Malley's (1992) work on crime prevention emphasized themes already noted, namely that risk strips away identity, and treats individual cases as members of risk categories. With respect to actuarial justice, the traditional model of individual justice was depicted as being replaced by sentencing based on statistical predictors of reoffending. Thus quite minor offences might result in long sentences under such models as "Three Strikes" legislation. At the same time, it was argued, the content of the sentence shifted away from therapeutic correctionalism toward simple incapacitation – a response interpreted by Feeley and Simon as reflecting a "pure" risk strategy of neutralizing sources of risk. With respect to crime prevention, O'Malley argued that the displacement of individualized justice and the promotion of a deterrence-based justice that assumed a rational choice offender, was linked to the rise of situational crime prevention (which also deployed rational choice offender models). While there were significant differences between these studies, both envisioned further risk-based developments in the governance of crime that eroded programs that delivered therapeutic correctionalism and/or programs of crime prevention that provided resources and remedial intervention.

However, the development of risk-based interventions took rather different courses. Rather than prisons becoming merely places of incapacitation, risk-needs programs have become widespread (Hannah-Moffatt 1999, 2001). These deliver therapeutic correctionalism, but target this by the use of risk schedules: the correctional "needs" of prisoners are provided for where risk techniques indicate that such interventions will reduce the probability of reoffending. With respect to crime prevention, while situational crime prevention has grown apace, it has been joined by developmental crime prevention. This identifies crime risk factors in the community and attempts to divert young people from future offending by targeting these factors. What is striking is that the nature of the risk factors reflects closely the kinds of problem that were the focus of the discredited "social crime prevention" of the period before the 1980s: low self-esteem, blocked opportunities, racial and ethnic discrimination, poor socialization, and so on. In both penal regimes and crime prevention, the expected erosion of "social" interventions has not occurred because risk techniques have unexpectedly shifted ground. This may be because there was a shift from a prevailing sense that "nothing works" to a "what works?" stance favoring evidence-led interventions. Early risk-based developments reflected the "nothing works" view that constructive interventions were ineffectual compared with simply making it impossible for offenders to offend by incapacitation or designing-out crime through situational prevention. As "nothing works" was displaced by a more optimistic policy environment, so risk has been deployed as a way of identifying "what works," producing more positive risk-based programs. In part, then, a key lesson has been not only that risk is a flexible and diverse technology, but also that the specific form taken by risk technologies will be shaped by the broader political environment in which it is set – an issue to which attention will shift in the next section.

Prior to taking up this discussion, there is one further feature to note about governmentality studies on the play of risk in the government of crime. Perhaps influenced by the "risk society" literature, there has been a tendency for a good deal of research in governmentality to chart the spread of risk, and to imply that risk will displace previous technologies. Given that there is little doubt that risk *is* being used in more and more contexts, such a view may be tempting, even though it tends toward the epochal and totalizing analyses inconsistent with first principles shared by most writers in the governmentality literature. However, much recent work has indicated limits to risk's empire. To begin with, there has been considerable resistance to actuarial techniques at the sentencing level. Freiberg (2000), for example, has pointed to the hostility of the judiciary to such developments, as they both affront the judges' sensibilities about their sentencing expertise, and represent a challenge to fundamental principles of justice that many regard as sacrosanct – such as proportionality between offence and sentence. While the intention of legislators may have been to sidestep such resistance by introducing risk-based sentencing tariffs, judges have many resources at their command to frustrate this. These include, for example, redefining an offence is such a way that it no longer falls into the range in which risk-based sentencing is mandatory. Or again, the work of Kemshall (1998, 2002) has shown that the social-science trained social workers and probation officers resist the institutional trend toward displacing their professional judgment in questions of parole and release, by making their judgments professionally and only then filling in the schedules in ways that reflect this. Even so, as more recent work (Kemshall & Maguire 2001) has shown, institutions themselves have curtailed the use of risk schedules, often specifying that they are only an *aid* to professional judgment rather than a replacement for it. In this way, something akin to the medical "case" model of risk emerges, where risk is only one element in a more complex ensemble.

The significance of such work is not only the point made already that we need to be cautious about projecting trends into the future. It also raises concerns about how we define the limits of governmentality. Rose's implied critique of Castel was based on an examination of contemporary risk schedules: in a sense, Rose remained at the level of blueprints. Freiberg, Kemshall, and Maguire, however, are now examining the active resistance of workers to these blueprints. In their landmark paper setting out the analytic of governmentality, Miller and Rose (1990) specified that the approach is not a sociology, at least in the sense of mapping out the empirical evidence on how governmental models are applied in practice (see also Barry et al. 1993). One response, probably acceptable to most of those working in the area, would be to say that there is no problem here. Governmentality is not a theory, in the sense of a consistent set of concepts and theorems developed for explanatory purposes. Rather it is at best a heuristic analytic and does not pretend to be all-encompassing. Other questions, such as those concerned with resistance to these blueprints, belong to empirical sociology, and there is nothing to stop researchers articulating governmentality with sociological analysis if that suits their purposes. But there may be more to it than this. Returning to Weir's work on risk and pregnancy, she stressed that there is a tendency of governmentality to make government appear univocal: as if the blueprints are the product of one mentality. In the case of pregnancy risks, however, she stressed that medical models of risk had been resisted by pregnant women and by midwives, who objected to some of the medical definitions of risk and to the corresponding ways of dealing with them. These resistances shaped existing risk techniques and practices. To interpret current techniques solely as reflecting "medical" governing mentalities would thus be both genealogically and politically problematic – silencing the subjugated voices that Foucauldian thinking aims to make salient – as part of a broader aim of revealing the non-necessity of what is (O'Malley et al. 1997). This suggests, therefore, that a governmentality that *refuses* any articulation with other research techniques and frameworks, particularly those centering the study of social and political relationships, might face problems in this respect. It is an open question, however, whether therefore this blind-spot constitutes a weakness characteristic of governmentality *per se*, or is simply a danger to which those using it should always attend.

Risk and Liberal Governmentality

It has been stressed several times that the ways in which risk is built into governmental practices will vary under differing governmental conditions – specifically, in relation to differing political rationalities. One of the most common themes in governmental analyses of risk has focused on the ways in which the genealogy of liberal governance has been associated with changes in the way risk has been constituted and deployed. Indeed, in some degree such analyses suggest that the differing approaches to risk *give shape to* different forms of liberalism (O'Malley 2004). Thus while great attention has been given to the "rise" of risk in the past few decades, something that stems in part from the risk society literature, those writing in the governmentality literature have stressed that if we look beyond the blanket characterization of risk as government in terms of probabilities, it is clear that we have been living through a period in which key institutionalizations of risk have *changed* in key ways. For much of the twentieth century, liberal governance relied extensively on socialized forms of risk, most notably the great social insurance schemes that were developed and implemented from about 1880 onward. Like most insurance, these spread risks across risk pools. But their distinguishing characteristics are that they operate at the level of the nation state and frequently are compulsory. Beyond that, it is rather difficult to generalize. In some cases (certainly most of the early models for dealing with health, unemployment, and old age), these operated as a conventional insurance in the sense that they were contributory. Members had to pay premiums, and were entitled to benefits that were linked to these payments. Indeed, this was a vital feature to understanding the early development of social insurance, for in this way it reflected prevailing "classical" liberal views on individualism, independence, and the virtues of thrift and diligence. These insurances did not give out charity but operated contractually. The beneficiaries did not receive something for nothing, and would not become dependent on the provider, since they had purchased a legal and contractual right to their benefits. Thus social insurance did not appear as an historical rupture, a radical and instant break with the past, but in many ways as a continuation or innovation within conventional liberalism. Certainly there were major concerns about the compulsory nature of these schemes, and equally prominent fears that they would lead to idlers freeloading off the system. It is important to see that both these factors were taken into account in the design of social insurance (Beveridge 1942), and that these critiques never disappeared – for they were to play a key role in the later shift to neoliberal risk techniques. What is equally important to note is that these schemes were no sooner in place than they began to be modified in unanticipated ways. For example, it was argued that housewives contributed to the social good, yet were unpaid and thus could not pay contributions. It was also argued that those who had worked and paid taxes through a long life had thereby earned a right to support in their old age. Gradually and unevenly the close connection between benefit and payment of premiums was eroded, and in the period after World War II many countries were adopting risk-management schemes – such as the British National Health Scheme – that were non-contributory. A right of benefit came to exist for all citizens by virtue of their membership of the social whole. Risk was still being spread, through taxation, but the connection to the insurance model outlined by Ewald was now only tenuous.

The calculation of probabilities itself was present but submerged in the more general processes of state finance management; contributions were often unrelated to benefits; the contract had been displaced by a right. Much of this has now changed with the rise of neoliberalism or "advanced liberalism."

Neoliberalism, as Rose (1996a) has argued, emerged out of both the surviving "classical" liberal concerns about welfare liberalism and the array of more recent critiques that were often leftist in their basis (e.g. Gough 1979). Many of these had little or nothing to do with risk (e.g. the criticism that experts had disrupted the authority of parents and eroded the nuclear family; Rose 1996b). While these processes have not advanced nearly as far as neoliberals would have preferred, the discourses of the new liberalism were uniformly in favor of new ways of governing life's risks. On the one hand, private insurance was to replace social insurances, especially with respect to risks related to health and old age (where private superannuation – and later share-market schemes – were preferred). Unemployment insurance was to be transformed into new schemes rendering their subjects no longer "beneficiaries" of social insurance, but "active citizens" making themselves "job ready." Risk management was being changed from a social or collectivized model to one focused much more on management by individuals on their own behalf, frequently in the name of "freedom of choice." With this shift, new self-governing subjectivities were being created, not only in these domains, but in such areas as crime prevention where individuals were admonished not to make it easy for criminals, and to manage their own crime risks with the assistance of government, police, and private sector (insurance) advice. This "new prudentialism" perhaps has been exaggerated in its reach (Dean 1995), but already it can be seen how risk is both shaped by, and shapes, the nature of liberal rationalities. However, it is at this point that a new complexity must be considered.

Let us return briefly to the nineteenth century, the era of so-called "classical" or "laissez faire" liberalism. To begin with, it is evident that risk-based techniques of government were developed during these years. As Tom Osborne (1996) has argued, this was the era of great programs that tackled issues of health risks by great engineering projects delivering pure water, establishing sewerage systems, and creating pure food and drug regulation. These programs exemplify yet another pattern of risk technology – which Dean (1999a) has termed "epidemiological risk" – in which individuals are not centered at all. The focus, rather, is on populations, unlike risks in the "case" model. The interventions are (like medical case-history risk) aimed at risk reduction rather than risk spreading, and obviously there is no capitalization of risk as in insurance. So, while this is yet another configuration of risk, it can hardly be argued that this era was not one characterized in important ways by risk. But perhaps other strategies were rather more central. Consider for example the tremendous emphasis on the poor governing their security through diligence and thrift; on the great imageries of the entrepreneur taking risks for the good of all; on the development of the police as a "preventative" force. Are these different forms of risk – for they would not seem to involve statistical, probabilistic modeling, or distributional modes of planning and intervention?

Risk and Uncertainty

In most contemporary approaches, risk is opposed to uncertainty. In Beck's (1992b) analysis, for example, uncertainty is the non-probabilistic family of ways in which government is based on *expectations* of how the future is likely to turn out. For Beck (1992b, 1999), uncertainty is the only way modernization risks such as that of global warming can be managed, for they are one-off processes that have never occurred before and cannot be the subject of statistical analysis. Uncertainty in this sense can be traced back through such other governmental thinkers as Maynard Keynes and Frank Knight (Knight 1921; Reddy 1996), who distinguished between the two in terms that basically correspond to Beck's: risks are statistical predictions of the future, uncertainty consists of other systematic forms of organizing of experience to predict – such as professional judgment, ordinary foresight, and rules of thumb. This is also how many in the governmentality field interpret the difference (Simon 1987; Ewald 1991; Ericson & Doyle 2004a). But others (e.g. Dean 1999a) have argued that the distinction is false, at least if we accept Beck's idea that uncertainty involves governing an "incalculable" future. As Dean rightly argues, all attempts to govern the future involve calculation; but clearly writers such as Beck mean by "calculation" *statistical* calculation. He is not suggesting that, for example, business people do not calculate when making investments on the share market; nor would he suggest that poor people practicing prudence are not calculating and making attempts to govern an uncertain future – even though both are resorting to techniques of uncertainty rather than risk. So we need to take account of the fact that risk is not the only predictive technology deployed in government. The point here, therefore, is not at all to challenge Beck's distinction between risk and uncertainty. Rather it is to stress that uncertainty is not simply a poor cousin to risk, nor is it merely "defensive" as Beck's work and the example of precaution suggest. Insofar as we live in an era of "neoliberalism" or "advanced" liberalism, then it is hard to ignore the fact that market models of competition, and visions of "entrepreneurialism" are extensively promoted in contemporary government as vital and constructive technologies (Giddens 2000). Indeed, some such thinkers even regard uncertainty as "making us free" – for when we engage in enterprise we create the future in innovative ways and escape the bonds of a statistically knowable future (Peters 1987; Bernstein 1996). Of course, in pointing this out, a governmentality of risk does not endorse either view.

This distinction, however, might appear confusing. The free market, of course, involves what many refer to as "risk" – the risks involved in competing. But "risk" is here being used to refer to techniques of uncertainty. Entrepreneurs "take risks" by calculating the future in much the same way that people do engaging in extreme sports (Simon 2002; Lyng 2005a): that is, by accumulating information, relying on experience, using practiced judgment and rules of thumb, and so on. As this makes clear, we now see a distinction between risk used as a term of discourse, and risk used as a technique. As with most things in governmentality, there is no hard and fast rule on usage, and some, such as Dean (1999a) and Weir (1996), prefer to group all those techniques that make calculated predictions – whether statistical or not – under the category "risk." Baker and Simon (2002) follow this route, but prefer to differentiate between "embracing risk" (as in entrepreneurialism or extreme sports) and avoiding or minimizing risk (as in insurance or health models). As governmentality is not a theory, and in its nature there is a resistance to laying down rules, these differences just have to be lived with!

Conclusions

While governmentality honed much of its cutting edge in analysis of risk during the early 1990s, it did not appear as a major presence in sociological journals until the last few years of that decade, while the first governmentality "textbook" (Dean 1999a) was published in the closing months of the decade. In that sense, governmentality is quite a new approach. It might be tempting to suggest that some of the inconsistencies noted above will be ironed out, and that some of the difficulties – such as the question of its relationship with empirical, sociological analyses of social and political relations – will be resolved. Perhaps this is so, for the work of some of its leading innovators (e.g. Rose, Ericson, and Simon) certainly has begun to examine *relations in* government in depth. Ericson, for example, has embarked on a major study of relations in the insurance industry (Ericson et al. 2003; Ericson & Doyle 2004b), while Rose has been engaged in studies of medical research and development that in a similar fashion take him away from the confines of governmentality as it once appeared (Rose 2003). But in this process, it is noticeable that the term "governmentality," and discussions of its characteristics – of the sort that characterized the early 1990s – are disappearing from this cutting-edge work, ironically just as a mass of new "governmentality" research is beginning to appear. Whether this means that the approach has achieved some sort of maturity and its characteristics can be taken for granted, or whether it means that it is mutating into something else in the face of discontents with its limitations, is a difficult question to answer. And perhaps this doesn't matter. As noted, not being a theory, it is not especially vulnerable to attacks on its central propositions, and research cannot show it to be wrong or internally contradictory – merely more or less useful for some purposes. Likewise, and mindful of Foucault's depiction of his own work as a "toolbox" with varied instruments for varied purposes and no necessary unity or systematic integration, it is proving to be readily deployable in tandem with other analytical approaches. Further, it does not – unlike a theory – have a research program to pursue, set out for it by its central propositions.

For such reasons it is difficult to talk with any precision of the prospects for further research and development. Much of the answer to this question simply will depend on how and in relation to which aspects or areas of government researchers choose to use it. Nevertheless, with specific reference to risk, it is possible to point to ways in which governmentality work in this area is becoming more sensitized to complexities of government. For example, the pioneering work of Ewald had few qualms defining insurance as a technology of risk, in the sense of actuarial calculation. However, it is now clear that this is simply inadequate as a general characterization. The recent work of Ericson and his colleagues (Ericson et al. 2003; Ericson & Doyle 2004a, 2004b), for example, shows that much insurance work is carried out without any reference to actuarial data and tables, but instead is calculated by "uncertain" experience-based techniques, and sometimes just plain hunches. Work by O'Malley (2003) and Kreitner (2000) indicates that the law of insurance – which governmentally defines what insurance is – on this issue is almost utterly indifferent to how premiums and benefits are calculated. Further, insurance currently is taking forms – as a "financial product" – that render it legally almost indistinguishable from gambling and business investment. Insurance, in this process (as Bougen 2003, and Ericson & Doyle 2004a also note), is perhaps being fundamentally reconstituted. For this reason also, it is likely that this will remain a key area of research for governmentality and its successors. A similar story can be told for criminal justice, as already indicated above.

More generally, both examples illustrate a tendency to move away from a focus on risk as though risk can be studied in isolation from the other predictive technologies with which it is almost invariably articulated. As well, this work is characterized by a more modest appraisal of the spread and influence of risk. Increasingly governmental research is showing that simply because risk is an element of a technology in a program or industry does not mean that it is the most important determination of its nature and implications (O'Malley 2004). Among the many benefits this may bring in its train may be a melioration of the perhaps exaggerated focus on risk and its impact which has typified not only governmentality but also sociology more generally.

Further Reading

Baker, T. & Simon, J. (2002) *Embracing Risk: the changing culture of insurance and responsibility.* University of Chicago Press, Chicago.

Burchell, G., Gordon, C. & Miller, P (eds.) (1991) *The Foucault Effect: studies in governmentality.* Harvester/Wheatsheaf, London (see especially papers by Foucault, Ewald, Defert, and Castels).

Economy and Society, vol. 29, no. 4. Special issue on *Configurations of risk.*

Ericson, R. & Doyle, A. (eds.) (2004) *Risk and Morality.* University of Toronto Press, Toronto.

O'Malley, P. (2004) *Risk, Uncertainty and Government.* Glasshouse, London.

4 | Systems Theory and Risk

Klaus P. Japp & Isabel Kusche

The way systems theory deals with the topic of risk derives from various general assumptions about the structure and processes of modern society. In contrast to other sociological theories, systems theory claims the status of a general theory of this society. It was Talcott Parsons who laid the foundations of this approach by distinguishing typical functions, which are fulfilled by societal subsystems, as prerequisites of a stable social order. The German scholar Niklas Luhmann (1982, 1995) took up the idea of society divided into subsystems and many other ideas of Parsons, but also introduced some major changes to the theoretical approach. Whereas Parsons understood the idea of subsystems as an analytical concept, Luhmann assumed that such subsystems are actually observable in modern society. He and the other proponents of this new form of systems theory regard communication as the basic social operation – in contrast to Parsons, who chose the concept of action as his point of departure. Society consists of a mass of communicative operations, immediately followed by other such communications. The major structural feature of modern society is the fact that most of these communications take on one of several distinct forms, which marks them as belonging to a certain subsystem of society. Each societal subsystem specializes in only one basic societal function and operates with communications the form of which corresponds to this function. For example, the continuous flow of specialized economic communications forms the economic subsystem of society, and in the same way other subsystems – politics, law, science, etc. – constantly reproduce themselves by processing their own specialized communications. There are, of course, other communications in society as well, which do not belong to such a subsystem. However, the specialization of much societal communication on certain functions is such a pervasive feature of modern society that systems theory talks about a functionally differentiated society. As society depends on the fulfillment of all these functions, no societal subsystem is more important than any other and there is no hierarchy between them. In contrast, the society of the early modern era was also differentiated, but according to social strata, primarily formed by birth rights, and not according to functions. Therefore it had the form of a hierarchy, with the top positions (nobility, clergymen) representing society as a whole. This difference between a stratified society and a functionally differentiated society is most important when it comes to the concept of risk, since systems theory regards risk as a distinctly modern phenomenon, inherently linked to functional differentiation.

The society of the early modern era with its stratified social structure still had social positions with religious and moral authority, and thus provided a general, binding frame for actions, not to be doubted by anybody. When a set of, in principle, equally important function systems developed and this functional differentiation started to dominate and replace the vertical stratification of society, these certainties dissolved and the phenomenon of risk appeared. Systems theory assumes that society no longer has any center or top and, instead of external references to religion that formerly guided actions, each societal system can only refer to its own logic and its own past in order to orient its operations. This self-reference of communicative operations, meaning that all communications of a functional system always primarily refer to other communications of this system, is the most important feature of function systems. For example, an economic communication dealing with the foundation of a new private university is bound to refer to investment costs, past and future interest rates, or similar aspects, but not to exciting results of scientific research. From the point of view of the economic system, the latter are only relevant in terms of possible financial returns. In other words, references to the outside of a function system are always internally constructed and therefore dependent on the structure of the system and on the distinctions it uses.

Systems theory describes this self-reference of modern function systems by using terms like *code* and *second-order observation*. A code is a binary distinction orienting the operations of a function system (e.g. truth/untruth for the system of science and property/no property for the economic system). As each function system uses its own code, the way it observes society is distinctly different from that of other function systems. The economic system observes everything in terms of consequences for liquidity and property; the scientific system observes everything in terms of consequences for knowledge recognized as true. Since all this happens in a continuous process of communications followed by other communications, every such observation is only momentary. A later observation within the economic system will thus identify another distribution of liquidity due to economic transactions that have taken place, and a later scientific observation may regard knowledge formerly believed to be true as falsified by new research. Moreover, a mode of observation which in this way focuses on the distinction used for an observation implies that there are no objective facts. Objectivity is a plausible idea only as long as observations take their own distinctions for granted, that is as long as they operate as first-order observations. But when distinctions themselves are observed, it becomes clear that the result of every observation depends on the distinctions used by the observer. The same event looks very different if one compares the perspective of the economic system with that of the scientific system. For example, the economic system will observe an earthquake with regard to the consequences for insurance companies, the stock exchange, and other similar aspects, which all point to questions of liquidity and property. In contrast, the scientific system will observe the same earthquake as an event that does or does not fit existing seismologic theories and thus offers hints as to their validity. If one takes this divergence of perspectives – multiplied by simultaneous and equally divergent observations of the other function systems – seriously, it implies that modern society does not have any common ground another observer could not question. In other words, second-order observation, focusing on distinctions, undermines all ontological assumptions. It is a mode of observation often found in modern society, and at the same time it is a basic technique of systems theory, used in order to question seemingly obvious facts and perceptions.

Based on its general description of modern society, systems theory develops a concept of risk distinctly different from other theoretical approaches in risk research. Systems theory neither assumes that risks are the result of an inherently dangerous process of modernization and its technological developments (Beck 1992b), nor argues that risk is associated with industrial capitalism (O'Connor 1984). But apart from dissociating risk and technology, systems theory distances itself further from conventional ideas of risk by opting against an understanding of risk based on action (Slovic 1992). Although it may be the easier approach to regard risk as something that results from people acting in a certain way,[1] this already presupposes relations between micro and macro structures about which we can learn very little by focusing on action. That is why such approaches tend to jump to very general statements about risk and society. In other words, an action-centered perspective misses the specific character of risk by linking it too quickly to other phenomena commonly regarded as typical for modern society, such as individualization (Sennett 1977), complex technologies (Perrow 1984), and globalization (Beck 1999). There is no doubt that these are relevant aspects when talking about risks, but by concentrating on them one underestimates how fundamentally risk is embedded in the structure of modern society. As a consequence, most risk research restricts itself to technological or other societal problems already framed by public discussion as concerned with risk. Instead of regarding it as a phenomenon associated with certain realms of society, systems theory places risk at the center of its theory of modern society.

In contrast, systems theory permits the application of the concept of risk to a wide range of topics. In doing that, systems theory takes up results of international risk research and concepts from New Institutionalism, but frames them in a particular way. It adds to the analysis of risk perceptions a perspective for which differing perceptions are not due to psychological mechanisms (Kahneman & Tversky 1984) or differences between lay and expert knowledge (Fischhoff et al. 1983); systems theory analyses them as results of communications using different distinctions (e.g. Hahn et al. 1992). With regard to risk regulation, the approach particularly focuses on the ways in which various function systems deal with risks according to the communicative logic of the respective system on the one hand and try to get rid of risk problems by shifting them to other function systems on the other hand (e.g. Hiller 1997; Schmidt 1997). Thus systems theory adds to the analysis of organizations concerned with risk regulation the sensitivity for constraints imposed on them by functional realms of society. Research using the approach deals with the perception and regulation of ecological and health problems, disasters, and the emergence of social movements, especially in connection with ecological conflicts. It is the interest in conflict as a social phenomenon anchored not in distinct group characteristics or value differences but in the consequences of functional differentiation that leads systems theory to broaden the scope of risk research. For systems theory, even problems like the conflict between Israelis and Palestinians can become the topic of an analysis in terms of risk.

Modernity, Decision Making, and Risk

As systems theory aims at a perspective that pays attention to the constitutive character of risk for modern society, it is careful not to interpret risks as objectively given dangers, like a first-order observation would be restricted to do. For instance, life in the Roman Empire or in ancient Athens was probably not less dangerous than life in modern New York. But the important question is whether it is also true that life was not less *risky* back then. The example of the daring merchant of the twelfth or thirteenth century, who decided to ship his goods without knowing whether they would reach their destination, points to the connection between uncertain and, in particular, negative consequences of a decision and risk.[2] Risk concerns consequences of a decision that will occur in the future but are unknown in the present. Without this uncertainty no decision would be necessary. In order to act toward the future, one must select from a horizon of possibilities. This implies that each selection made from this infinite horizon of possibilities could have taken place with another result. Luhmann (1995) uses the term *contingency* for this typical situation, in which all sorts of selections are possible, but not any one of them is necessary. This term is so general that it applies to every instance of decision making and therefore does not restrict the concept of risk to the realm of technology or health or to aspects of globalization. Insofar as all acting and decision making is based on a selection from a set of alternatives, it is always contingent and therefore always risky: It is risky to get married, to choose a career, or to live in the proximity of a nuclear power plant. One must decide about everything without any safe point of reference in the future. It is impossible to be certain and it is necessary to deal with this uncertainty.

By referring to contingency, one avoids haphazardly focusing on the next best aspect of risk and mistaking it for its core. Commonly, it seems that risk depends on the probability and severity of a future damage (see Japp 2000a: 6f.). In fact, modern risk-taking behavior relies on elaborate calculations of probabilities, which are primarily based on experience with similar risks in the past (MacCrimmon & Wehrung 1988). But it would be a mistake to regard this reliance on insurance companies and mathematics as the key to the role of risk in modernity (see Ewald 1993). The fact that the merchant who left his goods with the ship and its crew to the rigors of the sea decided without being able to rely on these instruments does not seem to be so important since we often experience this acceptance of an uncertain future in everyday life. Research about decision-making behavior in organizations shows that the attention paid to estimations of probability even decreases with increasing relevance of the decision (March & Olsen 1995).[3] What is important about the ship owner – no matter what he himself actually thought about his actions – is that he acted on his own account. He took responsibility for the success or failure of his project (see Brunsson 1985) and this self-attribution of consequences of decisions is a key feature of modernity.[4]

Risky decision making leads the way to, and at the same time accompanies, structural shifts from transcendence to immanence,[5] from nature to subjectivity, from external ties to internal motives: from external reference to self-reference. The concept of risk corresponds with diagnoses of modern society which state the loss of certainties and an accelerated dynamic of information and knowledge.[6] More precisely, contingency and the resulting need for decisions is an effect of the formation of functionally differentiated social systems. The existence of function systems which are in principle all equally important for society implies that there is no outside superior authority determining the course of action within a function system. In former societies, religion had this role of guiding actions, but now each societal system can only refer to its own logic and its own past in order to orient its operations. The self-reference of social systems replaces external references. It is this self-reference and the corresponding lack of externally determined references that produces the infinite horizon of possibilities and the resulting necessity of selection and decision making in modern society. As soon as societal operations are no longer anchored in external and binding references to religion or morality, they become self-referential and produce, on the one hand, an excess of options and consequently, on the other hand, a need for self-organization. Contingency is then the background of all societal operations and one could take every decision with another result and other consequences. This is the ever uncertain basis for decisions and the reference to "binding" information of any kind cannot reduce their risky character.[7] External ties, which protect against open futures, have to be "invented" (experience, routines, proper channels, hierarchy). However, they lose their substantial character, become themselves contingent (subject to decisions), and allow ever new futures, which keep the same circle of self-produced need for decision making going.

To say that there are few opportunities to change society (see Offe 1985) is not an argument against contingency as decisions are required in any case, which implies an open future.[8] Even when there is enormous resistance against change in a society (which means consequences of decisions made coalesce to structures resistant to change), it remains risky to act both in accordance with these structures and against them. Both options bear consequences which one cannot calculate in advance. However, there are tendencies toward self-reinforcement of decisions once they have been taken (Janis 1972; Japp 1992), which counter – although only temporarily – this self-production of indeterminacy. It is common to cling to past decisions, in spite of a growing amount of evidence pointing to negative consequences. This tendency toward reinforcement of past selections is one of the most important problems of learning organizations (Brunsson 1985). It is not less risky to opt against change, but the risks of the implied incrementalism are less visible than those of structural reform. In a sense, the orientation toward risk aversion (as the seemingly safe side of proved and consented practices) replaces the orientation toward goal achievement. This attempt to deal with an unknown future is risky itself, because possibly the damage is the missed opportunities due to not taking any risk (March & Shapira 1987; Wildavsky 1988).[9] Thus, in any case society encompasses so much non-knowledge (Japp 2000b; Japp 2003a) that it is impossible to avoid the "mystery of decision-making."

The terms shortly introduced here help to reframe the term "risk" in a way that, in contrast to other available sociological concepts of risk, fosters an understanding of modern society in general (see Luhmann 1993; Japp 1996, 2000a). They point to the structural contingencies that modern society has to deal with more clearly than other theories. Binary codes and self-reference of functionally specialized communications are the keys to an understanding of these contingencies. Societal communication is about legality or non-legality, about truth or untruth, about power or non-power: that is, about self-referentially established orientations for "correct" operations. The dominance of self-reference makes anything the system takes into account from the outside dependent on internal decisions, since there is no external authority that could impose its consideration.[10] Systems theory implies that modern society depends on decision making and therefore on risk as a fundamental fact. Risk is the modern form for observing decisions. Like all social meaning, decisions have implications in three dimensions, which are of course intertwined: the material dimension, the social dimension, and the time dimension. In the material dimension, decisions bear consequences for objects and their attributes: for example, the quality of housing in an area or the level of pollution in a river. In the social dimension, decisions affect people, and usually different groups of people in different ways. Finally, in the time dimension, they mark a difference between what was before the decision and what will be after it is taken. The following sections will deal with the relevance of risk in these three dimensions.

The Time Dimension: Modernity

At the beginning of the modern era, semantics of time emerge which replace the idea of the *unity* of past and future by the idea of the *difference* of past and future. A primarily cyclical concept of time (repetition) changes into a primarily linear concept of time (novelty) (Shackle 1976; Nassehi 1993). Inventions like the printing press and other innovations in art and science accompany this change, which is part of a transformation of the societal structure toward functional differentiation. Once the leading role of religion and nobility in the society is undermined and the specialized societal distinctions (codes) of politics, science, education, art, economy, and law begin to establish their functionally specified claims to autonomy, this change releases societal communication from an overarching religious frame into an open process of momentary communications. Modern society is no longer based on institutions that ensure redundancy, like the court or the integrative households of former centuries, which fused politics, religion, the economy, education, and law. These anchors of communicative integration vanish; a mass of decisions made in functionally specified contexts replaces them and produces variance. This requires open futures, which are at the same time produced in the course of continuous decision making: Decisions are only possible if the future is not identical with the past. Therefore only self-constructed criteria can limit such an open horizon of possibilities. On the other hand, no decision knows its consequences in advance, which is why it reproduces further open horizons of possibilities and the need for further decisions. The difference between past and future thus replaces the former unitary, cosmological concept of time (Shackle 1976; Luhmann 1993: 33ff; Nassehi 1993.).

The new concept no longer prescribes the future eschatologically, but triggers its explosion into an open horizon of possibilities. Functional differentiation – and that always means: self-referential communication – leads to a multiplication and inherent flexibility of the time horizons of the various social systems. The present is reduced to a fleeting moment, in some way the blind spot of the ever shifting difference between past and future. The future is unknown and each step from a present future into a future present can only confirm the difference. Each step toward a present future is already a modification of what has been the case. Having got married, the future of this marriage already looks different compared to the time before the wedding. Having realized an economic innovation, new problems already emerge. The present is only the switching point between these time horizons that shift from each present to the next. Neither revelation nor information can determine the passage from past to future, which will then already be a past future – one must decide it. In consequence, events and structures of modern society depend on the attribution to decisions made and not on tradition, custom, or habit. For example, the law refers to past legal decisions in order to decide a case and not to any other framework. This attribution to decisions is common even for aspects about which nobody seems to have decided. For example, in the aftermath of the hurricane Katrina a public argument developed in the USA with regard to the responsibility for the extent of damage: Was the inexperienced director of the Federal Emergency Management Agency (Fema) to blame? Or the inefficient local and state governments that did not manage to state clearly what kind of help they needed?[11] Nature does not play any role in such a discussion, apart from the connection made to climate change. But the latter is, of course, also the result of decisions: for example, about whether to enforce energy efficiency and to invest in alternative sources of energy. This structural drift of societal communication toward a focus on decisions and their consequences is the fundamental basis for a concept of risk in the context of a theory of modern society. Such a concept of risk takes into account the centrality of an unknown and unknowable future. One can only fake or imagine certainties and con-tinuous presents, but not avoid the necessity of decision making. It may be possible to deceive oneself about these conditions of modern society, but an observer could attribute even this to a decision.

Decisions make the difference of time visible. But this means that time is nothing substantial; instead one has to understand it as an opera-tional phenomenon. Using certain distinctions allows one to observe time; other distinctions would lead to other observations. Only the continuous stream of formerly unknown novelties that become known (technologies, medicine, art, etc.) draws attention to the old, a past soon distanced as simple tradition, thereby constituting the distinction between old and new. This distinction is certainly important for modern society, as its prominence in mass media and science illustrates. On the other hand, people get used to what is new – it must be really very new in order to still provoke amazement. And compared to the myths of progress typical for the nineteenth and the beginning of the twentieth century it is primarily the failures, the catastrophes, which elicit a public response. Progress is nevertheless everywhere, but it becomes increas-ingly invisible due to the continuous re-evaluations of changing time horizons (e.g. as a result of discussing so-called "unintended conse-quences" or "collateral damages") and loses its "given identity" (Nassehi 1993). People tend to observe the difference of past and future no longer with regard to whether it produces "progress," but with regard to whether it produces risks in the sense of disadvantages or damages attributable to decisions made. Risk is the most important scheme for observing time in modern society (Hiller 1993).[12]

Decision making integrates past and future in a selective way, which means always contingently or according to criteria themselves fixed by decisions. These criteria depend on the operationally constituted past and on projections of the future one can link to this past.[13] Based on such criteria, the open contingency before a decision is transformed into the fixed contingency after a decision (Luhmann 1995: 294ff.). After the decision (to get married or not, to innovate or not, etc.) there remains only to accept the selectivity of the decision, perhaps to regret it (Harrison & March 1984), and to identify new need for decisions. New Institutionalism argues that under such circumstances it is crucial to construct enough certainty about expectations in order for decision mak-ing to take place at all. Vaughan (1996) shows with regard to the fatal Challenger launch in 1986 how the NASA engineer teams converted uncertainty into certainty before each decision to launch a space shuttle. The constructed character of this certainty became obvious only with the Challenger accident. Not always is the uncertainty in the background of decision making so strikingly revealed, but it remains a problem for every decision. The consequence of constructing certainty concerning a decision is an almost inevitable regret, because the result cannot fulfill expectations. Risk implies *post-decisional regret*. From the point of view of systems theory, this regret is due to the irreducible contingency or irreducible selectivity of decision making. Decisions can never obtain certainty, because it would always have been possible to decide otherwise and one can never know whether another option would have been the "better one" after all. In that sense, decision making is risky: one cannot rule out disadvantageous consequences in advance. Only against one's better judgment is it possible to claim the "correctness" of a decision.[14] Mechanisms that compensate for this loss of certainties (see Japp 1992; Zey 1992) have to rely on a degree of fatalism or on the adaptation of preferences to the results of a decision.

As we have seen, the semantics of risk refer to a temporal difference characteristic of modern society in general. But the functional differentiation of the latter implies that each function system deals with risk according to its own communicative structures and code. Therefore an important field of systems theory research on risk is concerned with analyzing the impact of this way to observe time on concrete function systems. A prominent example is the legal system, because law is supposed to be a central mechanism for regulating risk. However, Luhmann (1993: 165ff.) himself is rather skeptical with regard to the capacities of law to deal with risk problems. Following him, Hiller (1993) points out that the main difficulty for the legal system derives from its own time orientation, which is very different from that of risk. Whereas risk refers to the future, law is primarily concerned with past events as triggering legal communication – someone has infringed a law and the legal system reacts to this violation. At a time when people tend to observe more and more problems as risks – that is, to attribute them to decisions – the use of law for risk regulation requires new concepts. In the field of environmental law, liability is an example. With the extension of liability to cases in which an endangerment of the environment was not foreseeable at the time the respective decision was taken, it is no longer possible to predict legal consequences of an action or a decision in advance. From the point of view of systems theory, this appears to be a contradiction to the basic function of law, which is the stabilization of normative expectations, and consequently a risky development for the legal system itself (see Hapke & Japp 2001). However, not all scholars agree with this view. In particular, Ladeur (1999) believes that it ignores the potential for flexibility within the legal system, because it concentrates too much on the role of court decisions. If one takes into account contracts as the most frequent form of legal communication, this function system seems quite capable of dealing with risks by developing conventions, which are anchored in contracts and not in court decisions. Apart from this theoretical argument, Ladeur believes that other scholars overestimate the example of liability as evidence for the difficulties of dealing with risks in the legal system. In his opinion, the extension of the respective laws may imply some dogmatic problems, but in practice their application poses no more difficulties than older rules for liability.

The Material Dimension: Risk and Danger

One of the most important conceptual changes Niklas Luhmann suggested in his works on risk concerns the term that is supposed to mark the opposite of risk. Commonly, one regards safety as this opposite. But observing the distinction between risk and safety – that is, seeing it *as a distinction* without ontological qualities – leads to the conclusion that safety never occurs, that it is only a goal worked toward but never reached. The term "safety" is similar to the term "health": both are terms for reflection in the sense that they mirror their opposite – uncertainty, illness – and none is achievable as a material state. From the perspective of second-order observation it becomes clear that safety itself is never certain, but always uncertain. By choosing the apparently "safe" option, one cannot know whether another option would have or would not have provided better opportunities. Every possible alternative in decision making is risky, at least in the sense that it is uncertain if by selecting it one throws away opportunities that could prove more advantageous.

As a consequence, Luhmann (1993: 19ff.) suggests replacing the distinction of risk and safety by a second-order distinction assuming uncertainty on both sides of the distinction. The general problem with uncertainty is that it may block decision making as a whole if it is too great. One is only prepared to decide if one believes that things are sufficiently under control, which then encourages one to accept responsibility for this decision although information is uncertain and incomplete. We are prepared to marry without really knowing the respective person or we allow the construction of nuclear power plants without being absolutely sure that they are reliable – we take a risk. Accordingly, making a decision and attributing its uncertain consequences to this decision implies risk. In contrast, negative effects regarded as caused by external events are mere dangers. In other words, the distinction between risk and danger does not refer to differences in certainty, but to a difference in attribution. Risk implies that the cause of possible damage is attributed to the system itself, whereas danger refers to the external attribution of a cause for possible damage.

This careful separation of the terms "risk" and "danger," otherwise often used as synonyms, is an important clarification. Instead of assuming a (possibly increasing) number of objectively given risks/dangers (see, e.g. Beck 1992b), it makes clear that whether we regard something as a risk is a matter of attribution. Thereby it leads to a further, closely connected distinction between decision-makers on the one hand and those affected by decisions on the other hand. This distinction derives from the question of whether the possibility of damage is voluntarily accepted or not. Of course, the respective degrees of acceptance or rejection differ according to whether something is seen as the result of own decisions or as an external danger (Starr 1969; Luhmann 1993: 104ff.). On both sides of the distinction, attribution works in a different way; some calculate a risk, whereas the others regard themselves as the victims of this calculation. The risks taken by some become dangers for others. It is the decision-maker who appears to have caused potential harm, since she could have decided otherwise. But the important thing is that it depends on observation who is held to be a decision-maker or, in other words, how risk and danger are attributed. Hilgartner (1992) in a similar way argues that established chains of causation leading to harm are the result of social construction. He talks about the construction of risk objects and draws on the example of Ralph Nader's efforts to change the perception of motor vehicle accidents. For a long time, the driver had been regarded as the dominant risk object in road safety policy or, as systems theory would describe it, the driver had seemed to be the decision-maker whose decision to speed or to drive drunk could become a danger for others. Nader pointed to several alternative risk objects with regard to road safety, especially unsafe cars. To the extent that he could establish this kind of observation, other entities, especially car manufacturers, suddenly appeared as decision-makers (Hilgartner 1992). It is possible to regard their decision to accept unsafe car designs as a danger for other people, who are simply affected by those decisions as they do not have any say in the design process. The example illustrates that the distinction between risk and danger is not objectively given. What is attributed to decisions depends on observation. That is why systems theory calls the distinction between risk and danger a second-order distinction. However, the first-order distinction between risk and safety remains important. Engineers and insurance experts have to use it if they want to meet expectations about their professional behavior. The fact that all communication depends on observation does not mean that anything goes. It means that the reference of observation, its context, is decisive. To deal with "safety" as an engineer is very different from observing these actions as a sociologist of risk.[15]

Hahn et al. (1992) apply the distinction between risk and danger to the case of AIDS and analyze how different groups of the German population perceive this disease. Adding ideas about individualization, the authors assume that the attribution of consequences to one's own decisions is something particularly practiced in contexts with many uncertainties. They suggest that especially people who are young, with high social status and an urban lifestyle tend to live in such contexts. Consequently, they assume that this group is more likely to show self-confidence in the sense of self-attribution, compared to older people with a lower social status and a rural background. Standardized interviews of a general population sample yielded the result that the latter group, although objectively the least likely to be infected, actually tended to perceive AIDS as an uncontrollable danger and to demand strict measures for the protection of public health. In contrast, the first group more often regarded it as a problem of individual risk and caution. Of course, in spite of such research, public health experts keep on informing the public about AIDS as a risk and about what each person can do to foster safety. They must remain first-order observers using the distinction between risk and safety. But the cited research as second-order observation is able to show that scientific enlightenment is not sufficient to convince all people that AIDS is a controllable risk instead of an uncontrollable danger.

If risk is a matter of attribution, this has consequences for the function systems of society, especially for the political system. It is, in particular, the political system which attracts all kinds of worries and expectations. As this system operates according to its own communicative logic, based on the code power/no power, such expectations gain relevance only when they seem likely to influence the chances of re-election for office. As long as this is not the case, the problem does not exist for the political system. People may see themselves exposed to all kinds of dangers, but this does not necessarily trigger any reaction in the political system. However, as soon as the political system takes care of a problem, it faces risks, because effects can be attributed to political decisions and thus influence public opinion and voters. Krücken (1997) analyzes the consequences of such a transformation of external dangers into internal risks of the political system by referring to the regulation of drugs. Drugs are scientific innovations aimed at reducing health problems, but their possible side-effects may themselves endanger health. Krücken argues that the regulation of new drugs implies that political decision-makers take on risks. They have to decide to what degree prevention is necessary. Depending on the situation, they could be made responsible both for prematurely approving drugs that later show serious side-effects and for delaying the approval of drugs in favor of further testing, although they could help many people. Comparing regulation regimes in Germany, Great Britain, and the United States, Krücken comes to the conclusion that regulation regimes are a reaction to this political problem. They are built in a way that aims not to minimize the technological risk of introducing a new drug but to reduce the political risk of being made responsible for decisions that later prove wrong. Consequently, they tend to include both scientific experts and drug producers in the process of regulation in order to diffuse responsibilities and thereby lower political risks. Krücken thus focuses on the shifting of risks between the function systems of politics, the economy, and science. On the level of organization systems, Rothstein et al. (2006) develop a similar idea: they describe how regulatory organizations come to regard their role in risk regulation as a risk for their organizational survival and react by shifting problems elsewhere, creating new risks for other organizations. Whether with regard to function systems or organizations, managing risks does not result in safety but in other kinds of risk.

The Social Dimension: Conflicts

The distinction between risk and danger and its equivalent in the social dimension, the distinction between decision-makers and those affected, also initiated research on conflicts (Luhmann 1993: 136ff.; see also Marshall et al. 2004). Its basis is the assumption, derived from these distinctions, that people reject decisions simply because it was not they but others who made the decisions. In other words, reactions are dependent neither on a special substantial identity of those being affected nor on the provision of "reasonable arguments." Instead they result from two fundamentally different perspectives of observation. In the social dimension, the distinction between risk and danger marks a boundary separating completely divergent expectations and communicative links concerning "the same risk." That is why there is so little understanding for the attitude of the other side and so much seemingly irrational resistance against probabilistic risk assessments of expert decision-makers. Any attempt to rationalize risk regulation by promoting methods such as cost–benefit analysis and to calm down public worries by pointing to the results of such calculations (see Sunstein 2002) cannot overcome the fundamental difference between those who decide about risks and those who have to deal with the consequences of these decisions. The problem is not one of rationality or its lack, but the general resistance against being affected by consequences for which one is not responsible. The decision-maker may strive for the most rational calculation of risks and opportunities; those affected are not the least impressed by the results, because their perspective is solely the effect of not *themselves* causing the consequences of the decision.[16] This alone is sufficient in order to reject any calculation or argument of the other side. At the same time, the decision-maker is obviously not able to agree to the perspective of those affected. The reciprocity that would allow a mutual understanding is clearly lacking. In fact, it is a modern form of a social divide, which is without predecessors in the sense that all common ways of integration, such as trust or authority (of experts), fail when it becomes relevant (Douglas 1985; Fowlkes & Miller 1987; Japp 2000a). The problem is one of divergent perspectives between self-attribution and external attribution of risks. Increasingly, there are cases in which all attempts to foster trust result in mistrust and all attempts to claim authority create opposition. The reason for this is not the issue itself, but the paradoxes of risk communication, which continuously produces the suspicion of hidden motives on the respective other side of the distinction (Otway & Wynne 1989). But how is it possible to come to agreements under such circumstances?

As the confrontation of decision-makers and those affected is due to a fundamental opposition of perspectives, the circumstances are reminiscent of what Miller (1992) calls an infinite conflict. An infinite conflict cannot be solved or dealt with, because the conflicting parties are not able to identify any common ground. They do not even seem to discuss the same problem. This is the typical situation in the case of a conflict between experts and lay-persons: for example, about biotechnology or genetic engineering (see Deckers 2005). Experts may discuss benefits and safety levels, but lay-persons who feel themselves affected by consequences of new technologies are not susceptible to this kind of argument. They do not care about probability calculations but simply perceive themselves as exposed to something *they* cannot control (see Luhmann 1993: 101ff.). This lack of common ground is normal in all cases of communication between functionally differentiated realms (economy, politics, science).[17] Since each function system operates according to its own logic and structures, there are no shared expectations of any kind. In this sense, functional differentiation encourages a tendency toward infinite conflicts. If this were the end of the story, all societal development would be blocked. Economically, it would be impossible to realize the construction of facilities believed to be dangerous. Politically, the collectively binding effect of political decisions would be undermined and the protest of social movements would remain unheard (Halfmann & Japp 1993). Miller hopes for structural change, which could bring about agreements nevertheless, primarily based on intermediary systems of negotiation (as bargaining, mediation, or participation). But systems theory points to the unavoidable difference in perspective between the conflicting parties. As a consequence, it clarifies that less ambitious attempts at an agreement are more likely to be successful. Communication aimed at consensus is bound to fail; instead only a pragmatic assumption of difference can provide the basis for discourse. Pragmatism means here abstaining from any attempt at "real" or "authentic" understanding. The typical result is that mutual understanding is simply assumed, and in this way it has actual consequences. What is needed are distinctions enabling the consideration of other perspectives, even if only in a tentative and provisional way. Infinite conflicts signal differences which do not encompass any opportunity for mutual consideration. From the point of view of participatory ideas, the involved preferences are autonomous – for example, purely economic – which is why they hinder the adaptation to preferences in the environment of the economic system, like political preferences or those of a social movement. Such situations require the creation of systems of negotiation, which specialize in the production of distinctions allowing temporary agreements between different perspectives (Miller 1992; Vollmer 1996)[18] or, in other words, multiple considerations (see Fuchs 1992: 237ff.; Giegel 1992: 106). A characteristic example from the recent German past (2000/2001) is the agreement about the shutdown of nuclear power plants. The economic and the political perspective on this issue were, of course, incompatible: in particular, the Green Party wanted to be able to point to the first closing of a nuclear plant as soon as possible, meaning at least before the next elections. In contrast, the nuclear industry preferred to run its plants as long as possible. An agreement became possible when the discussion switched from limiting the time nuclear plants were allowed to operate to limiting the amount of current allowed to be produced by nuclear plants. The latter provided an incentive for the industry to close down smaller and older plants, which was welcome from the political point of view, in exchange for longer terms of operation for the remaining more efficient plants, an advantage from the economic point of view. Another example are the various instances of resistance against refuse incinerators. In the long run, protests are often abandoned in favor of temporary agreements about incineration temperatures.

The assumption of understanding, of a common ground, works in spite of fundamental, but virtualized dissent. Such agreements come close to Miller's "finite conflicts." A finite conflict reproduces existing structures since no social change is necessary in order to create the common ground. The examples show that temporary agreements are possible, although nothing similar can be achieved concerning the basic difference in perspective or the divergent codes of the economy and of politics.[19] It is not possible to simply balance political acceptability of a nuclear power plant with economic profitability. The main function of agreements is accordingly their temporality, their potential for correction, and not their authenticity. This dominance of limited solutions shows the relevance of time for risk also in the social dimension.

Regardless of the degree of complexity such agreements show, they remain *pragmatic* forms. They are based not on (temporal, material, and social) certainty, but on uncertainty about the foundation of an agreement. They only work for this reason. Claims supported by certainty about one's argument lead only to self-reinforcement of exclusionary effects. This is especially true for any form of moral self-assertion. As soon as the communication exceeds a critical threshold, it breaks apart into first-order observations incapable of mutual consideration. Negotiations demanding too much consensus are prone to fail. It is also important to remember that even the most complex multiple considerations (of politics, the economy, science) are always based on internal processes of a system (e.g. the economy or a protest movement). All external considerations cannot eliminate this condition. Before enabling further information processing, all multiple considerations allow one only to consider the otherness of other distinctions and consequently to see the contingency of the own distinctions. A complete consideration of the other perspective remains impossible. Bora (1999) analyzes the attempts of the German legal system to combine administrative decision making with participative procedures. The law regulating the release of genetically modified organisms in Germany provides opportunities for the public to participate in legal decision making by attending a public hearing (see Bora 1999: 130ff.). Bora diagnoses systematic difficulties of such an arrangement. According to him, it ignores the inherent differences between legal communication, scientific communication, and political demands of protest movements. Whereas the procedure is defined as a legal one, the public hearing tends to be a mixture of arguments often ignoring the code of the legal system and the law on genetic engineering. Instead communication focuses on political preferences or moral evaluations. These communications are bound to remain without much impact on the decision in the end, as the logic of the legal system precludes invoking moral standards that ignore the distinction between legal and illegal in favor of certain values. On the other hand, the idea of the public hearing seems to suggest that everyone's view on the matter is treated as relevant. Participants are soon disappointed and the hearing becomes laden with conflict, since it cannot fulfill expectations. As a result, the procedure does not solve conflicts about the release of genetically modified organisms but even fosters them (see Bora 1999: ch. 6).

In sum, decision-makers and those affected can come to an agreement by keeping latent that the dissent in principle is insoluble and realizing the partial consideration of the other perspective instead. Any form of substantial consensus is unreachable. Agreements are negotiated, provisional arrangements, which imply nothing for the chances of consensus or rationality. Systems theory suggests that the basis for agreements is the irritation of decision-makers by those affected (and vice versa) rather than the rationality of arguments. Irritation renders one's own certainty relative and suggests self-imposed constraints in "discourse," if those involved regard the lack of agreement as not attractive. Because of the general incongruence of perspectives, ratio-nality or force could not create these self-imposed constraints. The fact that the constraints are only provisional – in the sense of finite conflicts which can surface again and again – points once again to the prominent role of the time dimension in risk communication. Compared to theo-retical approaches favoring participative procedures as the way to solve risk conflicts, systems theory emphasizes their limitations. All hopes for more social rationality as the key to risk regulation (e.g. Bradbury 1989) miss the point that general authentic consensus in a functionally differ-entiated society is impossible to achieve. Instead of lamenting the lack of reciprocal understanding, systems theory suggests lowering ambitions and focusing on pragmatic solutions in spite of continuing dissent.

Referring to the Parsonian version of systems theory, Münch (1996) criticizes this skepticism. He argues that function systems overlap in zones of interpenetration, in which negotiations between representa-tive actors of the system allow an actual coordination, whereas the Luhmannian strand of systems theory can only see different modes of observation and latent or manifest conflicts. In the end, this controversy goes back to the choice between "action" and "communication" as the basic term for a sociological theory. Conceiving of society as composed of actions, there remains the possibility of regarding the actors as those who have to reconcile all societal heterogeneities and differences, although one may wonder how they can be expected to succeed. In contrast, focusing on communication implies a heightened sensitivity to the divergence and incommensurability of societal realms and their necessities. Consequently, current social systems theory hesitates to count on rational coordination. However, the degree to which scholars regard weaker forms of coordination between function systems as possi-ble also differs within the community of new systems theory. Some scholars (Teubner & Willke 1984; Willke 1992) are more optimistic than others concerning this question (Luhmann 1989; Japp 2000a).

Beyond Classical Topics of Risk Research

Since systems theory reflects distinctions such as risk/danger and decision-makers/those affected as connected to the temporal and social structures of modern society in general, it is able to apply these schemes to problems and conflicts of this society that risk research does not usually discuss. One interesting example is the parallel structure of the distinction between risk and danger and the distinction between culprit and victim. Waldmann (2003) points to the public relevance of the latter distinction. On the one hand, all parties in a violent conflict tend to describe themselves as victims. The semantics of the victim create empathy and public recognition. On the other hand, Waldmann draws on the example of Israel in order to illustrate a general wish to take over a superior position and to control the others instead of being helplessly exposed to the force of others. In other words, there is a preference for being the culprit instead of the victim. The population of Israel includes many descendants of holocaust survivors and the foundation of the state of Israel itself is linked with the long history of persecution and discrimination of Jews. In that sense, one might expect familiarity and empathy with the perspective of the victim. Nevertheless, Israel deals with the Palestinians in a way that seems to ignore this past. Therefore, many first-order observers refer to questions of morality and guilt when discussing the conflict between Israel and the Palestinians, and suspect an inexplicable irrationality on one or both sides. But a second-order observer, who observes how distinctions are used, is able to see that the sides of distinctions such as rationality/irrationality and guilt/innocence are interchangeable between the conflicting parties. Both parties are entangled in a dynamic conflict, which permits them to see the respective adversary party only in terms of the harm they can do to them. That is why the conflict is no longer soluble without external intervention. The scheme of rationality is exposed as nothing more than a scheme for denigration in the context of the conflict dynamic in the Middle East.

Compared to this distinction between rationality and irrationality, the distinction between culprit and victim or, in other words, between decision-makers and those affected is far more interesting. The culprit decides and takes risks, whereas for the victim these decisions become dangers on which she has no influence. Applying the distinction in the case of Israel, it points to the political distinction between superiority and inferiority in power, implying positions of decision-makers and those affected by decisions, which moral distinctions cannot turn around.[20] In their history, the Israeli people were victimized to an extreme degree. Now they are decision-makers to an extreme degree, because they take risks they are not forced to take thanks to their superiority in power. In contrast, the Palestinians operate from a perspective which appears to them as a state of being affected that is without alternative, exposed to the consequences of the decisions of others. The conflict is not about irrational reasons of desperate fanatics on the one side and rational reasons of state on the other side. Already the relatively high degree of organization on the side of the Palestinians and certain operations of Israel that obviously contradict the idea of reasons of state are evidence for this. It is the scheme of risk and danger or its corresponding social scheme of decision-makers and those affected which provokes the Palestinians to try and reach the side of decision making and animates the Israelis to defend the position of decision-makers with all means. The fact that both parties attempt to stage themselves as victims in public only confirms the social fascination of the scheme. Everybody aims to become the subject of the consequences of decisions. In other words, everybody aims at autonomy. And what would be irrational about that?

A second interesting field for the application of systems theory in the context of risk is the "war on terror." In contrast to the case of Israel, it does not concern a conventional conflict about the control over a specific territory, but seems to be an effect of a cultural conflict on a global scale. After 9/11 the topic of terrorism has certainly emerged as a new important issue for risk research in general. From the point of view of systems theory, however, the first aspect to be noted is that the distinction between risk and danger, which works so well for western civilization, does not seem to fit in the case of global terrorism (Japp 2003b). Following the strict definition given at the beginning of this chapter, on the side of risk no risks are taken! The suicide bomber appears to execute an act without alternative, in the sense that he does not think about himself as a decision-maker. Suicide makes the consequences of his action certain: for him there is no future that could suggest an evaluation of his decision different from the present one; consequently, there is no post-decisional regret (Harrison & March 1984)![21] On the other hand, observers of world politics and the world public attribute to risk nevertheless. For example, they attribute bombings to entities with the assumed ability to act, primarily al-Qaida. For these observers, the temporal, material, and social uncertainties of organized and globally operating terrorism are a danger that can be attributed to a concrete enemy. Consequently, the political system is expected to deal with the problem, which thus is transformed into a political risk. That is why massive (military, diplomatic, intelligence, and economic) investments in proactive risk management take place. The "alliance against terror" is supposed to reduce the primary risk and does in fact shift it, particularly in public presentation, to dependence on structures of prevention.[22] Decisions about prevention reproduce the primary risk (see Wildavsky 1988), which consequently becomes a danger for those affected by them. Critical voices point to the loss of liberal rights as an effect of extended security measures, to negative consequences for the integration of minorities, or to the questionable support for authoritarian regimes joining the "alliance against terror." The world-political system transforms the risk of organized terrorism into the self-produced political risk of prevention.[23] If this is right, who is to blame when terrorist actions occur? In the long run, the endangered institutions themselves or, more precisely, their organizations which take defensive or preventive action will be blamed with taking risks by trying to constrain terrorist action. In western culture (i.e. in modern society), those will take the blame who could do otherwise – who are perceived as decision-makers. One strategy of political decision-makers to counter this tendency is the denial of any alternative course of action. But authoritative statements of "having had no choice" (e.g. to make war on Iraq or not to make war on Iraq) are bound to provoke public distrust sooner or later, followed by further assertions about the lack of choice. The result is a kind of authenticity trap, because those who are assumed to be able to choose may not admit it, as they have to legitimate extraordinary measures, such as a war. This trap may produce severe problems with respect to public trust.

Another interesting point concerns the terrorists themselves. Although suicide bombers are not risk-takers in the sense explained in this chapter, systems theory can offer ideas about the background of this seemingly irrational phenomenon by referring again to the distinction between decision-makers and those affected. Enzensberger (1994) developed the thesis that in a society emphasizing responsibility for one's own actions, the lack of social recognition leads to violent discharge. But deficiencies in recognition are universal. How are we to explain that only in very few cases are the results acts of violence? It would be necessary to specify a sort of threshold beyond which violence is likely to occur. Beneath this threshold the usual mechanisms for the production of normality are working. If recognition in modern society is related to individual autonomy, the self-attribution of consequences of decisions is a main source for social recognition. Vice versa, one could assume that violence becomes likely where being affected by the decisions of others predominates. In fact, this is the line of argument of most observers: they diagnose the dominance of western values and the result of being affected by this on the part of people living in Islamic countries (Waldmann 1998; Tibi 1998; Kaldor 1999). But for a specification of the assumed threshold this is not sufficient or at least is too general, since most reactions to being affected remain nonviolent. Who is most susceptible to a lack of recognition would then be a psychological or moral question.

Interesting from a sociological point of view is the impression that violent acts are often related to a simultaneity of contradicting consequences of decisions. For example, people with a non-western background encounter pressures to act under the premises of self-attribution when entering western educational systems or those oriented toward western values. They must decide about their choice of career instead of letting origin determine it. But accepting such pressures contradicts the cultural and religious background of people from regions dominated by Islamic heritage (see Bruce 2000). As a result, they perceive themselves as being affected by the requirements of individualistic norms. They attribute consequences of decisions to a hostile environment. They take decisions, but are forced to do it! Risk and danger fuse with each other. Decision-makers and those affected are identical. One could say that a conflict becomes a drama in that way. It seems plausible that it leads to attempts at liberating oneself from the pressures of such a paradox. It is the paradox of the simultaneity of self-attribution and external attribution, of liberty and constraint. This heuristic application of a systems theoretical distinction must, of course, be validated by further research. But it would imply that violence is not an irrational reaction of backward people (as not only the media often tend to suggest), but a collective "liberation" from a social form with high – and sometimes unbearable – imposition (Bruce 2000' Japp 2003b).[24] In addition, the fact that the scheme of self-attribution is culturally embedded in values of individualism and liberal subjectivity, but also responsibility, can explain the middle- and upper-class background of many suicide bombers (Hoffman 2003).

In sum, even those who turn to violent action in contexts commonly interpreted as irrational still remain connected with the main value of modernity: the risk of modern autonomy versus the danger of external constraint. However, modernity does not seem to be capable of liberating itself from a "dialectics of enlightenment" in this respect either. Because the difference compared to the Palestine conflict is evident, how could any form of temporary, provisional "agreement" be possible in this case?

Conclusion

From the point of view of systems theory, risk is a form of observing modern society, and it is a very important one. Using this form, one observes all events according to the difference of past and future. Apart from the measurement of time with chronometric devices, only the observation of risk generates time as the qualitative, non-linear, and *irreducible* difference of past and future in the vanishing present of decision making. The importance of the category of risk consequently lies in its denial of transparency and the lack of opportunities to control it. The common forms of risk observation aim at compensating this lack of opportunities for control by "risk management" (Wynne 1987) in the material dimension (system/environment) and "risk dialogue" (ibid.) in the social dimension (ego/alter or consent/dissent respectively). Risk management can mean such diverse measures as the establishment of an emergency plan for a chemical production plant and the "war on terror." In parallel, risk dialogue does not only encompass forms of participation such as local public hearings before a refuse incinerator is built. In fact, one could regard nation building as a form of risk dialogue in the context of the risk of terrorism. To rely on such mechanisms inevitably leads to temporary illusions of control that may suddenly break apart and to disappointment if the expected consensus does not form. But to do without the compensations (e.g. by relying on purely "neoclassic" market solutions) would mean leaving oneself to the abysses of the form risk. And this option is ruled out by the preference for the position of decision making, for control, which is inherent in all aspects of social communication.

The perspective of systems theory on risk obviously differs from other approaches, such as reflexive modernization, cultural theory, and organizational approaches, in this ambition to link a theory of risk with a general theory of modern society. As a result, it does not take for granted the term "risk" itself, neither as usually associated with technologically induced risks nor as a commonsense term that does not need further elaboration. Instead it interprets risk as inherent in decision making and sees decision making itself as a question of attribution in communication. The resulting distinction between risk and danger, or rather its equivalent in the social dimension, the distinction between decision-makers and those affected, corresponds to distinctions often made in risk research, especially the one between experts and lay-persons (see Otway 1992). But whereas such distinctions usually have an ad-hoc character, derived from empirical cases of risk conflict, systems theory helps to clarify that they go back to fundamental structures of communication in modern society.

This way of describing risk problems provokes a number of critical objections. Scholars emphasizing the urgency of risk problems and hoping themselves to contribute to practical solutions strongly oppose the suggestion to conceptualize risk as a matter of attribution and observation. For them, systems theory implies several unacceptable consequences. By rejecting theoretical approaches that start with the assumption of actors, systems theory seems to distance itself from the realm of practical action in favor of passive observation. Although the previous sections have provided a number of examples which actually imply practical consequences for risk management, the approach faces a lot of opposition. The main reason for this is probably the fact that the practical implications of systems theory predominantly point to difficulties of dealing with risks instead of offering positive solutions. Systems theory points to barriers against enlightenment and mutual understanding that are embedded in the basic structures of societal communication. It draws attention to factors that prevent the overall success of information campaigns striving for a more rational attitude toward health risks. It shows why participative procedures introduced with the best of intentions may fail nevertheless. But, most importantly, it argues that such failures are not due to a lack of good will or appropriate methods, but are inevitable consequences of the way modern society operates. A theory yielding such results can be interpreted as an apology for the existing social structure, blocking the attempt to search for alternative societal arrangements by stating its hopelessness (see Habermas 1987: 353ff.). An important aspect contributing to this impression is the skeptical view of systems theory on the potential for rationality in a society that has become so complex that all efforts at control create a cascade of unforeseen effects and thus imply new risks.

Critics stress that the basic need of a democratic society to influence its own future (see Habermas 2001: 59f.) precludes abandoning the possibility of rational or at least more rational decision making.

Thus it does not seem surprising that, apart from those scholars with a clear preference for systems theory, risk research in general rarely takes up its concepts. Sometimes ideas from systems theory are used: for example, the assumption that social systems are closed communicative networks following their own logic and not very susceptible to external expectations (see Hood & Rothstein 2001) or the observation that modern society does not face more "actual risks," but tends to frame more and more events as risks (see Rothstein et al. 2006). But they merely provide interesting ideas on a special aspect of a problem and do not form a part of a consistent application of systems theory to this problem. The emphasis on second-order observation may seem a disadvantage for those who aim at contributing to actual reductions of risks or to more participative modes of decision making. However, the skeptical view of systems theory on the possibilities of realizing such objectives may be useful at least as a corrective and reminder of the limitations that a complex modern society implies for planned change and enlightenment (Japp 2004). But the most important reason for its hesitant reception in the wider risk research community is at the same time (paradoxically) the strength of the approach: its embeddedness in a complex theory of modern society in general. This theoretical background of a sociological systems theory implies a number of access barriers due to specialized terms and concepts contradicting common sociological wisdom: for example, concerning the role of the actor in social processes. Therefore it remains an important task for the scholars explicitly applying systems theory to foster its diffusion in the field of risk research. In order to achieve this, future research must on the one hand take up current risk debates, even if one strength of systems theory lies in its ability to point to the ubiquity of risk beyond public worries. On the other hand, empirical studies which include an international comparative perspective are necessary in order to increase the relevance of systems theory in risk research.

Further Reading

Luhmann, N. (1982) *The Differentiation of Society*. Columbia University Press, New York.

Luhmann, N. (1989) *Ecological Communication*. Polity, Cambridge.

Luhmann, N. (1993) *Risk: a sociological theory*. De Gruyter: Berlin and New York.

Luhmann, N. (1995) *Social Systems*. Stanford University Press, Stanford.

Rasch, W. (2000) *Niklas Luhmann's Modernity: the paradoxes of differentiation*. Stanford University Press, Stanford.

Notes

1. See for example Brunsson's (1985) concept of risk in the context of organizational research, which refers to individual motives, responsibilities, and tolerance for uncertainty in order to make risks comprehensible.

2. For the historic origin of the term "risk" in overseas trading and insurance, see Bonss (1995) and Clark (1999).

3. Except for organizations dealing with a great number of similar risks (e.g. car insurances), which are able to statistically "normalize" their calculations.

4. Of course, this self-attribution is fictitious in a way. After all, there are lots of decisions in the environment of the decision-maker, which he cannot control as they take place at the same time (e.g. decisions of the ship's crew). But it is the function of self-attribution to permit holding someone responsible or answerable in the case of failure. Otherwise nobody would be prepared to join a risky operation. This is true for all kinds of undertaking. For example, nobody would punish the American soldiers in Iraq if the project of democratisation failed, but it is likely that the American people would hold political decision-makers responsible for it. Accordingly, a success would also be attributed to the responsible decision-maker. It is because of this other side of possible failure – the chances – that one can expect self-attribution of risk at all.

5. Transcendence here means a world view that places all meaning of existence beyond the mundane world, whereas immanence implies a world view that sees life itself as the central aspect of existence.

6. The latter always change quicker and are more complex than information technologies would be able to compensate for.

7. In other words, uncertainty means that the *correct* choice (of an alternative) can never be certain. This is due to the contingency of choices and the contingency of distinctions used to make a choice. Consequently, information is only a necessary, but not a sufficient condition for the reduction of uncertainty: the selection of the "right kind" of information is itself contingent and therefore risky.

8. Even if one does not decide, another one can observe this as a decision (the decision to postpone and decide not), including all possible consequences.

9. This is reminiscent of the insight that organizations do not attain goals, but search for them (March & Olsen 1976). But this preference for search (risk) is countered by a dominant preference for the risk averse limitation of search options: for example, with the help of substantiated organizational goals. As one can see, there is no way out since one must decide between risk and risk aversion.

10. That is why modern society is so dependent on organizations, which process decisions.

11. One function of attributing blame is to affirm the general possibility to decide "correctly."

12. Of course, this is not meant as an abstract statement only. Each decision-maker calculates – whether implicitly or explicitly – the difference of time according to his or her goals in order to achieve the lowest risk load possible. In other words, he or she observes time (see also Shackle 1976).

13. See, for example, Marcel Proust's *In Search of Lost Time*. The identity of the narrator remains curiously latent exactly because it produces itself as an attempt at self-ascertainment in the process of narration.

14. Therefore March and Olsen (1989) talk about "appropriate" decisions. The political system, in particular, creates a huge apparatus for continuous reconstructions of decisions, the negative consequences of which have to be "normalized." The effect is usually further decisions (Japp 2004).

15. The sociologist of risk observes that the engineer relies on mechanized operations (established causal plans). To the extent she follows these plans, she does not make a decision but just does what seems necessary (not contingent). When such causal plans run into difficulties – for example, when the foundation for a pillar is unreliable – decisions are necessary. But in such a case, the "safe side" is no longer accessible, because the irreducible contingency of decision making infects all that follows. The engineer takes a risk, even if she herself does not see it like that. For the special case of "high technology," see Perrow (1984), for whom the aspect of decision making comes into play due to the susceptibility of complex causalities (e.g. in nuclear power plants) to technical faults. Contingency and risk reproduce themselves in the case of a fault, which cannot be mechanized (for a case study of the incident at Harrisburg, see Japp 1990).

16. One could suspect that the pressures of modern individualism with its strong expectations about individual autonomy are behind this attitude.

17. The difference between decision-makers and those affected is certainly applicable here. Each function system can observe decisions made in another system as affecting its own operations.

18. The formation of these systems is certainly a very complex issue. In any case, it is not the result of simple externally steered self-regulation of organized interests (see Leiss 1995). This would be an overestimation of

the capacities of social systems for reflection and self-constraint. Usually, intermediary systems of negotiation solve socially relevant problems only when the state has plausibly threatened with intervention ("shadow of law"). Provided that, negotiation actually works better than directive regulation in many cases (see Japp 1997; Eichener et al. 1991).

19. The observers are on different sides, but of the *same* distinction. This does not imply consensus, but the possibility to fake it (Hahn 1989).

20. Those who dispose of superior means of power may be able to interpret the difference between decision-makers and those affected in favor of themselves and to present themselves as victims. With regard to the difference in power, such a strategy is not available.

21. Except when the terrorist is found before his attack. Even then he does not regret the action, but the fact that he has not been allowed to die (see Juergensmeyer 2001).

22. The relevant distinction then is between exaggerating a threat and not being sufficiently prepared for it.

23. Wildavsky regards an anticipatory preventive strategy as appropriate only in very few exceptional cases. Instead he prefers resilience. "What matters is understanding that a strategy of anticipation should be accompanied by a recognition of its costs. Applying such a strategy in a very few areas of life is feasible. Applying anticipatory strategies in a wide range of activities would involve prohibitive costs. Anticipatory actions do have their place in a sensible safety strategy; the difficulty is to know what mix of anticipatory and resilient measures is optimum" (Wildavsky 1988: 85).

24. A common description refers to "hatred." Many authors then look for plausible reasons for this hatred (deprivation, victimization) or do without any explanation at all. But if the problem is one of hatred, it is a correlate of an insoluble social paradox, whatever "reasons" the latter might have.

5 | Edgework, Risk, and Uncertainty

Stephen Lyng

If there is such a thing as a Durkheimian *conscience collective* existing on a global scale, it is perhaps best represented by the widely held sentiment that we are living in a time of unprecedented danger. Although the chances of early death or disability are probably no greater today than in any other periods of human history, the dangers we currently face are unique in two respects: they are largely humanly produced and they impact us collectively rather than individually. Confronting the possibilities of nuclear annihilation, ecological catastrophe, pandemic diseases, global economic collapse, and the disruptions of rapid social and political change, we are increasingly aware of the dangerous consequences of the current global political economic relations and the advanced technologies of our scientific culture. Moreover, since these dangers are of our own making, we cannot draw on our ancestors' faith in divine forces to harmonize social and ecological imbalances and ameliorate the threats.

Many of the dangers we face today emerge as unanticipated consequences of economic and scientific progress, but we face additional threats to health and well-being that derive from our willingness to embrace risk taking as a positive virtue. This has occurred on the collective level in the form of broad-based political changes in western societies toward "neoliberal" policies and programs, which have shifted more of the responsibility for dealing with life challenges (unemployment, health and aging problems, etc.) from collectivities to individuals. At the same time, many individuals are adopting riskier lifestyles in their choices of occupational careers and leisure activities. New forms of high-risk or "extreme" sports (skydiving, hang gliding, rock climbing, etc.)

have emerged in recent decades, dangerous occupations (police work, firefighting, rescue work, etc.) have become a source of fascination for film and television producers and job seekers alike, and nontraditional relationships and lifestyles have flourished. Consequently, the voluntary pursuit of activities that involve a high potential for death, serious physical injury, or psychic harm – activities that I have termed as *edgework* – has acquired special cultural significance in the contemporary western world. In this chapter, I discuss the edgework model of voluntary risk taking, describing the origins and development of the model, its application to various empirical domains and substantive issues, and the intellectual problems, controversies, and possibilities it has spawned.

Voluntary Risk Taking in Late Modernity

The edgework model was initially introduced to account for the growing popularity of high-risk sports within the USA and other western nations during the last three or four decades (Mitchell 1983; Lyng 1990; Simon 2005). Although high-risk leisure sports are not an entirely new phenomenon in western society – Alpine mountain climbing has attracted sportsmen and reading audiences since the middle to late nineteenth century (Simon 2005) – the number and variety of these sports and rates of participation in them has greatly increased in the postwar period. Since the 1960s, major advances in technology and knowledge have created a wide range of new leisure risk-taking sports. People today jump out of airplanes (skydiving), scale high cliffs (rock climbing), explore the depths of the oceans (scuba diving) or the heights of the tallest peaks (mountain climbing), suspend their bodies from large kites (hang gliding), race motor vehicles of various kinds (motorcycles, cars, boats, etc.), and participate in a host of other risky activities. With the explosive growth of these new varieties of "extreme sports," it is not surprising that entrepreneurs have looked for ways to mine the economic potential of this leisure trend, which has spawned a new "adventure industry" devoted to such things as whitewater rafting, ropes courses, commercial skydiving operations, and the like (Holyfield 1997, 1999).

While edgework research initially focused on risk taking in the leisure realm, the research program quickly expanded beyond the leisure world to include other institutional domains and empirical problems. The initial leisure-time focus was dictated by the decision to make *voluntary* risk taking the primary conceptual issue, since people experience a certain amount of free choice in their leisure activities (choice delimited by class, race, gender, and other economic, social, and cultural factors). However, since there is an element of choice in occupational pursuits as well (delimited by the aforementioned factors), some researchers have suggested that certain high-risk occupations hold the same attractions as high-risk leisure activities for some people. Occupations like firefighting, police work, search and rescue operations, combat soldiering, and test piloting, and in the financial sector, stock and bond trading and other high-risk financial dealings (mergers and acquisitions, arbitrage, etc.), may also possess an alluring quality for their practitioners. As I discuss below, ethnographers who have studied these occupations describe a risk-taking experience almost indistinguishable from the edgework encounters of participants in high-risk sports (Wolfe 1979; Abolafia 1996; Knorr Cetina & Bruegger 2000; Lois 2005; Smith 2005).

Another area where the edgework model has been applied is in the study of certain forms of crime. Although criminologists have long recognized that many criminal acts involve a significant degree of uncertainty and risk, theorists have generally ignored risk taking as a motive for criminal behavior. The groundwork for conceiving of certain kinds of crime as a special form of edgework was laid with the publication of Jack Katz's (1988) book *The Seductions of Crime*. By assembling and analyzing qualitative data relating to the emotional and sensual dimensions of "doing evil" in criminal encounters, Katz demonstrates the primary importance of "moral emotions" in criminal conduct. At the same time, his data also reveal many of same empirical patterns found in the study of edgework activities (see Lyng 1993), which suggests that the sensual and seductive character of many criminal projects may be related to the risky nature of these endeavors.

For example, criminal acts often involve a relatively high degree of unpredictability due to possible resistance by victims, the chance that bystanders will intervene, and the unpredictable actions of co-offenders. Thus, by choosing to enter the alien worlds of victims, bystander interveners, and co-offenders, the robber places himself very close to the edge separating order from disorder. Efforts to conceptualize these criminal projects as distinct forms of edgework have been undertaken primarily by "critical" and "cultural" criminologists (Ferrell 1993;

Hayward 2005; Milovanovic 2005) who have joined Katz in focusing on the sensual attractions of criminal endeavors.

As revealed in this brief review, the range of empirical phenomena that can be classified as edgework has expanded considerably since the initial introduction of the concept. Some empirical studies have used edgework primarily as an analytic concept to distinguish key characteristics of practices or behaviors that involve danger, risk, or uncertainty (Holyfield & Lilian 2003; Smith 2005). However, as I demonstrate below, by attending to both micro- and macro-level structures relating to risk-seeking activities in contemporary western societies, the edgework model functions primarily as a general theory of voluntary risk-taking behavior.

One thing that sets the edgework perspective apart from other general theories of risk is the unique status of the concepts of risk and uncertainty within this framework. While most academic and policy perspectives on risk and uncertainty emphasize the negative connotations of these terms, the edgework approach focuses on the positive consequences of risk taking and the experience of uncertainty for social actors. Adopting the standard conceptualizations of "risk" as the probability of an adverse effect of a hazard[1] (Short 1984: 711) and "uncertainty" as the probability of events that are unknown or unknowable (Heimer 1988: 493), the edgework perspective employs both concepts to account for the positive attractions of high-risk leisure activities, occupations, and other dangerous pursuits. As explained below, edgeworkers of all types engage in risk management practices in their extensive preparation for doing edgework, in their reliance on sophisticated equipment, and other activities devoted to reducing the likelihood of serious injury or death. At the same time, however, this perspective reveals the importance of uncertainty in all dangerous activities that can be conceptualized as edgework. Confronting and responding to uncertainty is what edgeworkers value most, even as they devote significant effort to managing risks in order to reduce the likelihood of hazardous outcomes. Indeed, it would perhaps be more accurate to describe the edgework perspective as a general theory of *uncertainty* seeking rather than a theory of *risk* seeking *per se*.

Thus, in attempting to explain the attractions of the edge, the edgework approach highlights the distinction between risk and uncertainty to a greater degree than most other perspectives. With its foundation in probability theory, the concept of risk presupposes a specific range of outcomes and therefore implies a certain form of determinacy that limits human agency. In contrast, uncertainty refers to unknown probabilities and therefore implies a form of indeterminacy that expands the creative possibilities for human agents (see Bernstein 1996: 230). By emphasizing uncertainty over risk and analyzing the social context in which uncertainty at the edge is experienced, the edgework perspective can account for the seductive character of dangerous activities in modern social life. As we shall see, the special allure of these activities can be understood in terms of the basic tension between spontaneity and constraint in human action, an issue of longstanding concern to sociological theorists.

The edgework model also offers an alternative to the strict objectivist and constructionist perspectives on risk by incorporating elements of both approaches. The model embraces a constructionist view of risk (see Douglas & Wildavsky 1982; Douglas 1986) by asserting that perceptions of risks by edgeworkers are influenced by situational and subcultural interpretations of the risk experience. As described below, edgeworkers often believe that they can control circumstances that are actually chance-determined and the model offers a number of propositions about the sources of these distorted perceptions of risks. At the same time, increasing participation in voluntary risk-taking behavior in recent decades – and greater overall risks that people confront as a result of this trend – is attributed to objective changes in the structure of modern societies. The greater willingness to take risks in various domains of social life may be a direct consequence of the changing nature of human agency in late modernity. That is, the increasing importance of risk in these different institutional domains may reflect a shift to a new kind of social order in which risk consciousness and action are ascendant. This possibility, along with other competing explanations, are discussed in more detail below.

Development of the Edgework Concept

Explaining the new trend in voluntary risk-taking behavior has created several conceptual and theoretical challenges. First, the salient features of a broad range of high-risk endeavors – undertaken not as means to other ends, but as ends in themselves – must be identified through the application of a unifying concept. Although several existing concepts could be used for this purpose, most notably Erving Goffman's idea of "action"[2] or Mihaly Csikszentmihalyi's notion of "flow,"[3] neither of these concepts captures the highly unstructured, chaotic conditions that often must be negotiated in extreme sports and similar endeavors. The concept of "edgework" specifically refers to the experience of managing these conditions. As a possible subcategory of *action* that may involve some elements of *flow*, the notion of edgework directs explicit attention to the most anarchistic dimensions of high-risk experiences (Lyng 1990).

The term "edgework" was first coined by the self-described "gonzo" journalist, Hunter S. Thompson, in his early books *Hell's Angels* (1966) and *Fear and Loathing in Las Vegas* (1971). As a journalist with little interest in the social scientific application of his term, Thompson never provided an explicit definition of edgework, although his powerful descriptions of his own risk-taking experiences conveyed a rich understanding of the phenomenon. Appropriating Thompson's idea for sociological analysis required that edgework be rigorously conceptualized in terms of its two component parts – the *edge* and *work*. On the one hand, risk-taking experiences classified as edgework all involve an encounter with a particular edge or boundary condition. At the most abstract level, this boundary condition consists of the line separating form and formlessness, order and disorder, expressed more concretely in terms of the distinction between life and death, sanity and insanity, consciousness and unconsciousness, or other consequential human limits. In confronting either the life and death challenges of Himalayan mountain climbing or the psychic dangers of hallucinogenic drug use, making sure that one does not "cross the line" into formlessness or annihilation is a critical goal of the enterprise. However, the real significance of the "edge" in these activities is reflected in how edgeworkers of all stripes ultimately seek to get as close to this critical line as possible without actually crossing it (Lyng 1990).

On the other hand, negotiating the line between life and death or consciousness and unconsciousness involves the use of skills and capacities typically associated with the experience of "work." The term "work" carries many different meanings in both its commonsense and academic usage, but the edgework model employs a sociological conception based on the Marxian distinction between *free* and *alienated* labor. Marx's conception of free labor, or "work" in the terminology employed in his early writings (Marx & Engels 1932), focuses on the dual function of this "activity" in creating "use value" and allowing human beings to objectify their human powers in nature. Under certain structural conditions, work serves as a vehicle for developing human potential because it requires the combined use of multiple human capacities. As the most demanding of all human activities, work or free labor can be described as "conscious," "purposive," "concentrated," "physically and mentally flexible," "social," "skillful," and "rational" (Ollman 1971: 120). This conception of work stands in direct contrast to the conditions of workplace alienation. "Alienated labor" – labor controlled and organized by capitalist employers for the purpose of maximizing efficiency and profit – possesses none of the potential-developing features of free labor. Thus, in its typical form, alienated labor is mindless, coerced, inflexible, competitive, deskilled, and often irrational.

Thinking of the "work" component in edgework in Marxian terms highlights the other crucial aspect of the risk behavior subsumed under this concept. Close encounters with the edge typically require high levels of concentration combined with an expanded awareness of the range of factors that determine the final outcome. One's actions are purposive in that they ensure one's survival or safety in the face of extreme danger. Edgeworkers also employ specific skills – those appropriate to the particular risk activity (skydiving, mountain climbing, motorcycle racing, etc.) and a generalized "survival capacity" common to almost all forms of edgework (see Lyng, 1990: 859). The latter ability is often seen as a form of mental toughness that is crucial for maintaining control over situations most people see as completely uncontrollable.

Finally, a crucial requirement for doing edgework is the capacity for mental and physical flexibility – the ability to "ad hoc" a response and avoid crossing the line between form and formlessness. Thus, except for the missing qualities of "sociality" and "rationality" (discussed below), edgework embodies all of the elements of free labor, the form of human activity most important to "the full development of human powers." This point is critical to a theoretical understanding of edgework as a form of self-creation and an "act of liberation" (Foucault 1991b).

The introduction of the edgework concept into the study of risk and uncertainty raises several critical concerns that should be addressed before describing the full theoretical model. First, it is important to acknowledge a certain lack of rigor in applications of the concept to risk-taking activities in recent years. In their eagerness to apply the concept to specific risk-taking endeavors, some researchers[4] fail to recognize their own distorted perceptions of risks. Thus, some are inclined to define activities like bungee jumping as edgework but not more common activities like driving automobiles, even though the dangers of the latter are much greater than the former. The usefulness of the edgework concept will depend on its rigorous application to empirical cases and the development of more refined conceptual distinctions between it and other concepts ("adventure," "thrill-seeking," etc.) related to activities differentiated by various levels of risk.[5]

A second criticism of the edgework idea involves a potential bias in the concept relating to gender, race, and class differences. Eleanor Miller (1991) initially raised this concern by calling attention to the race-, gender-, and class-specific nature of the qualitative data from which the model was inductively derived. As Miller points out, the original edgework model was based on evidence collected on prototypically white male pursuits – "extreme sports" and occupational pursuits numerically dominated by white males. By ignoring the risk experiences of females, nonwhites, members of the underclass, and other minority groups, this approach presents the practices of white, middle-class males as the standard for defining "normal" or "typical" edgework, implying that divergences from this model do not constitute true edgework. In the case of women, the model could lend implicit support to the popular view of females as innately risk-adverse, a view that is contradicted by recent research (see Walklate 1997).

In recent years, the empirical base of the model has expanded to include the risk experiences of a wider range of social groups (Wacquant 1995; Lois 2005; Miller 2005), although much more work remains to be completed on this front. One important development in this regard is the growing literature devoted to the exploration of gender variations in risk taking (Walklate 1997; Hannah-Moffat & O'Malley 2007), which opens up several exciting new avenues for research on the gendered nature of edgework practices (see Lyng & Matthews 2007).

Theorizing Edgework

As we have seen, the edgework perspective challenges a number of traditional presuppositions about risk-taking behavior. Individuals who are inclined toward high-risk behavior are often assumed to be psychologically exceptional in either a positive or negative sense. This assumption has inspired psychologists to propose a wide range of different personality characteristics, intrinsic motivations, or pathological conditions as sources of risk-taking behavior (see Lyng 1990: 853f.). By conceptualizing risk taking as a form of "work" – that is, work undertaken in negotiating the line between life and death, safety and serious injury, or other consequential boundaries – edgework can be analyzed in social-historical terms. The nature of work activity is always structured by historically specific system of economic production, as implicated in the Marxian contrast between "free" and "alienated" labor.

Thus, the edgework model focuses on the broader social-historical factors that compel and shape risk-taking behavior. This shift in focus is empirically justified by one of the dominant social trends of the post-industrial era – the fact that voluntary participation in high-risk activities has steadily *increased* in the last half-century (Lyng 1990). Combined with other evidence of wide variation in voluntary risk taking across different societies and social groups, these patterns cast doubt on the claims by psychologists that the attraction to risk taking reflects an individual's predisposition to take risks – a personality trait, an intrinsic risk-taking motivation, a pathological psychic condition (such as an inclination for "indirect self destructive behavior" (Farberow 1980)), or other psychic tendencies. If such core predispositions are uniformly distributed across different societies, historical periods, and social groups, then focusing on these factors cannot explain the social-historical variations in risk behavior.

As a structurally oriented theory, the edgework model locates the motives for risk taking in the interrelation between the general action orientation of human beings and the social context in which they act. This motivational approach avoids the reductionism and circular reasoning of psychological models of risk. In this respect, it is similar to the economic, rational choice model of risk, which assumes that decisions about risk taking are based on estimations of the potential benefits of one's actions against the probability and costs of failure. Structural reasoning within this latter perspective deals with the influence of the social-cultural context on the definitions and distributions of the benefits and costs of risk taking. Consequently, rational choice theory can account for historical, cultural, and social group variations in rates of risk participation by showing how structural factors impact the perception of risks, the value of risk outcomes, and the management of the costs incurred in risk taking.

While the rational choice approach and the edgework perspective share a common structural logic, the two approaches differ in a fundamental way. What proponents of rational choice see as the principal strength of this perspective – the rigor and parsimony of its model of individual action – is the source of its failure as a multidimensional explanation of risk-taking behavior. If social actors are motivated in their actions by perceived rewards relative to potential costs, there is little to be gained from a close examination of the details of the immediate risk-taking experience. In spite of what actors may say about their attractions to risk behavior, their perceptions cannot hide the fundamental truth about risk taking – the fact that people are willing to take risks when expected rewards outweigh the expected dangers. An all-encompassing definition of "rewards" ensures the robustness of this concept and shifts the analytical focus to the problem of determining how social structural factors impact risks and rewards confronted by different social groups. Thus, despite the individual-level point of departure in rational choice theorizing, this approach functions chiefly as a structural-level form of analysis.

In contrast, the various permutations of the edgework approach give equal priority to the individual and structural levels analysis by connecting the immediacy of the risk experience with the broader structural forces that shape this experience. Drawing on the theoretical traditions of pragmatism and phenomenology,[6] the edgework approach views human actors not as calculators of risks and rewards, but as symbolic beings transacting with the material relations of their physical and social environments. In this framework, a search for the motives behind any course of action must begin with a detailed examination of the actor's lived experience and attend to the embodied emotions, sensations, emergent human capacities, and humanly constituted objects of the actor's environment. These aspects of the actor's experience are not relegated to the abstract categories of costs and rewards, but are treated as elements of a sensual event that attract or repel the people involved in actively constructing this reality. By analyzing rich ethnographic descriptions of lived experience on the edge, this action orientation promotes the development of an empirically based theory of voluntary risk taking.

The edgework model has much in common, in this respect, with Jack Katz's (1988) pioneering work on crime. Katz's phenomenological approach rests on a similar theory of action, which explains why Katz's perspective has been linked to edgework by sociologists and criminologists in recent years (Young 2003; Hayward 2005; Miller 2005). In assessing the dominant criminological paradigm, Katz makes a strong argument for why this analytical framework must be inverted, an argument that applies equally well to the sociological study of risk taking.

Like the rational choice model of risk, the traditional criminological paradigm devotes primary attention to the macro structural factors that shape the life conditions of potential criminals and influence their decisions about the costs and benefits of engaging in criminal acts. Katz challenges this approach by suggesting that we look for the motivations of criminal acts in the experiential "foreground" rather than starting with the structural "background" factors and working forward to a rational criminal actor seeking to achieve material and culturally valued goals. As Katz (1988: 312) states,

> [I]t is not necessary to construct the field [of criminology] back to front. We may begin with the foreground, attempting to discover common or homogeneous criminal projects and to test explanations of the necessary and sufficient steps through which people construct given forms of crime. If we take as our primary research commitment an exploration of the distinctive phenomena of crime, we may produce not just ad hoc bits of description or a collection of provocative anecdotes but a *systematic empirical theory of crime* – one that explains at the individual level the causal process of committing a crime and that accounts at the aggregate level for recurrently documented correlations with biographical and ecological background factors (emphasis mine).

The "systematic empirical theory of crime" that Katz constructs directs us to causal significance of powerful sensations and feelings located in the foreground: in particular, the "moral emotions" generated in criminal endeavors. In his descriptions of "sneaky thrills," "righteous slaughter," and "ways of the badass," Katz demonstrates how sensations of transcendence, the emotions of humiliation and rage, and the dialectic of chaos and control lend a kind of magical character to the criminal experience. A careful examination of this experiential space reveals "the dynamic that people create to seduce themselves towards deviance," which functions as a more powerful motivation of criminal behavior than any desire to secure material rewards (1988: 321).

Indeed, Katz presents documentary and ethnographic evidence that demonstrates how truly insignificant material gains are to understanding what drives many criminals to pursue a life of criminal action (1988: 314f.).

Thus, as systematic empirical theories constructed from front to back – that is, from the phenomenal foreground to the social structural background – Katz's theory of crime and the edgework theory of risk both seek to privilege actors' own accounts of human activities devoted to the pursuit of moral and existential uncertainty and chaos. In doing so, these two theories avoid the empty abstractions of existing perspectives on risk and crime. While there is certainly an important place for abstractions within a comprehensive theory of risk taking, they should not be used to hide or distort the powerful causal forces at work in the immediate experience of individuals making decisions about highly consequential courses of action. The strength of the social structural level analysis of such behavior is clearly dependent upon a valid understanding of the forces compelling action at the individual level.

Conceptualizing the foreground of edgework activities

So, what is the nature of those forces operating in the foreground of high-risk situations? As previously indicated, we find some important similarities in the phenomenological data on certain forms of crime (stick up, righteous slaughter, etc.) and the edgework experience, suggesting that these criminal endeavors may be conceptualized as distinct varieties of edgework action (see O'Malley & Mugford 1994). The most significant empirical patterns here are those relating to the sensual pleasures and aesthetic arousal experienced by participants. In all edgework activities, including the criminal forms described by Katz, one confronts an "other-world" experience that transcends the mundane reality of everyday life. These other-world features include time and space implosions, in which time passes either much faster or slower than normal and spatial boundaries collapse as the edge is approached. For example, combat soldiers engaged in pitched battles lasting many hours often describe the experience as seeming to last only a few minutes, while skydivers experience 60 seconds of freefall as lasting an eternity. Edgeworkers who employ various forms of technology (racing cars or motorcycles, high-performance airplanes, surgical tools, etc.) describe the blurring of boundaries between themselves and these technologies, leading to a sense of mental control over the machines or tools they use.

Other strong feelings and emotions contribute to the seductive appeal of crowding the edge. Time and space implosions give a "hyper-real" quality to edgework activities, which are experienced as more "authentic" than everyday reality. The feelings of authenticity are accompanied by a sense that the experience is ineffable – words cannot adequately describe what it is like to approach the edge. Participants confront additional intense emotions that must be managed. Paralyzing fear must be overcome or transformed into something that is sensually appealing. Consequently, edgeworkers convert their fear into something positive by focusing on the corporeal reverberations it generates. The goal is to cultivate a mindset that allows them to act skillfully and competently by combining intense bodily arousal with a focused attention and creative responses to the immediate challenges at the edge. Such powerful and unusual sensations acquire a special allure that draws edgeworkers into a reality that stands in stark contrast to the normal routines of daily life. This is why they claim that being on the edge is when they feel most alive.

Other foreground features contribute to the attractions of edgework, but identifying these features requires that we move beyond the phenomenological data to empirical issues important to pragmatist inquiry. The edgework model's incorporation of pragmatism, particularly the ideas of one of the best-known pragmatists, George Herbert Mead, accounts for a certain social psychological emphasis not found in Katz's phenomenological theory of crime. What pragmatism encourages is greater attention to the self and body as important foreground elements in edgework and a unique way of connecting these two elements to mind and society.[7]

The sense of omnipotence and control that flows from successfully managing fear when negotiating the edge leads many edgeworkers to see themselves as members of an elite group. They believe that the power to control seemingly uncontrollable circumstances is innately determined and transferable from one form of edgework to another (Lyng 1990). Their capacities for control are sometimes viewed as deriving from a basic "survival skill" that distinguishes true edgeworkers from those who are attracted to risk taking but lack the "right stuff" (Wolfe 1979) to conduct it successfully. In an interesting tautological twist, they view instances of people dying or being seriously injured in risk-taking endeavors as evidence that these individuals lacked the core survival skill of a genuine edgeworker. This way of accounting for negative risk consequences also provides them with a sense of confidence about the likely outcomes of their own high-risk pursuits.

Possessing strong feelings of confidence bordering on omnipotence and experiencing themselves as innately skilled in managing fear and controlling chaotic conditions at the edge, edgeworkers are drawn to high-risk activities as a way to achieve a sense of self-determination. In this respect, the edgework experience differs from the set of sensations that Csikszentmihalyi (1985) conceptualizes as "flow." While flow involves distortions in one's experience of space and time, feelings of transcendence, and a state of focused attention, the flow state produces a loss of self-consciousness or an "annihilation of the ego." In contrast, edgework generates a heightened sense of self that subjects describe as a form of self-realization or self-actualization. This represents another dimension of the "authentic" character of edgework experiences: in addition to confronting an exaggerated, transcendent reality (a "hyper-reality," as it were), participants also experience an exaggerated sense of self at the edge, which they often describe as their authentic or "true" self.

Finally, a full description of the foreground elements of edgework practices must also include some attention to the *embodied* character of these practices (Wacquant 1995; Lyng 2004). Edgeworkers often refer to the innate capacity of their bodies to respond appropriately, immediately, and automatically in life-and-death conditions, which they see as a non-cognitive capacity. This belief in the primacy of the body in the spontaneous and creative responses relates to other aspects of edgework previously discussed, including the ineffability of the experience, the sensual arousal generated by many forms of edgework, and the authentic sense of self that emerges in edgework projects. Understanding the embodied nature of edgework along with these other facets of the experience requires that we consider the impact of social factors on the lived reality of edgework practice. In other words, having described the immediate foreground of edgework activities, we must now extend the analytical framework in the direction of background influences. The pragmatist ideas of G. H. Mead will be most useful for taking this first step from front to back.

Conceptualizing the social in the edgework experience

As we have seen, the key premise of the edgework model is the assertion that the motivational basis of risk-taking behavior is found in the seductive power of the risk experience. Rather than responding to psychological predispositions to take risks or a desire to attain external rewards through calculated risk taking, participants are seduced by the transcendent and intensely authentic nature of the experience. As edgeworkers themselves often say when prodded to explain why they put their lives on the line, "we do it because it's fun!" Although the present analysis reveals that this statement is a gloss for a complex pattern of experiential elements, it can be taken as further evidence that risk-takers are pulled into the experience rather than pushed by intrinsic psychic factors or the desire for extrinsic rewards. However, the remaining challenge is to account for *why* edgework is experienced by its practitioners as self-actualizing, authentically real, and creatively satisfying.

To address this problem, we must examine the most proximate "social" forces at work in the social psychology of risk taking. In the original treatment of this issue (Lyng 1990), the self that emerges in edgework activities was conceptualized in terms of Mead's "I/me" dialectic. In this formulation, the "me" can be understood as the social self, or as Mead (1934: 175) defines it, the "organized set of attitudes of others which one himself assumes." This component of the self can be considered as the "voice of society" involved in normatively assessing and interpreting one's self-actions and the actions of others. The "I" refers to spontaneous, unpredictable, and creative elements in the *overt* phase of the act, standing in contrast to the *covert* phase of interpretation and assessment undertaken by the "me." Most human action is rooted in a dialectical interplay between the "I" and the "me" phases, with the "I" experienced only through the mediating influence of the "me" and the "me" overtly expressed only through the continually emerging "I." However, under some unusual circumstances – such as the conditions prevailing in edgework encounters – this dialectical interplay between the "I" and "me" is disrupted. The primary effect of this disruption is a radically different experience of self and reality.

As the critical "line of consequence" is approached, one must ad hoc an immediate, almost instinctive response to the rapidly changing situation. Under these conditions, it is not possible to draw on the interpretive capacity of the "me" to formulate a strategy for avoiding death or serious injury. The requirement for instantaneous action terminates the process of "imaginative rehearsal" involved in normal voluntary action and problem solving, which silences the "voice of society" and annihilates the "me." What remains after the social component of the self has been displaced is a residual, "acting" self that responds without reflective consciousness (Lyng 2004: 362). The collection of sensations, emotions, and self-feelings of the edgework experience form the residue left by the annihilated "me."

Although it would be incorrect to say that the residual self found at the edge exactly corresponds to Mead's notion of the "I,"[8] this form of self-action possesses many of the same characteristics of the "overt phase" designated by the "I" concept. The spontaneity, creativity, unpredictability, and impulsive/instinctive nature of edgework action accords with Mead's descriptions of the "I," even though these features arise not as a dialectical expression of the "me" but as an immediate consequence of its extinction. There are also important similarities between these "I"-like qualities and the "work" component in edgework. If work is conceptualized in terms of Marx's notion of free labor, the phenomenal features of *working* the edge can be viewed as extensions of the Meadian qualities described above: the action is "conscious,"[9] "purposive," "concentrated," "physically and mentally flexible," and "skillful." The only free labor characteristics missing from edgework are "sociality" and "rationality."[10] As I discuss below, accounting for the absence of these last two characteristics in edgework will contribute to a better understanding of the broader social and cultural significance of this practice.

We see then that edgework allows its practitioners to experience a fully embodied form of human action in which the usual processes involved in interpreting and managing the external world have been fundamentally altered. The embodied nature of edgework practices accounts for many of the defining features of the experience. Alterations in the perception of time and space, the sense of mental control over environmental objects, and the ineffable nature of the experience are produced by the diminution of the social mind and immediate projection of a contingent body into the flow of action. As edgeworkers "body forth" in response to the threat at hand, they experience the indeterminacy of the natural world in completely novel ways – "terminating indeterminacy" and breaching the culturally mediated "consentient set" normally used in constructing reality. Consequently, they discover authentic selves rooted in the objective uncertainty of their bodies and an alternative reality in which culturally defined time and space distinctions are dissolved and reconstructed.

In short, the application of Meadian theory to the edgework experience offers a way to connect the phenomenal foreground and the social background at the point where these two regions meet most immediately. Examining the impact of edgework practices on the most proximate social forces involved in human action yields a partial understanding of how high-risk experiences draw people in and inspire an intense commitment to exploring dangerous edges. However, a complete account of the sensual attractions of edgework requires that we take additional steps in the direction of the social background and consider the relevance of broader social structural factors in the edgework experience, moving from the proximate to the ultimate social forces that constrain human action. The next section extends the analysis in this direction.

The Structural Context of Voluntary Risk Taking

In shifting the analysis to the macro structural level, we seek some insight into how broad-based structural forces either push or pull (or both simultaneously) individuals into the pleasurable pursuit of risk. The range of potentially useful frameworks for extending the analysis in this direction is extensive, considering the interpretive nature of our analytical task at this point. Consequently, this section reviews a number of theoretical possibilities for exploring the link between the risk-taking experience and the key structural imperatives of contemporary western societies, drawing on both modernist and postmodernist perspectives.

Alienation, reification, and experiential anarchy in late capitalism

The earlier discussion of the edgework concept highlighted the "work" component of this compound term and discussed a theoretical rationale for conceptualizing voluntary risk taking as a form of work. As we have seen, the experiential dimensions of edgework correspond very closely to the phenomenal elements of Marx's notion of free labor. While it is unlikely that Marxian theory influenced Hunter Thompson's choice of the term "edgework," his decision to employ productivist terminology suggests a way to analyze this phenomenon from a socio-economic perspective.

The Marxian project to critically analyze the structural logic of capitalism begins with a clear theoretical and political baseline, a point of reference that reflects Marx's vision of actual historical possibilities for human freedom. Examined at the most abstract level, this baseline rests on the dialectical conception of the relationship between the "spontaneous" and "constrained" dimensions of human action, a concept that Marx shared with George Herbert Mead. Indeed, this common metatheoretical link opens the door to a synthesis of the Marxian and Meadian frameworks, which can serve as an integrative theory oriented to both micro- and macro-level sociological analysis. The first effort to theorize edgework in sociological terms made use of this synthetic framework (Lyng 1990).

In their shared conception of the dialectic between spontaneity and constraint in human action, both Marx and Mead see spontaneous, creative, and self-affirming forms of action emerging only under a particular set of constraining conditions. For Mead, the constraining conditions that foster free action are found in the "I/me" dialectic discussed above, such that the creative potential of the "I" can only be realized in the presence of a fully developed "me" capable of taking the attitude of the entire social community. Marx asserts that spontaneous, creative action arises in "work," but a form of work that expands human capabilities rather than blunting their development. In addition to producing useful products for human consumption, work can be undertaken to develop human capacities for concentrated effort, planning, and multiple skill use, which allows for the full expression of human potential. Of course, work can be organized in this way only in a system of economic production that gives priority to the human interests of workers over the managerial goals of efficiency and profits. Marx's critique of capitalist society is devoted to analytically unraveling the structural relations that maintain the dominance of the profit motive and other capitalist managerial interests over the interest of workers in achieving full creative freedom as human beings.

The Marxian and Meadian perspectives, linked through their common foundation in the dialectic between spontaneity and constraint, offer a way to conceptualize the varied and mutually reinforcing social forces that inspire the search for edgework opportunities. The Marx–Mead synthesis highlights separations, contradictions, and conflicts in socially constrained action that result in diminished prospects for spontaneous, creative behavior. The social conditions that sustain human beings who possess a broad range of skills for mastering their social and material environments cannot be found in a social order characterized by alienated labor, class conflict, oversocialization, and radical individualism. Consequently, an unremitting search for self has become one of the hallmarks of the modern age, as people struggle for a greater sense of personal agency in their institutionally determined lives. One of the most alluring destinations for those seeking a sense of self-determination is the mystical space at the edge, where one's individual skills, powers of concentration, capacities for control, and will to survive are the most critical determinants of one's continued existence. This encounter stands in direct contrast to the perfunctory performance of institutional roles that seem impervious to the individual's creative powers.

Thus, by expanding the analytical framework further in the direction of the structural background, it is possible to develop a more comprehensive understanding of the transcendental character of edgework experiences. Although many distinctive edgework sensations are consequences of immediate survival demands that extinguish the social "me," the experiential anarchy of these high-risk encounters also provides a powerful contrast to institutional experiences conditioned by alienation and reified social structures: while labor becomes increasingly deskilled in many occupations, skilled performance is always demanded in edgework; while most workers have little control over the conditions of their labor, "controlling the seemingly uncontrollable" is experienced in edgework; while forced concentration or mental detachment is often required in performing occupational roles, highly focused attention occurs automatically in edgework; and while the self involved in performing institutional roles often seems artificial, an authentic, fully embodied self arises in edgework.

Analyzing the structural context of edgework practices in terms of the Marx–Mead synthesis takes us a good distance in explaining the seductive attractions of doing edgework. Although the Marx–Mead lens reveals powerful background forces that push people toward the edge in the contemporary social order, other contextual features of modern life may also give impetus to risk taking as means of personal transcendence. The next section expands the focus beyond the domains

of work and community to consider the significance of "rationalization" as a background force shaping the edgework experience.

Rationalization, disenchantment, and the mystical edge

If Meadian theory connects the immediacy of edgework with a social
mind ontologically rooted in community life, and Marxian theory situates edgework in the political economic relations of capitalist society,
Max Weber's ideas provide a way to contextualize edgework at a level
extending even beyond the particularities of western individualism and
capitalism. Weber's analysis focuses on the principle of formal rationality as the central imperative of the modern social world. This principle
is reflected in a broad range of human actions in the western world but
is also embodied in external social structural forms. Thus, while formal
rationality involves means–ends calculation on the part of people
engaged in everyday problem solving, it extends beyond people's pursuit
of pragmatic self-interests to encompass the "universally applied rules,
laws, and regulations" that dominate bureaucratic organizations and
govern affairs within economic, legal, political, and scientific institutions
(Ritzer 2000: 132). Although Weber generally rejected evolutionary
models of world historical change, he did discern a rationalization trend
in the modern Occident, with an expanding number of institutions
configured to achieve formal rational standards of calculability, predictability, efficiency, and control.

The Weberian framework offers an encompassing vision of the background forces that shape social actors' role performances. While Marx
and Mead give priority to constraints imposed by modern economic
relations and community life, respectively, Weber emphasizes a broad
range of institutional environments that shape people's daily affairs,
irrespective of their class locations and their community interactions.
The rationalization process has relegated people to an "iron cage" of
routinized behavior and diminished opportunities for creative action,
but extends even further into the actual experiential conditions of daily
life. By eroding traditional values and reconfiguring people's connections with nature and the cosmos, rationalization also produces a sense
of meaninglessness and existential sterility.

The experiential consequences of the rationalization process are captured by Weber's notion of "disenchantment." Members of traditional
societies live in close contact with the mysterious powers of nature and

are regularly confronted with the revelations of religious or magical practices. In modern society, however, these traditional sources of enchantment are steadily displaced by the expanding rational imperative. Uncertainty and surprise give way to predictability and boredom. Spiritual abandonment is replaced by rational control. Sensual involvement in the natural environment is shunned in favor of insulated protection from nature's disturbances. Thus, what is lost in the modernization process are those enchanting qualities of human experience that generate meaning and inspiration in people's lives. As Weber put it, a social world purged of sacred mysteries and vibrant experiences comes to be dominated by "specialists without spirit, sensualists without heart" upholding a "nullity [that] imagines it has attained a level of civilization never before achieved" (Weber 1958: 152).

Weber was clearly concerned about the spiritual dead-end that awaits people in their disenchanted worlds, but he failed to consider the possibilities for achieving enchantment through nontraditional means in modern societies. This problem has been taken up recently by several theorists who have modified the Weberian framework to account for the growing importance of consumption practices in postindustrial societies (Campbell 1989; Ritzer 1999). George Ritzer makes a compelling argument for why the rise of the "new means of consumption" may offer possibilities for re-enchanting the postmodern world. He describes the enchanting qualities of the "cathedrals of consumption" (shopping malls, chain stores, casinos, cruise ships, etc.) that attract millions of shoppers and vacationers seeking some escape from the stupefying conditions of rationalized work environments and other bureaucratic iron cages. In these postmodern cathedrals, people experience implosions of space and time, explosions of simulations that blur the lines between the real and the unreal, and a wide range of manufactured spectacles that leave them awe-struck and inspired. Thus, the enchanting character of consumer experience stands in stark contrast to the rationalized reality of most other institutional realms.

While we may question whether Ritzer's cathedrals of consumption actually captivate many of the jaded consumers who occupy these spaces today (see Lyng 2005c), the suggestion that alternative avenues to enchantment exist in the bureaucratic-capitalist social order has obvious implications for analyzing edgework. As previously noted, a key problem in understanding the motivations for doing edgework is to explain how this experience acquires its sensual, almost erotic appeal.

Considering the profound contrast that the edgework sensations offer to the dominant reality of the rationalized social institutions, it is little wonder that many people experience this boundary domain as a transcendent space and often describe it in otherworldly terms. The implosions of consumer spaces pale in comparison to those found in the immediacy of edgework experience, where the collapsing and expanding of time and space occur in unexpected and uncontrolled ways. If cathedrals of consumption and electronic media generate hyperrealities with sophisticated simulations, personal perceptions rather than simulations mediate the hyperreality of edgework. As an experience that is deeply embodied, largely ineffable, and resistant to techniques of rational control, edgework is an especially powerful way to re-enchant the most disenchanted specialists of modern society.

This interpretation has some advantages over the Marxian-inspired analysis discussed above. In the Marxian interpretation, participation in edgework should be highly correlated with alienation in the workplace – the greater one's alienation (lacking control over the conditions of one's work and having little opportunity for the development and use of skills), the greater one's attraction to edgework activities. If alienation is most pronounced at the lower end of the class structure, we would expect most edgeworkers to be lower-class individuals. However, the data on participation in high-risk leisure activities indicate that few lower-class individuals are involved in leisure edgework, which is not surprising considering the importance of discretionary income to one's engagement in many of these sports. Although a broader view of the kinds of risk activity that qualify as edgework may lend support to the Marxian interpretation, the growing participation of middle- and upper-class individuals in high-risk "extreme" sports and related activities still raises an important question: why are individuals who generally experience control and empowerment in their work and broader social circumstances attracted to edgework?

One possible answer to this question would direct us to the highly rationalized and bureaucratized character of the professional and managerial work environments of many middle- and upper-class people. However insulated these individuals may be from alienating work conditions, they still confront the disenchanting consequences of a work world dominated by the principles of formal rationality. Consequently, they look for other opportunities to infuse magic and mystery into their lives, either in the pursuit of leisure forms of edgework or, for some, in high-risk occupations that offer high drama combined with the potential for large economic rewards. The latter form of "financial edgework" has been described in a growing body of ethnographic research on stock, bond, and commodities trading, especially Abolafia's (1996) work on "hyper-rational gaming" in the bond trading business. Similar studies of high-risk financial occupations (Knorr-Cetina and Bruegger 2000; Smith 2005; Zwick 2005) reveal many of the same experiential patterns that typify leisure edgework.

Thus, the Weberian perspective adds another dimension to the modernist interpretation of edgework practices, broadening our understanding of edgework as a transcendent experience that emerges against the background structural conditions of modern society. Adding to the deforming influences of alienation, reification, oversocialization, and individualization, the rationalization trend and its disenchanting effects push people to explore alternative realities where they can experience themselves as self-determined, soulful human beings. Thus, the various classical theoretical interpretations of edgework focus on the fundamental opposition between the institutional world and the alternative space of edgework practices. In considering the possibilities for experiencing human and spiritual agency, these modernist perspectives emphasize the compensatory character of edgework, seeing it as filling a void created by the dehumanizing forces of modernity.

This interpretation offers a useful way to link the structural background and the foreground features of the risk experience, but it also points to another logical possibility for connecting these two dimensions. Rather than asserting that edgework acquires its seductive appeal through its *contrasting* power and compensatory value in the modern context, we could consider how edgework might actually *align* with emerging structural forces and allow for a deeper expression of the kind of agency demanded by the new structural configuration. I conclude this chapter by considering this latter possibility.

Risk society, risk agency, and the ethic of self

One of the most recent perspectives on modern social development has been introduced by the risk society theorists led by Ulrich Beck and Anthony Giddens. Since the idea of risk society first appeared in the 1980s, the body of theory associated with this concept has been elaborated in several different directions by Beck and others inspired by his original idea. As Beck (2002: 5) notes, "risk" is a distinctly modern concept: "It requires decisions and attempts to render the unpredictable consequences of civil decisions predictable and controllable." Thus, to describe the contemporary global social system as a risk society is not to imply necessarily that the world is more dangerous today than it was in earlier times (although, in fact, it may be). Rather, the concept captures a cultural shift where the uncertain and potentially harmful consequences of human decisions have been increasingly subjected to the calculus of risk analysis. The result is a growing acceptance of the dangerous side-effects of *human* products and practices. Beck and his collaborators describe this historical shift as the process of "reflexive modernization." With scientific and technological advancement and the expansion of markets, modern societies "turn back on themselves," leading to escalating risks of human-made disasters and increasing disruption of core social institutions.

In a further examination of the "second modernity" dominated by the risk society, Anthony Giddens (1994a: 96) sees the central structures of the "first modernity" being transformed by two interrelated dimensions of reflexive modernization – globalization and "the excavations of most traditional contexts of action." Globalization and the "detraditionalization" process (1994a: 100) erode traditional institutions in both core advanced western nation states and periphery non-western societies. The defining feature of the second modernity for Giddens, as for other risk society theorists, is the phenomenon of "manufactured uncertainty," which makes for a "genuinely new social universe of action and experience" (1994b: 106). Thus, while reflexive modernization produces increasing threats to human survival, it may also offering new opportunities for human freedom.

What are the consequences of this new social universe for individual actors? For one thing, sociality is no longer strongly dependent on institutional roles. The risk society "is one where social bonds have effectively to be made, rather than inherited from the past" (Giddens 1994b: 107). Trust is no longer dictated by traditional role relations but is "active" insofar as one must win another's trust and actively maintain it through "a process of mutual narrative and emotional disclosure" (1994b: 107). This reflects a developing "emotional democracy" between parents, children, and friends, in which individuals negotiate interpersonal relationships outside of traditional institutional definitions (1994a: 192). Beck (with his co-author Beck-Gernsheim 1995) sounds a similar note, describing the "chaos of love" in the second modernity. Ironically, such chaos is normal and predictable in a certain sense – separated from traditional roles, love becomes predictably unpredictable.

For Scott Lash (2003), subjective experience in the second modernity is captured best by Manuel Castells' (1989) notion of the "logic of flows," which stands in contrast to the "logic of structure" governing personal relationships and experience in the first modernity: "Beck's chronic indeterminacy of risk and risk-taking, of living with risk is much more of a piece with, not the determinacy of structure but the partial, the elusive determinacy of flows" (Lash 2003: 49). This gives us a new way to think about human agency and edgework in the risk society.

While the earlier structural analyses of edgework practices highlighted the *contrast* between institutional routines and the risk experience, such a contrast cannot be found in a social context where the "logic of structure" has been replaced by the "logic of flows." In the risk society, indeterminacy and uncertainty are the overriding qualities of the dominant social reality and successfully negotiating the uncertainties of daily life becomes the key challenge for many social actors. Doing edgework in this context is not focused on transcending the dominant reality, when the reality of everyday life bears a fundamental resemblance to the reality found at the edge. Rather than representing a form of "counteragency" in late modernity, edgework must be seen as the purest expression of the agentic qualities demanded by the risk society.

So, what draws people to the most extreme forms of risk taking when managing risks is at the center of their daily experiences? As a theoretical project in the early stages of development at the time of writing, the risk society perspective does not offer a definitive answer to this question. In a more speculative vein, we could posit that edgework may offer special opportunities to expand and hone people's risk management skills. Several analysts have suggested this possibility in recent years, most notably Jonathan Simon (2005), who has pointed to the increasing demand for edgework skills in the risk society. As Simon suggests (2005), edgework and "center work" begin to blur in the late modern context: "The polarity between institutional life and edgework collapses. Edgework is increasingly what institutions expect of people."

With the growing fragmentation of the "classic institutions" of the state, class, the nuclear family, ethnic group, etc., the subject moves from a position of *reflection* to *reflexivity* in the second modernity. As Lash (2003: 51f.) notes,

> Beck often describes today's non-linear reflexivity in terms of, not the 'I think therefore I am', but instead in terms of 'I am I'. 'I think, therefore I am' has to do with reflection. 'I am I' has more to do with reflex ... Reflexes are indeterminate. They are immediate. They do not in any sense subsume. Reflexivity, Beck notes, is characterized by choice, where previous generations had no such choices. What Beck often omits to say is that this choice must be *fast*, we must – as in reflex – make *quick* decisions ... The subject relating to today's fragmented institutions instead has moved from a position of reflection to one of being reflexive.

Edgework can be seen as the prototype of *reflex* action demanded by the risk society. In conducting edgework, one must act immediately in order to avoid serious injury or death. Consequently, edgework is reflexive in the sense that Lash describes: responses are fast and often occur without reflective consciousness. Action comes to mimic the spontaneous, instinctive character of the "I" as the "me" is extinguished by the demands of the moment. If we are indeed witnessing a shift from *reflection* to *reflexivity* at the level of individual consciousness and action in the risk society, then edgework represents the most dramatic expression of this transformation.

Thus, a strong argument can be made for viewing the attraction to edgework activities as indicative of a broad desire to explore and refine a form of agency demanded by the risk society. I will conclude by turning to another problem of agency that emerges in the second modernity. In developing this final point, I will expand the concept of reflexivity even further by exploring how edgework may contribute to projects of *self-reflexivity* in the risk society. This formulation relates to an empirical phenomenon at the center of the classical theoretical interpretations of edgework discussed above – the experience captured by the terms "self-determination" and "self-actualization."

As reported in the original edgework project (Lyng 1990) and subsequent studies, one of the most prominent empirical patterns found in the field data on a wide range of edgework endeavors is the magnified sense of self that participants experience as they approach the edge. This phenomenon is important to the Marxian, Meadian, and Weberian analyses of edgework because all three perspectives assert that the core structural dynamics of the modern social order (alienation, the decline of community, rationalization) undermine self-development. A primary attraction of doing edgework in these interpretations is the experience of a fully determined self, which cannot be found in normal institutional routines. In the risk society, however, the self cannot be "lost" in one domain of experience and "found" in another. Rather, producing a self becomes a personal project that takes place in a context of general uncertainty and unrestrained possibilities for exploration and innovation. Thus, agents within the risk society are both compelled and inspired to pursue projects of *self-reflexivity*, in which subjects actively create themselves in the risk experiences they negotiate in all aspects of their lives.

Among the many risk challenges that people confront in this context, doing edgework may offer the greatest opportunity for self-creation. This claim is supported by the classical Meadian interpretation, which also conceptualizes edgework as a project of self-reflexivity. By committing themselves to exploring dangerous edges, actors discover the creative possibilities of an "acting self" that has been liberated from the constraining influences of reflective consciousness and the social self (the "me"). As I have argued elsewhere (Lyng 2005c), the convergence between Michel Foucault's concept of the "limit experience" and edgework suggests the possibility of a poststructuralist version of this argument. Drawing on published personal interviews with Foucault and certain strands of his work, James Miller (1993: 30) has captured Foucault's sense of the limit experience as an enterprise in which one

> deliberately push[es] his body and mind to the breaking point, hazarding … 'an actual sacrifice of life … a voluntary obliteration.' … [so as to] breach, however briefly, the boundaries separating the consciousness and unconsciousness, reason and unreason, pleasure and pain – and, at the ultimate limit, life and death – thus starkly revealing how distinctions central to the play of true and false and pliable, uncertain, contingent.

The limit experience differs from edgework in certain ways (see Lyng 2005c: 44), but this passage clearly reveals that the two concepts refer to the same essential experience – the process of negotiating the most consequential boundaries one can possibly confront as a human being. Moreover, recent scholarship on Foucault's use of the limit experience demonstrates that he viewed this experience as a vehicle of self-creation (Miller 1993; Duff 1999; Warfield 1999). While Foucault's discussion of power-knowledge in *Discipline and Punish* and *The History of Sexuality* implies that the self does not exist outside of discourse, he shifted in his later works to viewing subjectivity as a pragmatic goal to be achieved by exploring the possibilities of the body. One pursues this "ethic of the self" by engaging in experiments of self-creation through the process of transgressing limits. The exploration of limits brings out corporeal potentials that remain unrealized in the "congealed subjectivities" imposed by previous social experience. Thus, in taking up the challenge of negotiating limits or edges, the actor initiates a project of self-creation, drawing on the indeterminacy of the body to identify new ways of being.

This treatment of the limit experience ignores fundamental differences between Foucault's conception of the "panoptic" society and the risk society model embraced by Beck and his collaborators (see Lyng 2005c). However, Foucault's insights about the "ethic of the self" do broaden our understanding of the nature of self-reflexivity in the risk society. Foucault was not specifically concerned with how the logic of risk has transformed the modern social order, but his conceptualization and use of the limit experience gives us a way to relate edgework to the broader risk imperative of late modernity. As social actors confront the risks and uncertainties of everyday life, they become increasingly aware of both the costs and opportunities of living on the edge. The certainty and security of institutionally based self-definitions steadily recede, but the loss of this security is accompanied by newly internalized skills of risk management. Armed with these skills and a growing sense of confidence in their ability successfully to manage risk, actors become more and more aware of the "liberating" side of living with uncertainty. Consequently, these experiences inspire actors to take up new projects of self-creation in the form of extreme risk taking – moving to the edge in order to do "work carried out on ourselves by ourselves as free beings" (Foucault 1991b: 47). As actors hone their edgework skills and discover avenues of self-construction not previously imagined, the allure of the edgework experience steadily increases, abating only when uncertainties beyond one's control transform a project of self-*construc*tion into one of self-*de*struction. Even with the threat of such negative outcomes, however, self-reflexivity has emerged as one of the key dimensions of the general process of reflexive modernization.[11]

Conclusions

My goal in this chapter has been to describe a form of "manufactured uncertainty" that arises in the experience of many members of contemporary western societies – the uncertainties that individuals manufacture for themselves through their pursuit of high-risk activities. I have described the common elements of a broad range of high-risk endeavors, from extreme sports and other risky leisure pursuits to high-risk occupations and interpersonal relations, and suggested that these common elements be conceptualized as edgework. I reviewed a number of theoretical approaches to the central empirical problem in the study of edgework – that is, accounting for the growing partici- pation in activities that pose a significant threat to the physical and psychological well-being of risk-taking enthusiasts.

In addressing this problem, I adopted an analytical approach that starts with the foreground of the risk-taking experience and attends to the powerful sensations and embodied pleasures that draw people into edgework activities. This approach has yielded empirical data that chal- lenge the traditional conception of voluntary risk taking (of the edge- work variety) as an activity governed by calculations of costs and benefits by rational decision-makers seeking external rewards. The phenomeno- logical evidence reveals that edgeworkers are seduced by the nature of the experience into exploring consequential boundaries. This foreground analysis was then linked to an investigation of the background factors that define the social context of edgework practices. The background analysis helps to explain how edgework acquires its seductively appeal- ing character for serious risk-takers.

One of the principal strengths of this approach is its empirical ground- ing in the lived experience of risk taking. By drawing on the subjects' collectively constructed accounts, the motivations for risk taking are treated as a topic of empirical discovery, thereby avoiding the problems associated with rational choice abstractions such as the "costs" and "benefits" or tautological conceptualizations like a "tendency to take risk" as motives for risk taking. As a sociological theory of risk taking, the edgework model also offers a more comprehensive understanding of the growing attraction of high-risk activities in the postmodern era. Contextualizing risk taking in this way allows us better to appreciate the social and historical significance of risk action and consciousness.

The qualities that account for this approach's primary strengths are also the source of its chief weakness as a perspective on risk and uncertainty. In seeking a comprehensive explanation of risk behavior by focusing on the interpenetration of foreground and background factors, the edgework model has relied, by necessity, on interpretive forms of analysis. While this approach offers many important insights into the problems of risk and uncertainty in the contemporary social order, it yields very little in the way of testable propositions relating to decision making in risk situations. In this sense, the theory of edgework contrasts with some of the most influential psychological and economic models of risky choice (Slovic et al. 1977b; Kahneman et al. 1982; Heimer 1988).

As the preceding review shows, one can view edgework either as an escape from the alienating conditions of modern life or as the most pure expression of the action orientation and skills demanded by the contemporary social order. Which of these viewpoints most accurately explains the edgework phenomenon, or whether we even need to choose between one or the other perspective, remains to be determined. In addition to resolving this issue, future research on voluntary risk taking must attend to variations in edgework practices related to gender, ethnicity, class, and other important social group divisions. There is much to learn about the various ways in which the logic of risk has come to dominate modern life and we have just begun this important investigation.

Further Reading

Ferrell, J. (2001) *Tearing Down the Streets: Adventures in Urban Anarchy.* Palgrave, New York.

Katz, J. (1988) *The Seductions of Crime: moral and sensual attractions of doing evil.* Basic Books, New York.

Lois, J. (2001) Peaks and valleys: the gendered emotional culture of edgework. *Gender & Society*, 15(3), 381–406.

Lupton, D. & Tulloch, J. (2002) "Life would be pretty dull without risk": voluntary risk-taking and its pleasures. *Health, Risk, & Society*, 4(2), 113–24.

Lyng, S. (ed.) (2005) *Edgework: the Sociology of Risk-Taking.* Routledge, New York.

O'Malley, P. & Mugford, S. (1994) Crime, excitement, and modernity. In: Barak, G. (ed.), *Varieties of Criminology.* Praeger, Westport, Conn., pp. 189–211.

Simon, J. (2002) Taking risks: extreme sports and the embrace of risk in advanced liberal societies. In: Baker, T. & Simon, J. (eds.), *Embracing Risk: the Changing Culture of Insurance and Responsibility.* University of Chicago Press, Chicago.

Notes

1. Hazards can be defined as "threats to people and what they value" (Kates & Kasperson 1983: 7027).

2. Action is behavior that is consequential for the individual, that has problematic outcomes, and is undertaken for its own sake (Goffman 1967: 185).
3. Flow is conceptualized by Csikszentmihalyi (1985) as a state of focused attention or deep concentration on a limited set of stimuli, accompanied by a distorted sense of time, a feeling of personal transcendence, and merging of the individual with the objects at hand. Flow is best illustrated by the experiences produced by certain meditative practices like Transcendental Meditation.
4. Although the author is not aware of any instance of this problem appearing in the published research on edgework, it has emerged in personal communications with other researchers and colleagues at professional conferences and other meetings.
5. Dragan Milovanovic's (2005) recent effort to construct a typology of edgework experiences is an important step in this direction.
6. Pragmatism can be briefly described as philosophical perspective that treats "reality" as the active creation of social actors engaged in collective efforts to solve practical problems. In this framework, subjects constitute themselves (develop human knowledge and capacities) as they create significant objects of the external world in active problem solving. The key classical theorists of pragmatism were John Dewey and William James and contemporary interpreters of this tradition include Hans Joas (1996), John Hewitt (1984), and Dmitri Shalin (1992). Phenomenology also derives from a well-established philosophical tradition, primarily the work of Edmund Husserl. In the original philosophical formulation, phenomenology was concerned with the nature and consequences of the human apprehension of "reality" through the senses. Alfred Schutz developed Husserl's idea in the direction of phenomenological sociology by focusing on the problem of intersubjectivity – how people come to understand the consciousness of others from their own subjective standpoint. In taking up this problem, Schutz developed a view of social life in which social actors actively construct social reality at the same time that they are constrained by pre-existing social and cultural constructions. The best-known contemporary elaboration of Schutz's idea is Peter Berger and Thomas Luckmann's *The Social Construction of Reality* (1967).
7. It is important to acknowledge that the body has been a focus of concern for a number of phenomenological perspectives, although the phenomenological approach to the body differs from the approach adopted here.
8. In the Meadian framework, the "I" cannot exist apart from the "me."
9. The term "conscious" should not be equated with the "reflective" nature of the "me."
10. The importance of "sociality" to both Marx and Mead's conceptions of

free action is the foundation of the Marx–Mead synthesis, as discussed below.

11. Although Ulrich Beck's work has been heavily referenced in this section, I should point out that the present interpretation of reflexivity is more closely aligned with Anthony Giddens' phenomenological perspective than Beck's institutional approach. Beck and Giddens employ slightly different interpretations of reflexivity, but these interpretations are generally regarded as complementary.

6 | Culture and Risk

John Tulloch

The sociocultural analysis of risk is a growing field, drawing on long overlapping interests in sociology, anthropology, criminology, cultural/ media studies, and literary studies. In particular, the notion of the "cultural turn" (and the "ethnographic turn") in the social sciences and humanities became very central to the thinking in many of these disciplines in the 1970s and 1980s.

On one hand, this was marked by an increasing interest in culture as everyday life – the notion that the meanings of cultures and subcultures are to be found in such active everyday activities as the clothing we choose to wear for different occasions, the media we engage with at different times, the beaches or football grounds we perform at, the different identities we shift through in any one day, the sexual or health or fitness practices we adopt, and so on – rather than in the more traditional idea of "culture" as expressing "timeless" or "universal" values through high arts such as canonical literature, or classical music and theater.

On the other hand, the cultural turn was marked by a profound rejection in disciplines such as anthropology and sociology of the notion that their research fields are objective or neutral. Denzin and Lincoln remark on the "traditional period" of qualitative ethnographic research (from the early 1900s to World War II) as believing it was focused on the study of "other" (alien, foreign, and strange) cultures via the " 'objective', colonizing accounts of field experiences" (1998: 13). They argue that anthropological research during this foundational stage was organized according to four beliefs: "a commitment to objectivism, a complicity with imperialism, a belief in monumentalism (the ethnographer would create a museum-like picture of the culture studied), and a belief in timelessness (what was studied never changed)" (1998: 14). They contrast this with the dramatic changes in the post-ethnographic turn anthropology of the 1980s toward the richly "thick description" of everyday life.

In contrast to the objectivist "monumentalism" of the early period, many anthropologists were admitting by now that all their writings were interpretations of interpretations. The "local situation" of every-day life had become the *subject* of anthropology, and at the same time there was a new emphasis on the *researcher* as the teller of "tales from the field." The traditional anthropological distinction between the researcher's "scientific" voice and the "objective" data extracted from her or his respondents' voices was now blurred, as was the distinction between expert and lay knowledge.

Denzin and Lincoln emphasize that the various historical phases of anthropological and ethnographic research they describe continued to coexist, leading to a range of choices in the theoretical position that researchers adopted. This encouraged multiple methodological approaches, competing criteria of evaluation, and a ferment of debate. After the cultural turn – with its more pluralistic perspective and focus-ing on cultural representations and their meanings – the "golden age of the social sciences was over, and a new age of blurred, interpretive genres was upon us. The essay as an art form was replacing the scientific article" (Denzin & Lincoln 1998: 19).

What this implies is that the *theory of knowledge acquisition* (or epis-temology) that researchers used became as important a part of their reflection as their choice of subject matter. We might not all, in the social sciences, have come to think we are writing an "essay as an art form" when analyzing our research, but nor do we think we are involved in objective scientific research either. Whatever we think we are writing, and whatever we choose to research, the power relationship we have with the people we write about becomes as much a focus of our atten-tion as the "raw data" we analyze. That is to say, researchers must be aware of themselves as *writers*, empowered to tell stories about the stories that their interviewees tell them. They must be reflexive. Consequently, a lot of work in different areas of the social sciences and cultural studies – dealing, for example, with media, power, class, ethnic-ity and gender, self and other, reason and emotions – focused on micro-analysis (of everyday life) and self-reflexivity.

It was in this post-cultural turn period of the 1980s that cultural theories of risk began to make a strong appearance in the academic literature. So it was no surprise to find that a representative book of the period, *Risk and Sociocultural Theory*, edited by Deborah Lupton in 1999, reflexively focused as much on the theoretical and epistemological positions adopted by the writers of the various chapters as on the substantive field of risk research. As Lupton described it,

> Three major theoretical perspectives on risk emerging since the early 1980s and gaining momentum in the 1990s may be distinguished. The first is offered by the work of Mary Douglas, who began in the early 1980s setting forth an influential perspective on risk ... that adopts a cultural anthropological approach (Douglas & Wildavsky 1982; Douglas 1985; 1990; 1992). The German sociologist Ulrich Beck's book *Risk Society*, published in English in 1992, has provided a major impetus to recent sociological examination of risk (...Beck 1992a; 1992b; 1994; 1995b; 1996a; 1996b; Beck & Gernsheim 1995). The English sociologist Anthony Giddens (1990; 1991; 1994b; 1998), adopting a similar perspective to that of Beck, has also influenced sociological diagnoses of the role of risk in society. A third perspective is offered by the several theorists who have taken up Michel Foucault's writings on governmentality (for example, Foucault 1991a,b) to explore the ways in which the state and other governmental apparatuses work together to govern – that is, manage and regulate – populations via discourses and strategies (Castel 1991; Ewald 1991; O'Malley 1996; Dean 1997) (Lupton 1999b: 1).

Lupton goes on to position each of these sociocultural theories of risk epistemologically; and in so far as her opening descriptions of "cultural/symbolic," "risk society," and "governmentality" perspectives go theoretically, Lupton's survey of "culture and risk" is extremely helpful, and I will follow them here. But they only go so far. First, because Lupton collapses (like many risk theorists) the notion of the epistemologically "real" into one catch-all category. This misses some of the more powerful risk theory since the 1980s: for example, within "Left realist" criminology, which is part of the broader tradition of critical realism. Second, because we need to take further the approach to cultural representations and their meanings, which I will try to do here by referring each of Lupton's three "sociocultural" theories (as well as my additional category of critical realism) to examples in media analysis. Third, despite the post-cultural turn emphasis on power, subjectivity and mixed identities (as compared with scientific objectivity and static roles), there has been little in the "culture and risk" literature which engages with the issue of subjectivity in *writing* about culture and risk, which I will try briefly to address in my final section on the "culture of fear" and terrorism.

Mary Douglas and Cultural Boundaries

Lupton is within the post-cultural turn tradition in making her preliminary distinction between, on one hand, all three of her sociocultural categories of risk theory and, on the other, techno-scientific approaches.

> For exponents of the technico-scientific perspective, which emerged from and is expressed in such disciplines as science, engineering, psychology, economics, medicine and epidemiology, risk is largely treated as a taken-for-granted objective phenomenon. The focus of research on risk in these fields is the identification of risks, mapping their causal factors, building predictive models of risk relations and people's responses to various types of risk and proposing ways of limiting the effects of risk. These inquiries are undertaken adopting a rationalistic approach which assumes that expert scientific measurement and calculation is the most appropriate standpoint from which to proceed. Such researchers may be described, therefore, as adopting a realist approach to risk. (Lupton 1999a: 2)

I will return later to Lupton's perception of a realist approach to risk. But what I have already said about the post-cultural turn in social sciences and humanities will indicate why Lupton is right to contrast "objectivist" accounts of risk (such as techno-scientific) with all the other "sociocultural" accounts. Each of the sociocultural approaches to risk that she discusses belong within the post-ethnographic-turn period of social scientific research that Denzin and Lincoln describe as one of "blurred genres" which saw qualitative researchers gaining in stature as they gave interpretive accounts of cultural representations and meanings, but at the same time having a very large complement of theoretical paradigms, methods, and strategies to choose from.

Within the internal history of risk theory, Mary Douglas's work tends to take a foundational place. But it is important to recognize the degree to which Douglas herself was part of this post-cultural turn ferment of ideas. Certain risks are singled out, according to Douglas, as the result of social and cultural influences. Because the perceptions of risk among people sharing the same cultural context are related to the group's legitimating moral principles, "other" (marginalized) groups are often identified as threatening the mainstream. Thus Douglas's "cultural risk" writing developed naturally out of her earlier anthropological work on purity and contamination, exploring the boundaries that cultures and communities construct between their own purity and the dangerous contamination risked by exposure to "Others." But as she described the construction of risk and "risky groups" – via the symbolic *meaning* of risk – within contemporary cultural discourses, Douglas was very much part of the "cultural turn."

A strength of Douglas's work has been her recognition that risk is both a meaning construction – so in this sense her work is "constructivist" in describing the use of risk as *discourse*, a "forensic resource" that *claims* scientific neutrality in explaining and predicting within western societies dangers arising from the more primitive "taboos" of Other cultures – and at the same time realist, in so far as her work with Aaron Wildavsky situates different cultural responses to risk within a structuralist "grid-group" model.

On one hand, there is the post-cultural-turn aspect of Douglas and Wildavsky which rejects "the wrong division between the reality of the external world and the gropings of the human psyche" still prevalent in the natural sciences and parts of the social sciences which "have allocated real knowledge to the physical sciences and illusions and mistakes in the field of psychology. Causality in the external world is generally treated as radically distinct from the results of individual perception" (Douglas & Wildavsky 1982: 193). Against this "scientific" position, the authors of *Risk and Culture* insist on the culturalist view that "Between private, subjective perception and public physical science there lies culture, a middle area of shared beliefs and values" (Douglas & Wildavsky 1982: 193).

But on the other hand, not *all* is culture, and a key element of Douglas and Wildavsky's grid/group analysis lies in checking characteristics of structural social organization at the "center" against the cultural beliefs and values of people at the "borders," as these latter both challenge and motivate the survival of social organization. Analyzing their notion of "grid," they draw our attention to structural "social distinctions and delegations of authority" (1982: 138) such as hierarchy and power. Analyzing "group" draws attention to the "outside boundary" values that people in religious, environmentalist, or other sects have erected between themselves and the outside world. So that while their analysis focuses on the indicators for "group" – they note the similarity of religious and environmentalist sects in having a global rather than local range, the sense of a regenerating moral fervor, an obsession with counteracting a global conspiracy of evil, a fear of infiltration from outside, and an emphasis on symbolic statements in rejecting "the larger society, especially its technology" (1982: 139) – Douglas and Wildavsky confess their "bias toward the center" (1982: 198) and toward the optimistic structural resilience of social organization against the global doom narratives of sectarian cultures.

So there is the sense of an "underlying" social-institutional basis in this risk analysis. Yet it remains culturalist too, in its emphasis on deconstructing the perceived "naturalness" of "expert" knowledge systems such as science and psychology, while focusing on the symbolic meanings and discourses through which "culture" is constructed in both everyday and institutional life. As Nick Fox notes of the Douglas and Wildavsky grid/group typology,

> What is considered as a risk, and how serious that risk is thought to be, will be perceived differently depending upon the organization or grouping to which a person belongs or with which he identifies, as will the disasters, accidents or other negative occurrences which occur in a culture (Douglas 1992: 78). The free-market environment (low grid and low group) will see competitors as the main risk, to be countered by good teamwork and leadership. In the bureaucratic culture (high grid and high group), the external environment is perceived as generally punitive, and group commitment is the main way to reduce risk. Finally, in the voluntary culture (low grid with high group), the risks come from external conspiracies, and group members may be suspected of treachery. (1999: 15)

Because of Lupton's tendency to reduce various "realist" positions to one (the techno-scientific), she finds Douglas's epistemological position somewhat ambiguous. She argues that Douglas's "cultural/symbolic" perspective is nearer the relativist pole of a continuum in which "a realist approach of the kind offered in technico-scientific approach is at one pole and a highly relativist constructionist pole is at the other" (Lupton 1999b: 5). Yet, Lupton also notes that

> Douglas does emphasize at various points in her writing on risk that she sees the dangers which are identified as risks as 'all too real'. She claims that her interest lies in elucidating the ways in which these 'real risks' are

singled out as important compared with other possible risks and how they are used in social and cultural relations: "this argument is not about the reality of dangers, but about how they are politicized." (Lupton 1999b: 5–6)

As I will indicate later, within a critical realist tradition of risk theory, Douglas's specific position on the construction and politicization of risk in the context of structural power is perfectly consistent. But for Lupton, Douglas's position seems to be lacking in logical consistency.

A major strength of Douglas's risk analysis is in its theorization of social uncertainty as that area where there is some symbolic blurring of, or transgression between, the known boundaries of cultural purity. A powerful example of Douglas's theory of cultural boundaries and uncertainty applied to cultural representation in media analysis has been provided by the Swedish research team of Boholm, Ferreira, and Lofstedt in their long-term research project on the Hallandsas railway tunnel-building fiasco. Acrylamide, a highly toxic sealant, was injected into the tunnel walls to prevent the flooding of the tunnel because of a high water table level, and this led to poisoning of local water courses and to significant economic and cultural breakdown in local farming communities.

The Swedish researchers draw centrally on Douglas's theories of cultural boundaries, transgression, and uncertainty in arguing that whereas newspaper readers were accustomed to the conventional image-assemblage of the "rural" as composed of "the dairy farm as an integrated whole including people (the farmers), animals (the cows), the landscape (pasture) and product (the milk)," in the case of the prolonged media coverage of the Hallandsas tunnel crisis, they were now facing something that looked very different, and revealed "the fundamental deviation from any supposed steady state" (Ferreira et al. 2001: 290). Now an assemblage of newspaper images showed a close-up of a deformed dead cow, a man squatting and pointing to a stream of polluted water, a farmer dumping milk into a urine reservoir, and a family posing next to their poisoned drinking well. Seen together, these images reflected something "Other," a new "testimony of disorder" (2001: 290).

> The kind of photographs that 'witness' the collapse of dairy farm imagery do not rely on notions of rationality ... but in the relation between how the imagery of order is culturally constructed and how its disruption is visualized ... Rather than being reinforced by the pictorial description, the factual and intended risk object (acrylamide/Roca-Gil) has been

metaphorically 'transformed' into the much more powerful and encompassing imagery of poison, concretized in polluted drinking water. Without delving in the symbolic imagery of 'poison' and 'water', we observe that they belong to two incompatible categories in human thought and that their mixing raises issues of purposeful human agency (or issues of negligence). Like the mixing of water and poison, the mixing of milk and urine ... plays upon one of the strongest 'taboos' in every society. (Ferreira et al. 2001: 291)

On one hand, this unexpected "taboo" cluster of images broke with long-established pictorial conventions of the "rural" and created uncertainty. On the other, a newspaper double page image-spread of the Hallandsas crisis conjured up and contrasted "the Swedish cultural imagery of 'open landscapes' and 'stone terraces' with the darkness, fear, and mystery of underground [harshly lit tunnel] imagery" (2001: 293). This explicitly evoked the contrast of order/disorder by juxtaposing two long-term visual metaphors that were not normally associated: the deeply resonant cultural memory of healthy Swedish landscape and the metaphoric image of the tunnel, which the researchers describe as a "risk event" in search of a new commonsense meaning.

Importantly, the Swedish researchers' culturalist analysis challenges here the rationalistic approach of techno-scientific theories of risk by arguing that "the potential of visual images to communicate emotive and intuitive knowledge, imbuing it with veracity and permitting projection of identification, makes them an effective medium for social constructions of messages about risks" (Boholm 1998: 126f.). This is to take Douglas's symbolic analysis of risk, contamination and the "Other" further into cultural media theory, while extending her culturalist critique of techno-scientific risk theories of rational choice.

> In accordance with a highly developed tradition of exegesis in Western cultures, we are taught from an early age to explain things and to check the logical exposition of our explanations. The tradition is deeply rooted – it is easy to think that we read sequentially and logically – and combines well with the idea of the "risk averse" individual ... The theory of rational choice, however, overlooks the fact that choices are made according to available alternatives that are themselves symbolic constructs ... The argument forwarded here is that stigma (its mark and visibility) ... is *implicated* from already existing ideas about how the world is socially constructed. Further, these ideas are embodied in concrete and recognizable risk objects that may not be the 'real' causes of the hazards or perceived threat. (Ferreira et al. 2001: 295, 297)

Thus as water (or milk) breaks its familiar contextual boundaries (of farms, farmers, rough stone walls, and healthy cows grazing in fields) in cultural representation, and transgresses into other visual contexts (dead cows, milk poured into urine pits, farm families squatting beside toxic water, hellish train tunnels beneath the fields), a major uncertainty is created for newspaper readers and viewers of these new "risk images," and a cultural hazard "flow" from one image-assemblage to another becomes "a main feature of risk events" (Ferreira et al. 2001: 297).

Ulrich Beck and Risk Society

Beck's "risk society" thesis became very well known first in Germany at the time of the upsurge of the Green movement in the late 1980s and then more widely in the 1990s once his book was translated into English. Whereas Douglas's focus is on the cultural construction of purity and the transgression of social borders, Beck's thesis focuses especially on the globalization of risks to the planet itself, quintessentially represented by the nuclear reactor disaster at Chernobyl which occurred shortly before he published *Risk Society* in Germany.

Beck argues that whereas the risks faced by people in premodern periods were as visible as their causes, and in industrial society were usually to do with class-based distribution conflicts of scarcity, the risks represented by Chernobyl represented something new. While environmental hazards in earlier times "assaulted the nose or the eyes and were thus perceptible to the senses," whether in the excrement-piled streets of medieval towns or in the squalid, cholera-threatened tenements of Europe's nineteenth-century cities, the "risks of civilization today escape perception and are localized in the sphere of physical and chemical formula (e.g. toxins in foodstuffs, or the nuclear threat)" (Beck 1992b: 21). Today's risks, such as global warming, the hole in the ozone layer, ionizing radiation, or the contamination of foodstuffs by pesticides tend to be invisible, and can only be assessed by scientific methods and culturally represented by scientific and media knowledge systems. Moreover, Beck argues, these risks often reflect the dangers posed by science itself.

Consequently, whereas science and technology were once seen as the motor force of economic growth and healthy well-being (as, for example, in the effect on water-borne diseases such as cholera of building sewers in mid-nineteenth-century London), they are now often seen in cultural representation as the problem itself. As Lupton says of Beck's and Giddens' notion of risk and reflexive modernity,

> This concept incorporates the notion that late modernity is character-
> ized by a critique of the processes of modernity, which are no longer
> unproblematically viewed as producing 'goods' (such as wealth and
> employment) but are now seen to produce many of the dangers or 'bads'
> from which we feel threatened (such as environmental pollution, unem-
> ployment and family breakdown). The central institutions of late moder-
> nity – government, industry and science – are singled out as the main
> producers of risk. An emphasis on risk, Beck and Giddens assert, is thus
> an integral feature of a society which has come to reflect on itself, to
> critique itself. (Lupton 1999b: 4)

Whereas Douglas's cultural focus on purity and pollution took her into issues of self and Otherness, Beck's particular focus on environ-mental pollution has led to a strongly ecological sense of planetary threat, and the notion that we are now all victims of a runaway world of scientific hubris and economic greed. Major risks such as Chernobyl or global warming now often affect the poor and the wealthy alike, and "smog is democratic" (Beck 1992b: 36). We live in a "world risk soci-ety," where environmental risks affect those who have produced and profited from them, as much as anyone else.

In this situation, people's intuitive experiential knowledge is less effective, and hazards are determinable by experts because of their mag-nitude and their invisibility to the senses. Yet, especially through the media, people have also become aware that experts disagree with each other (as over global warming or weapons of mass destruction). Ordinary people often see science and industry as producing the risks about which they are concerned. Consequently, much of the belief that existed in early modernity on the links between science, industry, and progress has evaporated, resulting in individuals having to seek and invent new certainties for themselves.

There are now a far greater number of uncertainties than ever previ-ously existed – not only those seen to be promoted by government, industry, and science, but in addition through related changes in the structuring of individual lives. Traditions which once shaped key aspects of our daily lives, such as the "job for life," the fixed work location, trade unions, marriage, and the nuclear family, have themselves also been weakened in the high-tech world of risk modernity and "under-employment." People have been forced to make themselves the center of the conduct of life, adopting mobile, multiple, and changing identities. Crises are more often seen as individual than as social problems; and people are expected to be reflexive in making decisions about their health or their sexuality or their employment to a degree that never happened before.

By emphasizing that risk-making institutions such as science, industry, and government have come under increasing public scrutiny from a "subpolitics" of advocacy groups, Beck points to the reflexive nature of modernity. But in his discussion of greater individualization, he also indicates how concern about risk has entered everyday life and how individuals are expected to seek knowledge about risks and make decisions based on that knowledge. For Beck, blame is both projected outward at governments, scientists, and industries as part of reflexive modernization, and taken inward, as part of individualization and "reflexive biography." Both processes are different sides of the same coin of reflexivity.

Not surprisingly, theorists working in the context of the "risk society" have come to focus on the cultural process of knowledge representation itself, challenging familiar binaries like "expert" and "lay" knowledge (Wynne 1996). For Beck, the "irrationality" which experts often ascribe to lay perspectives is often a perfectly rational response to the uncertainties, political processes, and media debates around risk which are such a central part of the reflexivity of risk society. On one hand, Beck ascribes a significant role to the globally standardized mass media as a cultural source of information for lay publics (1992b: 133). But, on the other, lay knowledge in Beck's thesis has become increasingly individualized. If we no longer trust scientists or industry or media as "experts," and at the same time lose many of the traditional authority structures such as class and "one-job-for-life," we are thrown increasingly on to ourselves in constructing our own risk narratives by way of local and mediated cultural representations.

For Beck, risks generated by institutional systems "continually produce frictions, disharmonies and contradictions within and among individual biographies" (1992b: 137); and sociocultural researchers extending Beck's risk society thinking to a focus on media have adopted as a methodological device his emphasis on individualization and the perceptions of "collective fate" which become deeply embedded within personal biographies. Thus, Tulloch and Lupton argue, "Risk biographies become the only map available in everyday life, as the individualized citizen chooses between daily knowledges, and much less often it seems, between social (sub-political) affiliations" (2003: 63).

Critics of Beck's "risk society" theory for being "too social" and not sufficiently cultural have represented two different aspects of the "cultural turn": one focusing on the aesthetic and affective dimensions of risk, the other on empirical studies of the cultural representation of risk in everyday life.

On the one hand, Scott Lash, like Mary Douglas, has emphasized the importance of aesthetic, affective, and cultural aspects of risk ideas. Like the Swedish cultural theorists, Lash has criticized Beck's risk society thesis for being too trapped by the "legislation of cognitive reason," and thus focusing too much on the institutional, normative, and hierarchical ordering of individuals in relation to their utilitarian interests. Lash prefers the notion of risk *cultures* which depend on substantive values rather than procedural norms, on symbols not rules, and on a "horizontal disordering. Their fluid quasi-membership is as likely to be collective as individual, and their concern is less with utilitarian interests than the fostering of the good life" (2000: 47).

Like Douglas, Lash contrasts the hierarchical organization and ordering of social institutions (such as the church) with the temporary, disordered nature of sects. Sects respond to "That part of ourselves in which we are incomplete and unfinished subjectivities, unfinished, lacking bodies. If in churches trust is in institutions or expert systems, in sects trust lies in the face-to-face or the mediated face-to-face of the affinity group" (2000: 59). Because of his focus on the relationship between face-to-face groups, unfinished subjectivities and "lacking bodies," Lash argues powerfully for a notion of aesthetic reflexivity especially emphatic in the "terrible sublime" (which is the gut-wrenching feeling of fear and trembling when we face some horrendous experience in our own life, or, more often, through art and popular culture). Thus he describes Robert Mapplethorp's international exhibition of violent homoerotic photos in the 1990s as presenting an affective aesthetic culturally representing "lacking bodies" and death in contrast to the probabilistic rationality of risk thinking.

> A number of viewers of the exhibition no doubt thought of Mapplethorpe's death from AIDS, and about AIDS more generally ... Surely this is a vastly different way of judging the bad, the event, the risk of AIDS than subsuming it under a set of statistics, under probabilistic logic. It takes the particular, i.e. the photographs which can potentially

open up a space of existential meanings. To consider AIDS through probabilities and statistics is a way of looking at risks via determinate judgment. The more aesthetic consideration of AIDS through the existential meanings of Mapplethorpe's images instead involves reflexive judgment. (2000: 53f.)

Lash's emphasis on face-to-face, temporary affinity groups within sects – in Mapplethorpe's case, the passing exhibition audiences faced with images of gay communities – and his aesthetic focus on the "fear and trembling," gut-wrenching existential experience of the "terrible sublime," together open up a range of research possibilities for the cultural analysis of audience meanings in the media and arts. Thus, Tulloch (2005) has drawn on Lash's notion of aesthetic reflexivity to examine the face-to-face situation of theater audiences' combination of "determinate understanding," "imaginative synthesis," and the "terrible sublime" in negotiating a strongly politicized, post-apartheid South African version of Chekhov's *The Cherry Orchard*, as fin-de-siècle nineteenth-century Russia meets end-of-twentieth-century South Africa in the "bodies with lack" of contemporary theater audiences (2005: 240f.).

On the other hand, a rather different sociocultural critique of Beck focuses on everyday construction of the meaning of risk. Tulloch and Lupton, commenting on Beck's work in relation to the media, note his "allowing the individual-everyday to drop out of both his theory and his (lack of empirical) method ... [W]hat is most needed in revision of Beck's theory is analysis of the ways in which reflexivity and individualization are experienced as part of personal biographies and how they are structured via such categories as class and gender" (2003: 66). Consequently, in their book *Risk and Everyday Life*, they bring together Douglas's interests in the risk, the liminality, and the tempting excitement of crossing borders – in this case, borders of geography, sexuality, aging, gender, class, and employment – with Beck's focus on individualization and risk biographies in a series of personalized case studies that indicate the ways in which we deal with media and cultural representation in our everyday lives. In one case study they trace the "risk biography" of a young, white male who was educated by South African media to fear blacks, left the country after a university education in critical sociology made him critical of apartheid, came out as gay in Thatcher's Britain, then went to work in Australia where he is more affluent and enjoying risky leisure pursuits, but also is more critical of media and institutionalized racism. In another case study, they compare the different media usage – and differentiated reliance on "expert knowledge" in relation to different risks like food safety and imminent redundancy at a car factory – of two former working-class but now quite affluent engineers, who are facing a multiplication of risks for their families as they contemplate redundancy, having to sell their homes and move into much tougher, more crime-prone areas with poorer schools and hospitals.

In contrast to these potentially downwardly mobile workers, Tulloch and Lupton describe the responses to risk of a 31-year-old IT manager who, confirming Beck's analysis of individualization, argues that people need to take much more responsibility themselves for the risks they face.

> I wouldn't trust the government that much; but at the end of the day, once something has become clear and cut and dried as a proper risk I think I would trust them then to come forward and to say it is a risk. I wouldn't trust big business at all frankly. I think it is in their interest to cover it up. The tobacco industry has been trying to cover up cancer things for at least 20 years. The media I would trust for a small while. I think they will take something that is a small risk and blow it up into a larger risk but at least with the media you know if they start shouting about something then there is something there and then it is up to you to find out what sort of level of risk there is … So at the end of the day [to find out about risk] I think I probably will go best with friends and family and then the media. (quoted in Tulloch & Lupton 2003: 87)

This IT manager is described as a "pragmatic capitalist" who, while blaming privatization in part for the Paddington rail crash (because "when there are 20 companies responsible, no one need take responsibility"), nevertheless thinks the media have blown the tragedy up out of all proportion. He believes, on capitalist risk-calculation lines ("Is one life worth the investment of a billion pounds?"), that probably the only possible solution for emergency signaling and breaking systems was reached, given the lack of rail investment earlier. "I think people consider themselves to be put at risk by other people when in fact you put yourself at risk. Nobody else does it for you most of the time" (Tulloch & Lupton 2003: 88).

The many risk biographies in Tulloch and Lupton's analysis tend to support Beck's emphasis on individualization and everyday reflexivity in relation to government, big business, science, and the media. But they also reveal the continuing importance of social-structural factors which Beck underplays: of gender, ethnicity, sexual preference, age, and socioeconomic background in the construction of cultural risk biographies. For example, like the IT manager above, men and women with high-tech education felt much more comfortable than IT-unskilled workers facing a life of short-term contracts. The IT-skilled made much greater use of a wide range of media in assessing personal risks, and in some cases even undertook extreme sports in their leisure time because they felt that the government and banks took too much of the risk out of their financial lives (Tulloch & Lupton 2003: 72). The focus here is on the cultural representation (within risk biographies) of the pleasures of risk.

Risk and Governmentality

The focus of Beck and other current risk theorists such as Giddens and Wynne on issues of "expert" and "lay" knowledge is given a different, Foucauldian interpretation within the "governmentality" perspective by theorists like O'Malley and Dean. Foucault's history of governmentality explores the power of expert discourses, ranging from the medieval confessionals of the Catholic Church, the theatrical public spectacles of sixteenth-century Elizabethan governance, and the tortured "guilt" admissions of heretics under the Inquisition, to the "panoptican" surveillance by growing scientific professions such as medicine and criminology in the nineteenth century. So, for example, the regulation of sexuality in lay "commonsense" life from that time was enshrined in official (scientific, medical, political, and moral) discourses, which together became the regulatory surveillance systems of modernity.

As Lupton says, in the case of the growth of twentieth-century modern liberal governments, which have emphasized the rule of law based on voluntary self-discipline rather than violence or coercion,

> Risk is understood as one of the heterogeneous governmental strategies of disciplinary power by which individuals are monitored and managed so as to best meet the goals of democratic humanism ... Several writers on governmentality have drawn attention to the increasing focus in contemporary neo-liberalism ... on personal responsibility for avoiding and managing risk. They have identified a 'new prudentialism' currently evident in governmental discourses and strategies, which moves away from older notions of social insurance as a means of distributing risks to

a focus on individuals protecting themselves against risk (see O'Malley 1996; Dean 1997). Like the 'risk society' theorists, therefore, some exponents of the 'governmentality' perspective have drawn attention to the importance placed upon the self-management of risk and the increasing privatization of risk (1999b: 4f.).

Lupton is right to indicate continuities between "risk society" and "governmentality" thinking. But the more sophisticated governmentality analysts of risk also pose significant differences between themselves and Beck's risk analysis. Mitchell Dean confronts the weaknesses of Beck's thesis of the incalculability and uncertainty of risk within risk modernity on three grounds.

First, he criticizes Beck's totalizing assumption that risk can be understood within a single cultural narrative of the modernization process, namely risk modernity. In contrast, Dean argues that "it is easy to show the virtue of focusing on the concrete and empirical and to analyze specific types of risk rationalities and practices" (1999a: 136). So, drawing on various analyses within the governmentality tradition, he describes (i) *insurance risk* (depending on specific quantitative and calculative techniques such as statistical tables and probability analysis); (ii) *epidemiological risk* (quantifying rates of mortality and morbidity within a population); (iii) *case-management risk* (qualitative assessment via face-to-face case analysis of "at risk" individuals in areas such as alcoholism, sexual, or welfare dependency); (iv) *comprehensive risk management* ("worst-case scenario" risk strategies in sites where disaster could get completely out of hand, as in chemical factory situations like Bhopal or nuclear reactors like Chernobyl, by way of emergency procedures such as evacuation plans, risk education, and other contingency management measures).

Thus while Lash's critique of Beck moves directly into a variety of aesthetic and affective representations which he contrasts to a single, rationalistic "determinate judgment," governmentality theories point to different discursive representations of meaning and risk amelioration *within* the deterministic rationality of risk thinking. Dean's point is that it is over-generalizing to speak of "risk society" being marked by its recognition of the incalculability of risk. For Dean, risk is always calculated and represented – as "an attempt to construct coherent programmes of government" (1999a: 145) – in the face of uncertainty, even if, as in some comprehensive risk-management scenarios, such calculation may be ad hoc, likely to fail, and primarily taken in order to be "seen to be doing something."

Second, Dean argues against Beck's notion of the uniformity of risks, as if they are all different instances of one type of instrumental rationality. Rather, "it is possible to demonstrate that risk rationalities are not only multiple but heterogeneous and that practices for the government of risk are assembled from diverse elements and put together in different ways" (1999a: 136). Thus,

> Epidemiological risk ... is similar to insurance risk in that the calculus of risk is undertaken on the basis of a range of abstract factors and their correlation within populations ... However, it has its own discursive rationality and set of techniques and interventions. It is not the loss of capital but of health outcomes of populations that are subject to risk calculation. Its technical means are public health interventions such as sanitation, quarantine measures, inspection of food supply, inoculation programmes, and so on ... In contrast to these two quantitative forms of risk rationality, it is possible to identify another form which is principally qualitative ... This kind of [case management] risk ... is linked to clinical practice in which certain symptoms lead to the imputation of dangerousness, e.g. of the likelihood of a mentally ill patient committing a violent act (Castel 1991). Here risk concerns the qualitative assessment of individuals and groups, as falling within 'at risk' categories. (1999a: 143)

In particular, Dean's governmentality analysis is strong in examining a variety of ways of "crossing risk rationalities and technologies with contemporary liberal political programmes" (1999a: 145). Thus, for example,

> Among the preferred models of the 'neo-liberal' prudential subject is the rational choice actor who calculates the benefits and costs or risks of acting in a certain way and then acts (O'Malley 1996: 197f.). As O'Malley points out, the prudential subject of neo-liberal programmes faced with health and crime risks overlays the responsible and the rational, the moral and the calculating (200–1) ... The responsible subject seeks to optimize his or her independence from others and from the state, e.g. by employing epidemiological data of health risks, and undertaking diet, lifestyle and exercise regimes recommended by private health and fitness professionals or publicly funded health promotion. As O'Malley has pointed out, it is not only unhealthy but some would say 'immoral' to engage in risky behavior such as smoking or lack of exercise. (1999a: 146)

In this kind of specification of the risk rationalities and discursive "technologies" negotiated between governments or private organizations and individuals, governmentality approaches specify much more clearly and historically what Beck describes as individualization, by, as Dean says, drawing attention to "the different types of agency and identity involved in practices of risk, and the political and social imaginaries to which these practices are linked" (1999a: 155).

Third, Dean engages with Beck's belief that "real riskiness has increased so much that it has outrun the mechanisms of its calculation and control. By this I do not mean that Beck fails to recognize the socially produced nature of risk but that he wants to treat risk ontologically. Thus we can talk of the reality of industrial risk society because it has produced massive, physical, incalculable, and illimitable hazards for which it can no longer provide precaution" (1999a: 136). Dean argues instead that "against the assumption of realism, it is easy to show the virtue of adopting a more nominalist position, i.e. one that analyses forms of risk as among the ways we are required to know and to act upon ourselves and others today in a range of moral and political programmes and social technologies" (1999a: 136).

In this part of his argument Dean's position is curious, especially as some of his more powerful examples – as when he discusses the success of social insurance as a political technology in nineteenth-century France as capitalist employers "sought to take over the mutual benefit societies of the workers, which often doubled as a source of strike funds" – are undoubtedly critically realist in both substance and epistemology. No critical realist would have theoretical, political, or substantive problems with Dean's statement, "Risk techniques are taken up under given historical conditions in the service of particular political rationalities and by various social forces and agents in the course of historical struggles" (1999a: 141).

A limitation of governmentality approaches to risk, as Mythen and Walklate point out, is in differentiating between the responses and media uses of different individuals. In particular, the "danger is that individuals are portrayed as insentient 'docile bodies' observing and obeying disciplinary discourses" (Mythen & Walklate 2005: 15; see also Tulloch & Lupton 2003). Thus, even though governmentality theory is concerned with cultural representation and meaning in very sophisticated ways at the level of the public production of regimes of risk meaning, it tends to ignore two decades of research within media and cultural studies on the "active audience."

But governmentality analysis of risk is especially strong where Beck's is weak, in specifying theoretically the regulatory regimes and discursive spaces within contemporary neoliberal states. In particular, cultural approaches to media analysis within a governmentality perspective tend to examine media as part of a set of assemblages of discourse acting together in order to police borders. Thus, Mythen and Walklate, writing (presumably) just before the terrorist attacks in London of July 2005, argued:

> It is … evident that understandings of terrorism are being discursively shaped by the agencies involved in risk definition. Forms of knowledge are being manufactured and circulated by an institutional matrix, involving the state, politicians, security experts and the media. In the United Kingdom, the public articulation of a series of 'near-misses' is symptomatic of an intertwining narrative of terrorist threat. Various terrorist plots have allegedly been foiled, including an aircraft attack on Canary Wharf Tower, explosive strikes on the Houses of Parliament and the detonation of a bomb at Old Trafford football stadium. Of course this is not to suggest that the terrorist threat is fictional – merely that it is being *fictionalized*. As Tudor (2003: 253) detects, interconnected expressions of fear carry greater weight than those which appear in isolation. The recurrent hot potato of the 'terrorist scare', passed from politicians to the public via the mass media, is unlikely to lessen public anxiety, nor to induce opposition to the hardening of domestic security. The dissemination of dominant discourses of terrorism can function as a tactic of disciplinary control through which right-thinking citizens are encouraged to order and adhere to governmental objectives. (2005: 11f.)

The strong sociocultural emphasis in this governmentality approach is on the way that assemblages of surveillance and risk discourses both (i) construct "subject populations" that are "dreamt up, marginalized and put under suspicion" (Mythen & Walklate 2005: 12) – thus potentially extending Douglas's emphasis on boundaries, impurity, and the "Other" via an analysis of the different techniques, interventions, and rationalities of different parts of the assemblage – and (ii) "normalize" the rest of the population, "inviting citizens to become security guards, spies and informants" (Mythen & Walklate 2005: 14). The rhythms of media production and circulation have a very important role in encouraging individuals to internalize the "gaze of surveillance" (Culpitt 1999: 147) and thus "design in" surveillance to "the flows of everyday existence" (Rose 1999: 234).

Critical Realism and Left Criminology

There has been a significant tendency in theorizing about risk – and especially in the debate around Ulrich Beck's "risk society" thesis – to caricature different traditions of realist theory, and to collapse together different versions of realism. In fact, what Nick Fox calls the "realist or materialist" position on risk (1999: 16), and Lupton refers to as technico-scientific realism (which she believes Beck tends to "waver" toward, 1999b: 5) is arguably naïve (empiricist) materialism.

Realist epistemology has quite another meaning in cultural material-ist analysis, as in Raymond Williams' work in literary, theater, and media analysis as well as in some feminist literature (e.g. Terry Lovell's work). Lovell sharply distinguishes naïve empiricism – an epistemology whose "world ... exists at the level of sense data, generated through observa-tion and experiment" – from realism whose "propositions of theory relate to the deep ontological furniture of the universe, rather than at the surface [of appearances] at which experience is located. Experience, properly interpreted, gives us access to that deep ontological layer because it is causally connected to it" (Lovell 1981: 19). Similarly, Tulloch (1990: 10–18) and Tudor (1995: 98f.) in media theory and Pawson and Tilley (1994: 292) in criminology, have argued for a philo-sophical realism that constructs explanations by seeking to identify "underlying causal mechanisms" that sustain patterned activity.

Much of the specific emphasis of critical realism – on the notion of ontological depth, surface appearances, and the causal mechanisms which link the two, as clearly argued by Lovell in her book *Pictures of Reality* (1982) – derives from philosophers of science, especially Bhaskar. However, within media, theater, and literary studies, cultural materialism has drawn much of its early inspiration from Raymond Williams and from the European historical-materialist theorists who influenced him, such as Georg Lukacs and Lucian Goldmann. In par-ticular, Williams adopted and refined Lukacs' distinction between natu-ralism and realism in his critique of what he called "Left formalism" in screen, media, and literary theory. What Williams called High Naturalism was a specific movement among nineteenth-century artists like Zola, Seurat, Ibsen, and Strindberg which employed positivist science to challenge the high cultural artistic conventions of the time, working this challenge through a variety of styles in the novel, painting, theater, and other art forms. However, for Williams, contemporary "habitu-ated" naturalism has lost its articulated roots in the philosophy of a particular history and become the dull, residual everyday values of prac-tice of conventional art and television. This kind of naturalism is involved in getting the "surface of appearances" right, as in the heritage televi-sion genre (see Poole & Wyver 1984: 145; Tulloch 1990: 181), and is embedded in precisely the same psychologies and individualized rational-actor universe which Lupton and other risk theorists describe as realism.

But though Williams is right to speak of a pervading naturalism in much contemporary media, the critical realist belief in underlying causal mechanisms has penetrated deeply into contemporary public consciousness, often via the media. For example, when journalists argued that the 2003 Iraq invasion by the "Coalition of the Willing" was not "really" about democracy but about US neo-con imperial ideology and oil, or when they argued that the scandals at Abu Ghraib represented the "reality" of a particular stage of US capitalism where prisons, not only in Iraq but throughout the USA also, are subject to privatization, they were invoking the notion of underlying causal mechanisms. Critical realists do not deny that risk theory needs to be interested "in investigating ... the forms of knowledge, the dominant discourses and expert techniques and institutions that serve to render risk calculable and knowable" (Lupton 1999b: 6). Indeed, the relationship between US neo-con political philosophy and current US foreign policy in changing the configuration of economic control over disappearing resources like oil in the Middle East or Africa, while invoking dominant discourses about "democracy" and "Make Poverty History," is of central interest to contemporary critical realists (see, e.g. Naomi Klein (2005) on the 2004 tsunami and the risks of "reconstruction" after natural disaster, and Harold Pinter's Nobel Prize for Literature acceptance speech). But the sedimented power of certain underlying structures and their hegemonic cultural representations (such as the neoliberal politics underlying international relief, World Bank directives to "failed state" and other supposedly "poor" countries in receipt of aid, and the current preference of international capitalism to establish policing rather than trading relations with "failed" or "rogue" states) means that critical realists want to examine the imbricated relationship between "discourse" and "causal mechanisms."

One of the stronger examples of critical realist work within the area of risk analysis has been left realist "fear of crime" research. At their best, critical realist criminologists and media researchers have embedded their analysis in culturalist "thick" descriptions of the everyday lives of media professionals or audiences (see, e.g. Schlesinger et al. 1992) on the one hand, and in historical and sociocultural analysis on the other (Young 2003).

For example, Ian Taylor has drawn together a range of qualitative, quantitative, and critical realist methodologies and theories to analyze together: (i) ethnographic study of everyday communication about uncertainty (corner-shop gossip, children's playground stories, local media tabloidization) within one affluent Manchester suburb; (ii) discursive analysis of local media and word-of-mouth campaigns representing the local community "under siege" from "city Others" who purportedly bring in drugs, ram-raids, and house-breaking; and (iii) comparative structural analysis of post-industrial capitalist cities' attempts to position themselves as "headquarter" sites for globalizing multinational corporations.

Taylor (1995) is thus able to examine local media differences and contrasting fear of crime "structures of feeling" (Raymond Williams' term) as between international "headquarter" post-industrial cities such as Manchester and an old industrial city in decline like Sheffield. In Taylor's analysis, "causal mechanisms" such as the shift into multinational "headquarter" city status (involving economic and discursive moves in Manchester like Olympic Games bids, establishing an international airport, building a cheap light-rail system, and promoting the "24-hour city" for shopping and leisure) help explain different media representations and individual fears about crime in Manchester and Sheffield.

If we move from this kind of critical realist analysis of risk fears to the familiar critique of Beck's "risk society" thesis for its supposed ambivalence and tendency to "waver between a realist and a weak constructionist position on risk" (Lupton 1999b: 5), we can see that it is possible for Beck as a realist to be perfectly consistent in claiming that risks are real as well as constructed. It is evident that Beck sees risk modernity as primarily "manufactured" (in both its ecological and high-tech "underemployment" modes) by the conjuncture of economics and science/technology discourses. Beck also suggests a number of times that a major motor (or underpinning "causal mechanism") of that conjuncture is the globalization within contemporary capitalism of its major discursive powers, such as politics, industry, and the media, and that this macro-assemblage impacts significantly at the micro-level of multiple identity formation and risk choice through the process of individualization.

However, from a critical realist position, Beck's "risk society" thesis is weaker in its macro-theoretical than in its epistemological consistency.

In particular, his emphasis on the politics of fear, uncertainty, and vengeance replacing in risk society a politics of risk in industrial society that emphasized progress and equality has been criticized on the basis of "underlying" social mechanisms. For Mythen and Walklate, "at an underlying structural level, it is improbable that the unsafe society has supplanted the unequal society. The correlation between class and risk remains tight, with those less able to acquire the goods being more adversely affected by bads (Scott 2000)" (2005: 10).

The Writer as Risk Victim and Academic

Post-cultural turn literature in the social sciences and media studies has emphasized the role of the writer in ethnographic research. Ang, for example, has argued

> for the urgency of rethinking the significance of ethnography ... as a form of storytelling, as narrative ... [O]ur deeply partial position as storytellers ... should be ... seriously confronted ... as an inevitable state of affairs which circumscribes the ... responsibility of the researcher/writer as a producer of descriptions which, as soon as they enter the uneven, power-laden field of social discourse, play their political roles as particular ways of seeing and organizing an ever-elusive reality. (Ang 1996: 75f.)

Valerie Walkerdine (1985), in the field of media audience studies, used this perception powerfully, examining her own role as a woman academic researching a working-class male viewer who ritually and routinely played and replayed the most brutal parts of the bloody boxing fights in the Hollywood film, *Rocky II*. Rather than adopt a conventional "objectivist" feminist position which reduces this one man's video viewing to gender, class, and age categories, Walkerdine uses a mix of theoretical approaches to examine her own surveillant power as an academic in seeking to avoid constructing her solitary male viewer as "Other" in the ethnographic situation of her research. In particular, her interest as writer in working through her own moments of gendered weakness (as a child in relation to her infantilizing father) as well as her adult discursive and representational power as an academic, encouraged her to blend psychoanalytical and sociological theory. In so doing, she was challenging her own power as one of Foucault's authors narrating a tale (about a working-class father watching *Rocky*) and questioning her own surveillant account of a pathologized family.

In the field of risk research, this kind of post-cultural turn reflexivity has been rare. But in recent work on suffering, Ian Wilkinson has focused some of the key elements of post-cultural turn thinking – the emphasis on researcher reflexivity, the critique of rational-technical discourse and its usefulness to those in power, the importance of emotions and cultural representation, and the need to focus on everyday lived experience – in relation to risk subjectivity and "the genuine voice of suffering" (2006: 4).

In a special issue of *Health, Risk & Society*, Wilkinson introduces a number of approaches to this issue: for example, by Andy Alaszewski extending post-cultural turn exploration of multiple and alternative methodologies to the examination of stroke survivors' diaries. Alaszewski considers reflexively the power of medical and social science discourse to "airbrush ... from the record patients' feelings of fear and distress ... [S]troke survivors experienced stroke as a failure of foresight; an event that occurred without warning. This was linked to uncertainty and anxiety about another stroke, undermined the taken-for-grantedness of everyday life and increased sensitivity to warnings about another stroke and reduced self-confidence" (2006: 43, 56).

A sudden, unexpected circumstance in my own life – my exposure at a distance of about three feet to a suicide bomber on a Circle line underground train in London on July 7, 2005 – forced me to begin to think about catastrophic risk both subjectively and in a new way, because, unlike Walkerdine, I was disempowered (as "victim") and empowered (as "risk expert") at one and the same time by the media in the months that followed. I was like Alaszewski's stroke survivors in so far as I was confronted by an assault without warning on my body which undermined the taken-for-granted nature of my everyday life, reduced my self-confidence, and was linked to anxiety about further attacks. Like the stroke survivors I found it therapeutic to write about my experiences, but unlike them I was a risk academic who was living each day risk discourses, technologies, and practices which I recognized theoretically even as they engaged with my personal suffering and loss of confidence.

The detailed, everyday subjectivity of that experience I describe elsewhere (Tulloch 2006). Here I want to focus on just one feature of the experience to try to bring together some of the thoughts in this chapter examining different academic approaches to risk and cultural representation. My focus will be on the transition I experienced between both empowered subject and disempowered object of media narration on terrorism and risk, exploring the "uneven, power-laden field of social discourse" (Ang 1996: 76) as my own image – bloodied and bandaged at Edgware Road Tube station immediately after the bombing – became, in the words of many media sources then and later, "one of the iconic images" of 7/7.

My image appeared internationally in the print and electronic media both immediately and then regularly over the next several months, as British and overseas media engaged with 7/7 according to a variety of new angles for public involvement: the "everyday" experience of July 7 itself, the hospitalization and slow recovery of victims, the regular media time-surveys of 7/7 ("one month, three months, six months, one year on," "end-of-2005" programming), the public compensation issue, Tony Blair's anti-terror legislation, the government's refusal to implement an official public inquiry, media reports on police forensic methods, the regular editorials and features about "terror and the British Muslim community," etc.

Early in this process, I had to think through my responses to the numerous international requests for interviews from the media, not least because the risk scenario that Douglas describes – where individuals, communities, and national media (and politicians) focused on cultural boundaries, constructing "risky groups" in terms of the threat they pose of transgressing "civilized western" cultural boundary markers – quickly became staple media diet.

A particularly powerful example of the imagistic transgression of familiar contexts of the kind Ferreira et al. describe, following Douglas, was the replaying by British media of the Al-Jazeera footage of the terrorist who bombed my Tube carriage on July 7, Mohhamad Sidique Khan. His pre-recorded video threatened the British public with blood because of their complicity in the Iraq invasion and other atrocities to Muslim people world-wide. Two major features of symbolic transgression and cultural uncertainty upset the British public at the time of this video, according to British media accounts. One was the fact that a speaker dressed according to familiar contextual boundaries for "terrorists" in international media footage (Muslim dress, violent words threatening violent deeds, "amateur" production values, etc.) spoke not only in English, but in a homely Yorkshire accent. The sense of terror "at home" was strengthened by that intimate, local detail of accent, and the symbolic boundaries of both "Britishness" and "homeland security" were transgressed. The second aspect of cultural transgression lay in the media's juxtaposition of two very different public images of Khan: the Al-Jazeera terrorist image and an earlier *Times Educational Supplement* photo of him as a teacher's aid listening to young children in a school in Beeston, Yorkshire.

In response to the Al-Jazeera and British television transmission of the Khan video, I was asked by BBC Radio 4's *Today* magazine for an interview, and this was just one example of a decision I had to make, and a media rhetoric I had to construct, in the direct context of thoughts I was having about Douglas-style analysis of "purity" and cultural boundaries. But there were many others.

As governmentality theorists would predict, different forms of risk "calculative rationality" were communicated technically and practically to me after the July 7 terrorist event.

1 Insurance risk regulatory discourse was employed in political and media terrains as an economic and financial technique (remunerating for risk), as a moral technology (enabling victims to continue in the face of the ill fortunes of life), and as a technique for the indemnification and reparation of damages.
2 Epidemiological regulatory discourse was employed quantitatively in a face-to-face specialist context to correlate percentage chances of many victims' shattered eardrums self-repairing or being restored by graft according to proportions of ear-drum lost.
3 Case-management regulatory discourse was employed by psychologists via cognitive behavioral therapy (CBT) assessments of post-traumatic stress symptoms (measured, as Dean suggests, via qualitative, face-to-face, and quantitative survey methods).
4 Comprehensive risk-management regulatory discourse was employed, especially in the mass media, to deal with the terrorist "festival of destruction" – in this case, via increasing emphasis on the severity of anti-terror legislation at the expense of civil liberties.

The mass media covered all of these areas of risk regulatory discourse, but whereas only one journalist I spoke with wrote a piece around cognitive behavioral therapy in the "war against terror," an entire media empire became involved in the anti-terror legislation debate on the British government's side when the *Sun* chose to use my image as 7/7 victim to support Blair.

I became aware of the negotiation needed in engaging with a variety of what governmentality theorists call the technologies of different risk rationalities, even as I was constructing, in Beck's phrase, my own "everyday" and individualized risk biography. But I was also experiencing reflexivity and individualization after my severe, career-stopping injury as a set of personal biographies, which were being structured via my academic and my political (intra-family) discussion, as much as by the therapeutic technologies of my professional counselors and carers. These, as Mythen and Walklate (2005: 15) emphasize, were the "cultural and biographical features which may encourage... resistance" to the "mentalities of rule and practices of governance" which have not been sufficiently delineated in governmentality theory.

I slowly realized, for example, that each of the surveillance technologies of governmentality that Dean describes was calling on different "interview" responses *from me*. For example, whereas I tried to avoid insurance risk discourses in media interviews, and tended to address epidemiological risk issues through exchange of personal emails with other victims, most of my media interviews were strongly inflected via case-management risk discourses. CBT's logic (of one-by-one short-term targets) and its "technology" became not only my reflexive rational-choice "recuperation" decision across all areas (extending from my bodily and psychological recovery to my strategy after returning to work after six months' sick leave), but also the center of my "recovering victim" narration in one media interview after another.

However, one particular angle that interested the media for a time was that an academic accustomed to analyzing risk was himself subject to the *media's* risk narration. This interest was cued when the *Sun* newspaper used my image in the UK to support anti-terror legislation which I personally rejected. Consequently, from that time on (in the *Guardian*, on BBC Radio 4's *Today*, on Australian Radio 5UE, and on BBC2's *Newsnight*) I could no longer, even had I wanted to, confine my responses to the "recovering" victim discourse of CBT.

But in any case, earlier than this, I had not felt physically or mentally strong enough to respond critically to all of these risk different rationalities. So I had already chosen to focus mainly on *comprehensive risk management*, such as issues of "war against terror," "Iraq," and anti-terror legislation aspects of 7/7. Comprehensive risk management in Britain since 7/7 had primarily chosen the terrain of government anti-terror legislation rhetoric (trying to calculate the "incalculability" of risk of terrorism according to sliding scales of "arrest without charge" time-frames, ranging from 15 to 90 days), and also of extra-parliamentary and initially secret strategies, such as the Metropolitan Police's shoot-to-kill policy, that only came to media attention after the shooting in an underground train on July 22 of the innocent Brazilian electrician, Jean Charles de Menezes. As Mythen and Walklate note, whether it is a matter of extremely conservative political groups carving out "economic and cultural inroads" (2005: 13) within nation states, or of the expansion internationally of western neo-imperialism, "terrorism is providing a political lexicon through which ulterior motives are being camouflaged and hidden agendas executed" (2005: 14).

The *Sun* newspaper attached to a huge front-page image of my face bleeding profusely on July 7, 2005 the words "Tell Tony he's right" to support Blair's anti-terror legislation by attempting to arm-wrestle dissident New Labour MPs via (my) "people's voice." The *Guardian* responded with four pages of coverage in riposte to the *Sun*, and this in turn gave me more opportunity to speak publicly in "critical realist" mode, as the media were alerted to this collision between members within its own profession.

Conclusion

My everyday "recuperation" risk biography, extending consciously but with physical and psychological difficulty, over many months after July 7, 2005, convinced me of two things particularly. First, it exemplified Dean's insistence that "risk rationalities are not only multiple but heterogeneous and that practices for the government of risk are assembled from diverse elements and put together in different ways" (1999a: 136). But it also confirmed Beck's emphasis on the link between individualized risk biographies and alternative practices of media intervention. Moreover, during my time of extreme weakness in hospital when I was unable to read newspapers, but scanned instead images of the post 7/7 events, Boholm et al.'s extension of Douglas's interest in the transgression of cultural boundaries to the notion of image-assemblages and the potential of the visual to communicate emotive and intuitive knowledge was clearly working for me. However, my encounter with a *News of the World* "victims' march" reinforced my views about the fuzziness of Douglas's cultural "group/grid" typology, in the absence of an underlying socioeconomic analysis.

Like Walkerdine, my evolving commonsense and academic under-standing of the media at that time interpellated different theoretical traditions, in this case mainly within the various fields of sociocultural analysis of risk. But these approaches are not theoretically commensurate in all their parts. More emphasis on the epistemological position adopted by any one piece of risk research is needed, which leads directly to fur-ther reflexivity about the writing (and power) role of the researcher.

The different discursive (and visual) calculative technologies employed culturally both by different genres of media and by risk victims like myself in engaging with them, need much more analysis. This is a major area for further research into both the symbolic construction of cultural forms and risk victims' use of and resistance to these. In the case of ter-rorism, for instance, this needs to focus on the array of discursive ratio-nalities (and of aesthetically reflexive image assemblages – cartoons as well as photographs) across different media outlets. It should also include the wide spectrum of political discourses adopted by British newspapers in relation to "new wars" like the Iraq invasion and the "war against terror."

The notion among governmentality theorists that certain technolo-gies of risk rationality, such as epidemiological risk, are better positioned than others to promote media public education campaigns needs to be interrogated in the light of the failure of the British government to do this in the case of potential terror attacks. Moreover, in the absence of these (or of government acknowledgment of "lay knowledge" in the case of further security on British transport systems), "risk society" the-orists' recognition of the rationality of apparently "irrational" lay knowledge (e.g. among those people post-7/7 who choose to catch buses rather than "deep" underground trains, even though both were attacked) needs to be acknowledged and further researched.

The sociocultural approaches to risk representation which have devel-oped over the last two decades clearly still have considerable power and provenance, as my brief discussion of my experience of terrorism sug-gests. Different parts of different traditions can be used together in future risk research, *provided* that two conditions are met: first, that the critiques of the risk society tradition and parts of the governmentality tradition for "meta-theory" are met via detailed local empirical research; second, that the theory of knowledge representation and the power of the researcher-as-writer becomes part of risk analysis as a norm of research practice.

Further Reading

Alexander, J. (1996a) Critical reflections on "reflexive modernization." *Theory, Culture & Society*, 13: 133–8.

Boholm, A. (2003) The cultural nature of risk: can there be an anthropology of uncertainty? *Ethnos: Journal of Anthropology*, 68(2): 1–21.

Cohen, M. J. (2000) Environmental sociology, social theory and risk: an introductory discussion. In: Cohen, M. J. (ed.), *Risk in the Modern Age: Social Theory, Science and Environmental Decision-Making*. Macmillan, Basingstoke, pp. 3–31.

ESRC Environmental Change Programme (1999) *The Politics of GM Food: Risk, Science and Public Trust*. Special Briefing No. 5, University of Sussex.

Irwin, A. (2001) *Sociology and the Environment: A Critical Introduction to Society, Nature and Knowledge*. Polity, Cambridge.

Lash, S. & Wynne, B. (1992) Introduction. In: Beck, U. (ed.), *Risk Society: Toward a New Modernity*. Sage, London, pp. 1–8.

New, C. (1995) Sociology and the case for realism. *Sociological Review*, 43: 808–26.

Rosa, E. A. (1998) Metatheoretical foundations for post-normal risk. *Journal of Risk Research*, 1(1), 15–44.

Strydom, P. (2002) *Risk, Environment and Society: Ongoing Debates, Current Issues and Future Projects*. Open University Press, Buckingham.

Tulloch, J. (2004) Risk. In: Ritzer, G. (ed.), *Handbook of Social Problems: A Comparative International Perspective*. Sage, Thousand Oaks and London, pp. 451–64.

Tulloch, J. & Lupton, D. (2001) Risk, the mass media and personal biography: revisiting Beck's "knowledge, media and information society." *European Journal of Cultural Studies*, 4(1), 5–27.

Van Loon, J. (2002) *Risk and Technological Culture: Toward a Sociology of Virulence*. Routledge, London.

7 | A Comparison of Sociological Theorizing on Risk and Uncertainty

Jens O. Zinn

The previous chapters have presented five different approaches to risk. In this chapter I compare them, examining their differences and similarities, implicit and explicit assumptions, and what advantages and disadvantages follow from them. None of these theories is homogeneous but it is not possible to do justice here to all their variants. Instead I refer to the main features of each approach or to one central proponent. In order to understand the different styles of theorizing and their underlying assumptions, the first section will highlight the *theoretical contexts* to which the different risk approaches refer and by which the respective theorists are influenced. Next I will discuss the *epistemological status* of risk which has caused strong debate. Since the one-dimensional opposition of realism and constructivism is often too narrow to understand the different approaches to risk, I examine them in terms of their *theoretical background*, their different *aims* of analysis, and their contribution to *critique*. This leads to a systematic comparison of the approaches which draws on five central aspects of risk theorizing: *knowledge, rationality, values, power*, and *emotion*. I conclude by discussing *promises, pitfalls*, and *perspectives* of theorizing.

Theoretical Contexts of Risk Theorizing

Mary Douglas's (1921–present) outstanding contribution to risk theorizing is her introduction of a *cultural symbolic* perspective into a discourse which was until then dominated by technical-scientific and cognitive-rational approaches. Having studied in the 1940s and 1950s, her anthropological approach is influenced by *structural functionalist* thinking, foremost that of A. R. Radcliffe-Brown and Émile Durkheim,[1] who were very influential in anthropology.

Douglas's early anthropological work on *The Lele in Zaire* (1963) and the analysis of ideas and rituals of pollution and cleanliness in *Purity and Danger* (1966) prepared the basis for her later analysis on risk. Douglas shows that the selection of dangers and the strategies to cope with them are fundamentally socially constructed (Douglas & Wildavsky 1982: 6f.). Concerns regarding dirt and pollution are less about bacteria, viruses, or pollutants than about socio-symbolic disorder and the lack of control of a group's boundaries. The control of the body and its margins serves as a symbol for controlling the rules which constitute a social group. Dangers become important for a community as a threat to its boundaries, orders, and values. Douglas draws on this work when she analyzes risk in modern secularized societies as functionally equivalent to danger, and when she develops her grid/group typology. Captured by the functionalist question of how social order is possible, her theorizing focuses on the stabilization and regulation of the social by institutions (Lash 2000) instead of conceptualizing social change. Consequently, she favors the structural advantages of "market" and "hierarchy" for their capacity to manage much higher complexity than voluntary forms of organization (Douglas & Wildavsky 1982: 198).

An even stronger functionalist contribution to risk-sociology is the work of Niklas Luhmann (1927–99) who studied structural functionalism with Talcott Parsons at Harvard (1962), but developed an independent approach later on. He aimed to develop a *universal theory* which could describe all social phenomena of the "world society." Luhmann adopted a strong sociologism, distinguishing rigorously between social and other phenomena, and instead of action he defined communication as the basic unit of the social (1995: 135ff.). Stripping the subject from social theorizing supported his aim of producing a *non-normative* sociology. The emotions, understood as embodied experience attached to a subject, are neglected in Luhmann's theorizing, which is concerned with the structural logics of the social. Unlike in Parsons' teleological perspective of human development toward a better society, Luhmann interpreted evolution as a "self-conditioning" selection which produces "highly improbable, unplanned complexity" (1995: 433f.). Thus, Luhmann's theorizing involves a high level of skepticism regarding the possibilities of steering a society or making an exact prognosis of the future. He aimed to disenchant common knowledge about the social by conducting systematic conceptual analysis against a background of a functionally differentiated society. In *Ecological Communication*, originally published in 1986, the same year as Beck's *Risk Society*, Luhmann regarded the value of his theoretical analysis as modest. He stated that theoretically inspired investigations, as opposed to more practical ones, would create ideas with a higher "probability of more serviceable results – above all, [they] can reduce the probability of creating useless excitement" (1989: XVIII).

Also indebted to grand theorizing, the work of Ulrich Beck (1944–present) is driven by the aim of tracking down and conceptualizing new social developments (1992b: 9f.), as identified in his theorizing on the *risk society* and *reflexive modernization*, and it involves a growing recognition of globalization (1999, 2005b, 2006). Beck most prominently refers to Marx and uses his theorizing as a background against which he unfolds his own ideas. For example, when he introduces the *relations of definition* as primary definers, organizers, and regulators of risk, he refers to Marx's concept of the relations of production (1999: 149), and when he examines the immizeration of civilization, he contrasts it to the immizeration of the working class (1992b: 51). In contradiction to Marx's class analysis, Beck emphasizes that social class loses its significance and has to be supplanted by risk as a new mode of social integration. But, influenced by critical thinking, Beck is still engaged with questions of political participation and conflict. He explains them as part of the historical process of modernization itself, triggered by new objective risks and the crisis of scientific expertise. Thus, Beck claims to provide us with an explanation for a general historical change. As in the historical inevitability of revolution as suggested by Marx, he argues that we are unavoidably "propelled" by side-effects of industrial modernization into a risk society (1999b: 73).

The *edgework* perspective was introduced by Stephen Lyng (1950–present), drawing on his research into skydiving (Lyng & Snow 1986; Lyng 1990). As part of a different generation of researchers and together with colleagues, he is actively involved in edgework activities himself (Ferrell 2005: 75). His work is driven by linking the real embodied experience of high-risk activities to risk theorizing. Even though others apply his approach to a far greater variety of voluntary risk taking – for example, in crime (graffiti writing, shoplifting, "righteous slaughtering") or in work (stock trading, firefighting, mountaineering; see Milovanovic 2005) – Lyng tends to bases the theoretical framework of edgework on high-risk activities on the natural boundary between life and death.

In contrast to "grand theorizing," Lyng does not start with a general thesis derived from a general theory of social change, but with a phenomenological-pragmatist analysis of the original experience of edgework. Against the Cartesian dualism of mind and body (O'Malley & Mugford 1994: 195; Milovanovic 2005: 52), the subject in edgework is understood as an integrated unit which is only partly socially included but a source of resistance and innovation originating from "beyond" the social.

Inclined to connect individuals' subjective experiences with general social changes, Lyng refers to concepts such as "alienated work" (Marx) and "disenchantment" by rationalization (Weber) which follow the mainstream interpretation of edgework as liberation from social over-determination (see the contributions in Lyng 2005a). But still, when Lyng refers recently to Beck's theorizing on the risk society and the idea that edgework expresses exactly what late modernity expects from its citizens, he brings back in notions of unpreventable logics of social change.

Clearly in contradiction to the claims of universal and grand theorizing is the *governmentality* perspective (Ewald 1986, 1991; Burchell et al. 1991; Foucault 1991a; Barry et al. 1996; Dean 1999a; O'Malley 2004), which draws on the work of Michel Foucault (1926–84). Foucault, like other French philosophers such as Gilles Deleuze and Jean-François Lyotard (1979), explicitly rejects utopian and revolutionary promises, as suggested by Marxism. Governmentality studies examine the phenomenon of governance in a broad range of societal domains, such as childhood, crime, health and illness, sexuality, and cyberspace (Dean 1999a: 3). Central to these analyses and the understanding of risk is Foucault's theory of power in modernity (1978, 1980, 1984a, 1984b, 1991a). The connection between *governing* and *mentality* in the term "governmentality" expresses Foucault's comprehensive view of power and domination, which includes the construction of realities through the practice of sense making, encompassing the multitude of societal organizations and institutions as well as self-governing practices. Liberal governance is no longer understood as regulation of natural liberty, but as constituting an artificial liberty. Freedom is produced by linking strategies which directly structure individuals' behavior (*power strategies*) and strategies which indirectly determine their way of living by empowerment of the individuals to manage their bodies, souls, and way of life in order to attain such goals as perfection, happiness, purity, or exceptional power (*technologies of the self*). However, governmentality studies focus on the different applications of calculative technologies (e.g. insurance risk, epidemiological risk, case-management risk, clinical risk; Dean 1999b: 142–4) and how they are embedded and connected to social sense making.

The critique of grand theorizing made by the governmentality perspective is shared by research inclined toward a *cultural turn*. This work emphasizes the significance of culture as mediating between action and structure. The *cultural turn* is a rather heterogeneous development. Its influence can be tracked down in the work of many authors and in different disciplines (principally ethnography, literature, media studies, and sociology). It focuses on the symbolic construction of meaning in discourses and narrations, but also on a more complete sense of the everyday, where risks become concrete embodied experiences differing from pure cognitive or rational risk calculation (Lash 2000). The cultural turn provides us with sensibility regarding moral issues and power relations, especially in the research process, accompanied by ideas of empowering the "research object" and a strong awareness of the researcher's position in the research process. Therefore thick descriptions are often preferred as well as a rather eclectic use of theorizing in order to go beyond mono-theoretical pitfalls to produce a kaleidoscope of perspectives and explanations (Tulloch in chapter 6 of this book; Denzin & Lincoln 2003).

Epistemology of Risk

It is common to distinguish theorizing on risk in terms of the epistemological status of risk on a continuum between pure realist and radical constructivist positions (see the introduction to this book; Renn 1992; Fox 1998; Lupton 1999a; Horlick-Jones 2000; Strydom 2002; Taylor-Gooby & Zinn 2006). Sociological theorizing is then opposed to technical-science perspectives as realist, and sociological approaches are identified as weak or strong constructivist. Even though this is useful for a general characterization of approaches, such a one-dimensional perspective tends to miss the more complex differences between the available approaches. Most prominent are differences in the object of theorizing and how risk is embedded in the respective theoretical context, as I will now examine in more detail.

The term "risk" is used in two connected forms. First, it is understood as a material or symbolic danger or harm, or an alleged negative future event. Risk theorizing is then about how such dangers or harms are managed, prevented, or attributed (or not) to decisions. Second, risk is also understood as a specific form of managing uncertainty – it is about the way uncertainties are (rationally) managed, and the theories vary regarding the degree of rationality, from a calculative practice to any form of purposeful management of uncertainty. The range of theories highlights different aspects and explanations which contribute to the explanation of these two fundamental understandings of risk as harm and calculative practice.

Differences in the definition of the object of research, and whether and how realism and constructivism are linked, are considered in the following. I will start with most constructivist approaches and will continue with approaches integrating more realist understandings of risk (an overview is given in table 7.1).

Systems theory (Luhmann 1989, 1993, 1995; Japp 1996, 2000a, and in this book) conceptualizes the social in terms of communication, and risk as communicated decisions. The social is understood as constituted by communications which make sense of the world or, better, which constitute the social world within communication. Therefore, in the perspective of society, there is no world "outside." Such a world exists only in so far as it is "communicated." As a result there is no longer an objective standpoint within or outside society from which to identify "real" risks. Instead, risks are "produced" differently and depend on the self-referential logic of functional systems such as science, law, religion, and economy. Therefore, as sociologists we would observe society as part of a specific functional system and construct society in our own sociological terms, which are different from other systems. In the perspective of systems theory, we as researchers "observe" how other systems observe, construct, and manage risks. This level of observations is called *second-order observations*. In contrast, many other approaches to risk are concerned with how to manage or reduce real dangers or harms. But the construction of "real" risks by science is only one way to describe risk problems as problems of objective knowledge. In other perspectives, risk decisions appear as problems of justice (law), morality (ethics), or money (economics).

Whereas other approaches to risk are concerned with how to manage real dangers or harms, systems theory interprets risk as immanent in *all decisions* and sees modern society as a society which mainly describes itself in terms of decision making.[2] However, systems theory is not thereby primarily concerned with the reality of dangers or harms, which is a technical-scientific way of observing risks. The central focus is on how society observes itself in terms of (risky) decisions, and how events are ascribed to decisions or non-decisions of social entities.

Another strong constructivist perspective on risk adopts the *governmentality* approach (Ewald 1986; Castel 1991; Foucault 1991a; Rose 1999; Dean 1999a; O'Malley 2004). Governmentality conceptualizes risk as being part of a specific technique to govern societies which developed in liberal states in early and late modernity, in western industrialized Europe (Foucault 1991a). Governmentality is about the constitution of social reality by discourses and practical techniques which guide the understanding of social reality and reasonable action. Even though there is a focus on discourse, governmental strategies are quite practical in terms of rules, the installation of surveillance technologies, direct force, and punishment.

Risk as a social technology for governing societies refers to the technique of probability calculation as applied in insurance (Defert 1991; Ewald 1991), in psychiatry (Castel 1991), or in other techniques to prepare for the future (Weir 1996; Garland 2003: 521; Dean 1999a).[3]

> Nothing is a risk in itself; there is no risk in reality. But on the other hand, anything *can* be a risk; it all depends on how one analyzes the danger, considers the event.   (Ewald 1991: 199)

Risk is therefore understood not as harm or danger, but as a specific way to manage such threats with the help of calculative technologies. A harm or danger "just happens." It only becomes a risk when it is brought into being as a probability of an event usually attributed to a person (with specific qualities) or a population.

For example, an accident is something that might happen, or not, to every driver of a car, but such an accident becomes a risk when the probability of an accident is calculated on the basis of our past experiences. Then we will see that the probability of having an accident is higher for young drivers than for middle-aged drivers. That says nothing about whether a specific young person drives in a riskier fashion than another. There might be young adults who drive very carefully, but as part of a group they are addressed by higher contributions to car insurance. The risk of having a car accident applies only for the population as a whole; it is identified by specific criteria and neglects others. It therefore produces an artificial reality. These techniques are applied differently, for example, in insurance, psychiatry, and criminology, in order to make an uncertain future accessible to human action.

But risk is not only a technique for managing an uncertain future. It is part of societal discourses which produce the knowledge to define reasonable action and decision making. Thus risk is unsolvable linked to normative and moral issues (e.g. Baker & Simon 2002; Ericson & Doyle 2003). Even when risk is introduced as "evidence based," as for example in criminology or medicine, whether and how such "objectivist" calculations are applied and which criteria are selected are necessarily confounded with moral judgments. For example, Viviana Zelizer (1983) has shown how the introduction of life insurance in the USA was delayed because of its controversial moral status. Life insurance was widely condemned by newspapers and religious leaders as sacrilegious and immoral. Only when the positive aspects of financial safety for the family were emphasized by priests and other important social agents, after the 1840s, did life insurance become a success in the USA.

While systems theory and governmentality claim constructivist positions, Douglas's *cultural symbolic* perspective brings together a realist understanding of danger with a constructivist idea of how such dangers are politicized. Even though Douglas noticed that "the dangers are only too horribly real," her argument is not about the "reality of the dangers, but about how they are politicized ... The debate always links some real danger and some disapproved behavior, coding the danger in terms of a threat to valued institutions" (Douglas 1990: 8). Real threats are always transformed into cultural-symbolic risks. But the sociocultural construction of risk is theoretically independent of its objective reality. Consequently, the quality of risk has no immediate impact on the forms of critique and resistance which are *functionally equivalent*. Instead the (chosen) social organization would determine which risks are selected and who has to be made responsible for them. Douglas (1990: 15f.) argues with the help of her grid/group typology that, in an *individualist* culture which favors free markets, the weak and the losers have to carry the blame for their failure. Social concerns focus on the risks for the competitive culture of markets. In a *hierarchical* culture, the deviants from the dominant social norms have to shoulder the blame, while the focus is on social risks. Finally, in an *egalitarian* culture, aliens and faction leaders are made responsible and there is the tendency to focus on natural risks.

In more recent cultural theorizing inspired by the *cultural turn* (see Tulloch in chapter 6 of this book) there is no homogeneous epistemological position. Having said this, there is a tendency to produce "thick description" (as against grand theory or assumptions regarding general societal changes), to adopt subjective and cultural constructions of risk in the everyday, and for self-reflexivity on the position of the researcher. Consequently, the recent work of Tulloch and Lupton (2003) emphasizes a constructivist position on risk and focuses on narrative/discursive constructions of meaning:

> Understandings about risk, and therefore the ways in which risk is dealt with and experienced in everyday life, are inevitably developed via membership of cultures and subcultures as well as through personal experience ... Our approach to risk adopted a social constructionist position,... acknowledging the importance of discourse in the construction of risk epistemologies and in emphasizing that all risk epistemologies are socially constructed, including those of 'experts'. Rather than drawing a distinction between 'rational' and 'irrational' ... risk assessments, we prefer to concentrate on the meanings that are imputed to risk and how these meanings operate as part of people's notions of subjectivity and their social relations ... We are drawing on the poststructuralist understanding of the importance of language in helping to constitute meaning and shape subjectivity. (Tulloch & Lupton 2003: 1, 12)

Thus, the *cultural turn* supports a perspective which conceptualizes the symbolic reality of risk in discourses and subjective experiences (Lash 2000; Wilkinson 2006) rather independently of the organizational structure of a social group.

In Beck's theorizing on the *risk society* (1992b, 1995b, 1999) the tension between realism and constructivism, or nature and the social, looms large. On the one hand, Beck understands risk as danger or harm – but unlike the approaches considered earlier, he assumes that the quality of new risks has a direct impact on the social. "In contrast to early industrial risks, nuclear, chemical, ecological and genetic engineering risks (a) can be limited in terms of neither time nor place, (b) are not accountable according to the established rules of causality, blame and liability, and (c) cannot be compensated for or insured against" (Beck 1999: 77). Therefore they cannot be managed by modern strategies of probabilistic calculation. This argument is very different from all the other constructivist approaches presented above, which concentrate on the social sense making of risks and try to explain it by the sociocultural organization (Douglas), functional systems logics (Luhmann, Japp), or power strategies (Foucault, Ewald). New risks are not just too horrible (as Douglas stated 1990: 8), they have, as Beck argues, a new quality and thereby cause specific knowledge problems to manage them.

On the other hand, Beck interprets risk as brought into being by social entities, such as science, law, politics, and the mass media, which define, select, and manage risks. Beck argues for the social construction of real and imagined risks. Since risk implies an uncertain future, real dangers as well as concerns, fears, or imagination are indissolubly parts of risk. Risks are always real and constructed.

Criticized for his mix of realist and constructivist perspectives (e.g. Alexander 1996a, 1996b; Hollway & Jefferson 1997; Lupton 1999a; Elliott 2002; Boyne 2003; Mythen 2004), Beck takes a rather pragmatic position (1999: 23–30, 134, 146). Instead of taking one perspective in principle, he claims to use these perspectives as means of expressing the complex and ambivalent character of risk which encompasses both risk as real events and risks as talk. Beck refers to Latour (1993) and Haraway (1991), who argue that the distinction between nature and culture (or real and constructed) is rather an artificial one introduced by modernity itself. They suggested, therefore, examining the world in terms of nature/culture hybrids which are neither pure nature nor culture. While their concepts are negative, saying "what is not," Beck conversely interprets risks positively as nature and culture or "man-made hybrids" (Beck 1999: 146), and the risk society as a "hybrid society" which "watches, describes, values, and criticizes its own hybridity."

The embodied experience of risk is central to the *edgework* perspective, which aims to explain the increasing number of people who are seduced into engaging in high-risk activities in (late) modernity (Lyng 1990, 2005c). The focus is on the individual's ability to manage high-risk situations or, as Lyng emphasizes, to go as close to the edge as possible without actually crossing it.[4] While the notion of edgework has been applied to a range of activities (crime, mountain climbing, share dealing;

Table 7.1   Understanding of Risk and its Embeddedness in Theorizing

	What is the aim of theorizing?	*How is risk involved?*	*What is risk?*	*Epistemological status of risk*
Systems theory	Understanding the logics of social "evolution" in functionally differentiated societies	"Risk" is the form in which modern societies describe themselves as decision-based	The attribution of an undesired event to a decision	Constructivist
Governmentality	Reconstructing the practices and changes of governmental strategies	Concerned with how calculative techniques (risk) are used and how they are embedded and constituted in social discourse and practice	A specific way to manage uncertainty by calculative techniques and a specific way to govern society by allocating responsibility to a prudent subject	
Cultural turn	Reconstructing the production and reproduction of culture	"Risk" describes the transgression of meaning (e.g. regarding identity, the constitution of social groups)	A danger for or transgression of symbolic orders	

Sociocultural theory	Explaining the constitution of societies and social groups	Risk is a real danger transformed into a transgression of social values of a social group	An objective harm transformed into a symbolic danger for a social entity	Weak constructivist
Risk society	Understanding the fundamental changes within modernization	New risks are unforeseen side-effects of modernization which contribute to the self-transformation of modernization	A hybrid or quasi-subject. It is a real danger, constructed as objective issues as well as a social construction of future possibilities and thereby hypothetical	Realist and constructivist
Edgework	Explaining the increase in high-risk-taking activities	High risk taking is a form of immediate embodied experience of a real self. The motivation to take high risks is increased by social changes	There is a real danger of crossing a material boundary (life and death)	Weak realist

Lyng 2005c), the strong argument in the original concept focuses on the natural boundary between life and death and practical embodied skills to manage emotions and risks. Consequently, the concept of risk is real in the individual's management of high-risk situations. Starting with the analysis of the excitement of risk taking in the phenomenological foreground, there is a tendency primarily to interpret this experience as anti- or pre-social desire, understood as an immediate body-experience of the world.

However, edgework originally explains the increase in voluntary high-risk activities by the lack of possibilities to experience and shape a satisfying self in an alienating, over-socializing, and disenchanting modern world. The desire and seductive character of edgework is therefore caused, on the one hand, by the activity itself, but on the other hand by the social context. Consequently, the increase in high-risk activities is interpreted as a response to general sociostructural and sociocultural changes. This dualism of the embodied experience and general social change is maintained in a recent explanation for edgework which interprets people's increasing involvement in high-risk activities as an adaptation to social change. Growing uncertainties in late modernity may socially reward the development of edgework skills (Simon 2005; Lyng 2005c; and chapter 5 in this book).

What follows from this for theorizing? Obviously the approaches differ not just in their positioning of the risk problem on a scale from realism to constructivism; rather each approach examines a specific domain of phenomena. Therefore critique and solutions offered for risk problems are structured by the theoretical positioning of risk in the wider context of theorizing.

The Theoretical Positioning of Risk

All approaches link risk somehow to the dimensions *values, knowledge, rationality, power,* and *emotion,* and normally take one of the dimensions as a fulcrum for their theorizing. The risk society's main focus is on knowledge and its limits, while systems theory refers to a general lack of an overall integrating rationality. The cultural approaches are about social values which constitute social identity, while the governmentality perspective theorizes on risk in a framework of power and domination. Finally, the edgework perspective focuses on the positive emotions involved in high risk taking. In the following I will examine in more detail how the approaches refer to the respective dimension.

Values

Many authors claim the relevance or even priority of culture in the understanding of risk in present-day society (Douglas & Wildavsky 1982; Douglas 1990, 1992; Lupton 1999a; Lash 2000; Tulloch & Lupton 2003). Cultural theorizing addresses social values and valuations which mediate between structure and action. In many disciplines a so-called *cultural turn* has led to a greater acknowledgment of the significance of culture as part of the social world (Tulloch in chapter 6 of this book; Bonnell & Hunt 1999; Denzin & Lincoln 2003). In what follows, I will focus on Douglas's cultural symbolic approach to risk, which takes something of a classical position in cultural theorizing on risk, and will add aspects and emphases contributed to theorizing by the cultural turn. Afterwards, I will show that the other approaches conceptualize culture in much more general terms.

Differing values and valuations are at the core of *cultural approaches* to risk, referring to the coherence of social groups and the identities of their members. Douglas (1966, 1982, 1990, 1992) (Douglas & Wildavsky 1982) emphasizes that the selection, perception, and response to risk is an inherently cultural process which depends on different *worldviews* which are connected to decisions regarding the kind of social organization (hierarchy, market, sect)[5] we like to live in. Members of a social group select dangers and harms symbolically transformed into threats to the respective form of social organization and respective group's values. Douglas and Calvez (1990), writing on AIDS, show that the dominant *hierarchical* culture would tend to exclude and marginalize others (i.e. homosexuals) when an epidemic such as AIDS takes place. The *sect-like* culture is constituted by the rejection of the center community and is suspicious regarding knowledge and practices provided. Instead, this culture tends to justify their risky attitudes by alternative beliefs and non-scientific practices which it is assumed would protect against AIDS (e.g. a specific diet). *Individualists* who favor a market culture are explicitly risk-takers and do not belong to a specific community. They emphasize the cultural project of free and independent risk taking and having control over their own life. In brief, it is argued that it is not the risks or their quality but the values which are connected to specific types of social organization which are responsible for how risks are politicized, selected, perceived, and managed.

Research inspired by the *cultural turn* rejects a strong link between socio-structural organization and meaning such as provided by Douglas and Wildavsky (1982), and prioritizes thick descriptions of everyday discursive sense making of the world as a starting point for theorizing. Research does then focus on the construction of identity in individuals' narratives and embodied emotional experiences (Lash 2000), and construction of meaning in social discourses (Tulloch & Lupton 2003).

While sharing with Douglas and Wildavsky the assumption of a general societal change toward individualism (Douglas & Wildavsky 1982, Douglas 1990) or individualization (Beck 1992b) respectively, the *risk society approach* addresses sociocultural values as risk culture and individualized culture. But the approach is rather indifferent regarding (sub-)cultural differences in perceiving and responding to risk. When Beck assumes that public solidarity and subpolitics would develop out of the shared and/or believed affectedness by risks (1992b: 36, 49f.), cultural differences are neglected. When complex and contradictory knowledge allows interest groups to refer to different kinds of knowledge, this is not about the cultural backgrounds of such groups. The focus is rather on affected citizens who try to enforce the scientific acknowledgment of the risks (1992b: 71ff.). When Beck argues toward individualization, he emphasizes the spreading of an individualized culture and a self-culture. Stating that the subject is constructed by the network of relations (Beck et al. 2003), he claims that the individual has to act as a "planning office" of his or her own life (Beck 1992b: 135), even though he acknowledges that individuals' individualization can fail (1992b: 131ff.). However, Beck does not systematically theorize the sociocultural or sociostructural factors which constitute the ability to act in the first place. He does not conceptualize specific sociocultural milieus and how they influence and are influenced by social changes or how old sociocultural and new individualized milieus mix or are mutually constitutive.

Governmentality similarly approaches culture on a rather general level, and assumes that good governmental practice mainly corresponds to the individual's interests and values of self-conduct, since governmentality constitutes individual's sense making by discursive power. Risk culture is therefore understood as being part of a liberal style of governance and social regulation. Even though a growing number of empirical studies describe the plurality of contradicting subcultures as well as the people's ability to resist governmental strategies, these issues are still neglected by theory.

Systems theory conceptualizes cultural values even more generally. Culture is understood as a source which delivers themes and semantics that can be used in societal communication (Luhmann 1995: 163). In this perspective, culture doubtlessly indicates proper and improper contributions to communication, but systems theory does not conceptualize the internal structure of cultural framing. Instead, it focuses on the functional logics of subsystems and the distinction between risk and danger. While the historical change of semantics is indeed a theme in systems theory, subcultural diversification might be addressed in (historical) research but is not a central focus of theorizing.

Finally, *edgework* focuses on sociostructural changes rather than subcultural diversity. While in the status nascent of the approach, *edgework* was identified as a specific subculture in skydiving, developed in relation to sociocultural changes in the USA in the late 1970s and 1980s (Lyng & Snow 1986), it is now theorized beyond the mediating instance of subcultural values. Referring to Marx, Beck, or Weber, the approach focuses on divergences and correspondences between individuals' needs and cultural expectations or circumstances of living. But the approach does not provide us with cultural explanations which could bridge macro- and micro-level analysis. The approach does not develop a number of ideal types of different subcultures which could increase understanding of the various responses to social change.

Knowledge

In social discourses on risk, conflicts regarding knowledge are central. Most prominent are the controversies about the epistemological status of lay knowledge in contrast to expert and scientific knowledge (Pidgeon et al. 1992). Wynne (1996) has shown the importance of laypeople's local and situated knowledge and that even expert knowledge is confounded with value decisions. Thus, many sociological approaches address risk conflicts not primarily as knowledge problems, but as problems of cultural values, functional differentiation, or governing societies. Even though Beck acknowledges the importance of such factors, his theorizing originates from knowledge and its production communication, and systematic limits (1992: 22ff., 26ff.).

Beck argues that *new risks* become problematic because there is not enough knowledge available from science and technology to control their occurrence or to deal with their negative outcomes by insurance (Beck 1995b, 1999: 77). The modern large-scale accidents at Bhopal, Harrisburg, and Chernobyl might bring these limits of knowledge and controllability into public awareness and therefore drive another question to the forefront. What are the risks we would like to take when we have to acknowledge that even the securest technology sometimes fails, and accidents are "normal" (Perrow 1984; compare also Beck 1992b: 177) even in (alleged) safe technologies? When the assumed consensus on technological and economic advancement is challenged by new risks the normative questions become a matter of public debate again.

In a further line of argumentation, Beck refers to *scientific knowledge* which is characterized by over-complexity, differentiation, and fragmentation. Science produces contradictory knowledge and therefore erodes its own authority. Questions of true knowledge can no longer be answered only by science, but need further consideration. That does not mean that scientific knowledge is irrelevant. It rather leads to a competition between different scientific views, while it is even more necessary to underpin one's own political position with scientific expertise (Beck 1992b: 167). Faith, values, and interests are additionally needed, and these lead to a blurring of boundaries between science and politics (1992b: 155–82). In this respect, the ability to define knowledge in social discourses with the help of the media is an important part of the power battles within risk societies.

The growing complexity and fragmented logic of modern knowledge production, which was so successful for quite a long time, not only supports its politicization but also systematically produces *non-knowledge*, which allows risks and dangers to develop unobserved (1992b: 34, 45). This assumption seems paradoxical, but all the knowledge we gain (e.g. regarding the genetic construction of life) produces new questions and awareness of what we do not know. Our advancement in knowledge is a result of specialized research, while at the same time the interaction between different domains of knowledge is limited.

Beck argues that in the risk society non-knowledge is produced as an unforeseen but not necessarily as an unforeseeable *side-effect*. Later would rather be the way in which risks are legitimized (1992b: 34). He is keen to show that non-knowledge is at the same time systematically produced by (accepted) ignorance (1992b: 34, 57–71). We are not just exposed to unforeseeable side-effects of modernization. We can do something about them (1992b: 170–82). Even though we cannot ultimately solve these knowledge problems, we can tackle them better. First, an acknowledgment of the fallibility of scientific and human knowledge is important (1992b: 177). Thus, we would be better off with decisions which keep open our human ability to act instead of burdening future generations with the unsolved problems of the present – for instance, how to deal with nuclear waste (1992b: 178). Furthermore, Beck argues that recombining fragmented knowledge using new learning strategies is necessary to manage the complexity of scientific knowledge (1992b: 179–81).

Finally, Beck explains how the erosion of traditional class knowledge by individualization challenges individuals' management of risks and uncertainties in everyday life. When one can no longer refer to traditional knowledge, short-term situated knowledge and individualized biographical experience loom large. The individual is dependent on secondary institutions such as the labor market and welfare state, and has to act even though the future is contingent and sufficient knowledge is no longer available (1992b: 131). Beck advises that it is necessary for individuals to plan and direct their life, in order to have any chance of shaping their life in their own terms, even though there is often no chance to do so (1992b: 135).

In *systems theory*, knowledge is understood against the background of a functionally differentiated society. Even though all systems produce their own knowledge, controversies about "true knowledge" are interpreted as part of the scientific functional system. Drawing on the concept of functional differentiation, the understanding of risk issues as a knowledge problem is seen as an important but only one specific perspective on risk. In the perspective of other functional systems, such as law, religion, politics, or economics, we would interpret risk as a problem of justice, faith, power, or money. Systems theorists do not narrow their analysis to the discourse on true knowledge, but focus on conflicts which result from the incompatibility of the distinctive logics of functional systems. For example, lay-people might claim that laboratory knowledge is limited because it tends to ignore the specific local conditions. Science can then improve its application by considering local knowledge. But conflicts regularly arise because experts present risk problems primarily as knowledge problems while lay-people frame risk otherwise: for example, as ethical risks. Consequently, such controversies cannot be solved only with the help of objective or true knowledge.

In the *governmentality* perspective, knowledge is seen as part of (discursive) power which guides individuals' self-conduct. Risk technologies such as probabilistic calculation produce a specific kind of "objective" knowledge which structures individuals' activities. But in fact, risk knowledge cannot be separated from the values involved, which frame the risk's production and application. For example, the medical advice given to pregnant women draws on empirical knowledge which is based on probability calculations. Such knowledge indicates what would generally harm the mother or the unborn child. The mother is urged to behave prudently and with responsibility for the unborn life, in accordance with this (probabilistic) knowledge. She is obliged by the moral imperatives attached to this knowledge to behave as a responsible mother, who is aware of the objective risks of pregnancy.

While governmentality approaches knowledge mainly in terms of its moral involvement, the problem of a lack of knowledge has recently been addressed. In contradiction to the constructivist notion of risk in the governmentality literature, Ewald (2002: 296) argues, similarly to Beck, that the quality of new risks – their catastrophic character – causes specific knowledge problems and leads to a change in the insurance principle from compensation towards precaution.

In Douglas's *cultural-institutional* perspective, knowledge depends in the same way as risk on the particular cultural organization (1992: 32f., 107–10; Douglas & Calvez 1990: 446ff.). This can best be exemplified with the help of Douglas's grid/group typology. In a *hierarchical* perspective there is confidence in the correctness of traditional knowledge. Knowledge production as such is seen as a long and slow cumulative process. The political system upholds the authority of scientifically proven facts and focuses on protecting the traditional system of knowledge which underpins its power (1992: 32). In an *individualist* culture the social world is mainly organized by market principles. Even knowledge would follow the logic of competition. New knowledge challenges and supplants old knowledge. Priority is given to the latest knowledge and thereby perforce discredits old knowledge (1992: 32). While these two cultures are ascribed to the center of a social community, at the social border professional knowledge is perceived with general suspicion. The sect (or egalitarian) culture is rather critical of, or even rejects, professional or scientific knowledge and the organizations which produce it (1992: 108f.). This culture approaches other forms of knowledge (e.g. alternative medicine in the case of health and illness) or develops its own group-specific theories, enforced by the charisma of group leaders rather than precise testing. For example, "there was a fashion among some California gay communities to believe that healthy eating and macrobiotic foods could prevent HIV infection" (Douglas & Calvez 1990: 451).

The *cultural turn* influences theorizing by emphasizing the cultural and subcultural constitution of knowledge in general. Rather than linking organizational forms to specific cultural knowledge, cultural turn literature follows a more descriptive approach which emphasizes the indeterminate number of cultural forms of knowledge. At a micro level, knowledge (production) is always understood as situated in specific and contradictory contexts of the everyday. Indeed, even the researcher's biographical experiences and affiliation to social groups, a specific generation, and a historical epoch, constitute the researcher's understanding and analysis and must therefore be reflected as part of research (Denzin & Lincoln 2003; Tulloch in chapter 6 of this book). Against cognitive understandings of knowledge, a stream of cultural turn literature emphasizes embodied knowledge, which includes pre-rational, aesthetic, emotional, affective, and intuitive aspects of knowledge (Lash 2000).

Edgework sheds light on this domain of embodied intuitive knowledge. Even though edgeworkers are highly trained and skilled, the application of their competences is not a rational balancing of pros and cons but an embodied and reflexive (in Beck's sense of reflex) response to situations where time and resources are restricted. Pre-rational and intuitive knowledge is applied, which refers to the ongoing debate about embodied, implicit, tacit, or intuitive knowledge (Polanyi 1958, 1967; Merleau-Ponty 1962; Reber 1995). But there is a tendency in everyday theories of edgeworkers to cross the boundary between high skilled competence and belief. Many assume that they have an innate competence which is necessary to manage successfully the uncertainties of high risk-taking (Lyng in this book). Lyng (1990: 859) refers to Tom Wolfe's (1979) study on test-pilot subculture to illustrate this point. While on the one hand test-pilots are highly skilled they do on the other hand believe in possessing "the right stuff" as an innate ability. A fatal crash then gives evidence that the respective person has never possessed it in the first place.

Rationality

There is no homogeneous understanding of the term "rationality" in social sciences. Some approaches irreconcilably stick to notions of instrumental rationality or statistical calculability, while broader socio-logical concepts include notions of *subjective* and *social rationalities*. The latter refer to a however subjectively or socially justified foundation of decisions, actions, or developments. All the approaches presented here share fundamental reservations regarding the concept of instru-mental rationality. Instead, they introduce a variety of institutional, cultural, and other factors which would structure the social.

Systems theory very fundamentally conceptualizes risk against the background of a functionally differentiated society which makes any substantive or teleological notion of rationality impossible and is thereby responsible for the increase in risk communication (Luhmann 1993: 174, 189). Luhmann draws on the historical change in semantics, from the antique normative rationality referring to nature (Aristotle) via the diversification into different kinds of rationality (principally, scientific and economical) up to a critique of rationality itself (compare Max Weber). Luhmann concludes that there is no longer a substantial or teleological idea of rationality available to regulate or integrate society as a whole (Luhmann 1997: 171–89; 1995: 472–3). Instead, all func-tional systems follow their own logic, while the application of their spe-cific rationality is loosely coupled to the other systems. For example, what is scientifically possible is not necessarily desirable morally, politi-cally, or economically. The other functional systems have to keep science within limits to prevent the otherwise uncontrolled and destructive power of scientific development.

Luhmann's criticism of the idea of an overall social rationality is accompanied by a critique of the notion of rational decision making. In his view, "perfect rational (optimum) decisions" are as impossible as "anticipating what will have constituted a decision" (Luhmann 1993: 189), because the rationality might alter before, during, and after a decision. One seeks a favorable constellation of action and expectation rather than a maximization of expected utility (Luhmann 1995: 296f.). Consequently, every decision becomes a risk! As a result, Luhmann observes a shift from "rationality" to "risk" (Luhmann 1993: 174, 189). When risk is understood as a fundamental problem of every decision, it is more interesting how decisions are attributed or how people, organizations, or functional systems try to get rid of such ascriptions of responsibility. But in systems theory these are contingent processes since no overall rationality is available (Luhmann 1989: 83).[6] Consequently, Luhmann changed the perspective from first- to second-order observation[7] and introduced the distinction between *risk* and *danger*. He calls events *risk* when they are attributed to one's decision and *danger* when they are attributed to the decisions of others or are not decision-based, as in natural events (Luhmann 1993: 21f.).[8]

Beck addresses the problem of rationality by using the distinction between *scientific* and *social rationalities*. Central is the breakdown of science's monopoly in defining risk (1992b: 29). The occurrence of new risks which cannot be managed in the modern way of rational calculation and insurance as well as the fragmented logic of scientific knowledge production has led to an erosion of the scientific rationale. It became obvious that risk questions always involve normative assumptions regarding the acceptability of risk (1992b: 58). Thus the monopoly claim of scientific rationality as an unquestioned fundament for decision making is broken and competes with *social rationalities*. As a result, scientific rationality becomes no less important, even though Beck sees the danger of a "feudalization of scientific knowledge practice through economic and political interests and 'new dogmas'" (1992b: 157). Quite the opposite is the case. Scientific support is even more important, but no longer sufficient to influence and legitimize (political) decisions (1992b: 71, 165).

The risk society perspective and the *governmentality* approach share the view that *"rational" rationalities* (scientific, instrumental) and *social rationalities* are indissolubly connected. However, Beck focuses on the conflicts between them, while governmentality rather emphasizes their complementary character. Therefore governmentality plays down the idea of a crisis of rationality. Instead, it interprets risk as part of a more general rationale by which societies are governed and govern themselves with the help of risk technologies and moral discourses. In contrast to Beck, research on governmentality emphasizes the range of calculative techniques applied in various areas (Dean 1999a) which constitute different rationales. Such techniques are used for calculating the effectiveness of treatments and medicine, for identifying the probability of reoffending of delinquents, or for the spreading of risk in insurance. Within this approach, some authors emphasize that risk will increasingly supplant other techniques of professional judgment (Castel 1991), while O'Malley emphasizes that other reasonable techniques necessarily remain to manage uncertainty, even though they do not rely on probabilistic statistical calculation (2004: 77). Risk rationales would rather complement than supplant other strategies to manage uncertainty (e.g. "ordinary foresight," "professional judgment;" see O'Malley in chapter 3 of this book).

The *sociocultural* types in Douglas's grid/group typology could be seen as different kinds of sociocultural rationale which structure the meanings in a community and thereby guide individuals' activities. Consequently, Douglas interprets culture as being prior to instrumental rationality, and contrasts cultural analysis to instrumental rationality (1992: 125ff.).

> The upshot of much anthropological research on cultural bias suggests that individuals do not try to make independent choices, especially about big political issues. When faced with estimating probability and credibility, they come already primed with culturally learned assumptions and weightings. One could say that they have been fabricating their prejudices as part of the work of designing their institutions. They have set up their institutions as decision processors which shut out some options and put others in favorable light. Individuals make the basic choices between joining and not joining institutions of different kinds. (1992: 58)

Douglas has no intention to exclude instrumental rationality from culture considerations. "Indeed, some sort of rational choice should enter cultural analysis" (1992: 125, 142), but as part of the cultural constitution of society. Instrumental rationality is in the core of the individualist market culture. Consequently, Douglas and Wildavsky (1982; Douglas 1990) interpret growing controversies on risk as an expression of the increasing dominance of individualist culture, which is characterized by the competition for best solutions.

The *cultural turn* literature also emphasizes *subjective* and *social rationalities* in opposition to instrumental rationality. Such rationalities are understood as logics of sense making in social discourse and everyday life. Cultural turn literature often focuses on the individual's management of the everyday and the embodied biographical or everyday life experiences of risk (Tulloch & Lupton 2003). The specific ways of perceiving and managing risk are explained by situated logics and/or biographical identities beyond instrumental rationality. In the context of media research, the literature is rather concerned with the cultural embeddedness of the understanding of media coverage and the cultural meanings which are endangered or violated by risk (Ferreira et al. 2001). The violation of cultural boundaries not only triggers attempts to re-establish or defend the original meaning; it can also contribute to the establishment of new meaning. For example, places such as Harrisburg and Chernobyl can become symbols not of the advancement of science but of the dangers and uncontrollability of nuclear power or new technologies.

In the *edgework* perspective, Lyng claims that the emotional excitement of risk taking contrasts with instrumental rationality and the idea that unnecessary risk must be avoided. Decision making during edgework activities is situated in a spontaneous application of intuitive rationality, typically applied in situations where time and knowledge are limited (as in skydiving, fire-fighting, and military combat). That does not mean that edgeworkers act irrationally, but that they follow a *situated rationality* which relies on body experience rather than on cognitive reflection (Lyng 1990). Furthermore, Lyng's argument (in chapter 5 of this book) for the occurrence of edgework in response to changing societal conditions of living draws on a *subjective rationale* which is ultimately rooted in the nature of the human being: the desire for self-creation as a "free being," to "discover the creative possibilities of an acting self," to "explore the possibilities of the body," or to develop a "self-determined, soulful human being."

Power

From the onset, considerations on power have been part of social science theorizing on risk. The new and growing political power of social movements, and resistance against nuclear power and advocating for an ecological style of living, were the background against which Douglas and Beck developed their theories. But power is more central in the governmentality perspective than in other theories. Drawing on various social theories, the approaches' concepts of power range from traditional ideas of top-down or legitimacy of power to more discursive concepts, while there is little theorizing on coercive power.

Unlike all the other approaches, the *governmentality* perspective fundamentally theorizes risk from a perspective of power and control. Risk is understood as brought into being as a technology (calculative practice) and as discourse (knowledge) by societal institutions and governments in a liberal style to govern modern societies (Foucault 1991a).

Governmentality studies draw on Foucault's *discursive concept of power.* Foucault significantly deviates from traditional understandings which conceptualize power in hierarchical terms as applied by governments to the public with a form of legitimacy or just coercion. His concept of power is much broader. It is understood as a discursive system by which power is allocated in society. Power as knowledge is disseminated everywhere in society and is generated by institutional and subjective production of meaning. That makes "power" a "catch-all" term. However, a pure discursive concept of power, which primarily interprets power in terms of communication, would mislead. Even in liberal states discourses are accompanied by very practical measures which stand ready to enforce obedience if necessary (O'Malley in chapter 3 of this book; Dean 1999a).

Governmentality distinguishes between *power strategies,* which try to determine individuals' behavior directly, and *technologies of the self,* which empower citizens to manage their bodies, souls, and way of life in order to attain such goals as perfection, happiness, purity, or exceptional power. Here risk comes into play as a power strategy and a technology. On the one hand, the individual is no longer addressed as a whole, but as part of a calculative practice which aims at populations defined by a specific combination of factors. Thus, the individual is no longer defined by his or her real characteristics but by probability calculations. One becomes an object of measures because of probabilities which are valid for a population but might not apply for a specific person.

On the other hand, risk technologies produce a specific kind of knowledge which defines what we should do. It is therefore closely linked to the liberal concept of the autonomous, self-responsible, and prudent subject which conducts itself. Risk knowledge identifies specific behavior as reasonable and socially desirable. In this way, governments structure individuals' behavior indirectly with the help of the production of a specific kind of risk knowledge. Thus, liberal government is no longer the regulation of natural liberty. Instead, it constitutes an artificial "freedom" for economically rational individuals (Burchell 1993: 271; Rose 1996a: 50–62).

Using a *cultural-symbolic* perspective, Douglas refers to different forms of legitimate *structural* and *symbolic power* which vary with the three ideal types of social organization (hierarchy, market, and sect). She argues that the kind of enquiry into disaster varies correspondingly. In the *individualist* culture, the authority of true knowledge is sought;

in *hierarchical* culture, the legitimacy of traditional institutions; and in *egalitarian* culture, the purity and goodness of belief systems as religion and ideology. "Each distinctive kind of regime will invoke a distinctive set of active powers in the universe to do three things, one cognitive, to explain disasters, one political, to justify allegiances, one system-maintaining, to stabilize the distinctive workings of the regime" (Douglas 1992: 60). In this way, Douglas approaches social conflicts through the forms of power provided by the various cultures and their social positioning in the center (hierarchy, individualist) or at the border (sect or egalitarian) of society. However, Douglas interprets the increase in individualist culture as something which we actively support or which we have chosen (Douglas 1990: 12f.) rather than as a result of conflictual social processes.

Thus, Douglas highlights different forms of legitimate power, while Beck starts from a traditional top-down model of power when he is focusing on social conflicts. In *Risk Society* he argues that top-down governance is eroded by the challenges to the scientific monopoly of defining risk and is increasingly complemented by situational coalitions of organized and individual actors. In the new arena of "subpolitics," the public discusses what was formerly decided within the formalized political system or in the nonpolitical spheres of decision making in laboratories or international enterprises. "Coalition of anxiety," which is based on people's concerns, assumptions, and knowledge of new risks (Beck 1992b: 36, 61) gain power in the subpolitical sphere. New interest groups and corporate actors develop which are able to inform, direct, and mobilize significant parts of the public and political consumers. "The 'heads' of the political system are confronted by cooperatively organized antagonists, with a 'definition making power' of media-directed publicity ..." (Beck 1992b: 194).

Systems theory addresses power on two levels. First, power as *political power* is attributed to the political functional system. On this level, Luhmann's position regarding new social movements comes surprisingly close to that of Douglas.[9] Both disqualify the Green Movement and the resistance against nuclear power as rather irrational. In his book *Ecological Communication* (1989: 84–93) Luhmann argues that the political system has problems in responding to the new movements, which are driven principally by anxieties and fears, because it is not possible to argue rationally against such emotions. Even the best argument can be disputed based on subjective anxieties. Communication regarding risks might even increase anxiety and fear. Consequently, the new movements tend to block decisions or "make trouble" (1989: 86) but cannot offer alternative political options. Their power is restricted to disturbing the otherwise superior processing of functional systems.

Second, *power* is also present in the relationships between all other systems. Power regarding risk is then about the ability to produce decision-making situations for others and thereby to produce risks for others. Environmental or other dangers as discussed in the risk society perspective (e.g. nuclear power, genetically modified food, bird flu) only become relevant when they are transformed into decisions: for example, when media coverage urges politicians or parties to take positions regarding a topic. Alternatively, the public can influence the decisions of the economic system, as when issues involve financial risks. A famous example is the public's response to Shell's plan to sink the Brent Spar oil rig in the sea in 1995. The public boycott of Shell's fuel stations was a financial risk which forced Shell to find a publicly more acceptable solution, no matter how "Irrational" the new solution might be in terms of threatening the environment. Shell, according to this perspective, responded in terms of the feared financial impact of consumer actions.

In *cultural turn* literature, power is understood as discursive power generated by social discourses in which different agents struggle about definitions of who or what is "at risk" or "risky." In this perspective, the researcher is part of societal power relations and has to take political responsibility for his or her research. This responsibility does not just lie in showing how the perception of risk is bound to the supported form of political organization, as suggested by Douglas (1992: 49, 50); researchers would also have to reflect on their own position and its influence on the discursive construction of reality. More self-reflexive research is suggested which acknowledges researchers' own experiences and social involvement. The aim is to return power to the "object" of research, which is seen as subjected to the researchers defining power in traditional research (Denzin & Lincoln 2003).

While recent cultural approaches tend to interpret power as culturally constituted in societal discourses, *edgework* focuses on forms of power which come from "beyond" the social. Drawing on Foucault's work on the *limit experience*, Lyng (in chapter 5 of this book; 2005c: 39ff.) argues that one can use the direct embodied emotional experience of high risk taking to disrupt the all-embracing institutional and sociocultural demands. High risk taking is a way of positively creating and changing the self and therefore a source of power to resist or to optimize the management of societal circumstances of living.

Emotion

"Emotion" and "affect" have been eclipsed for a long time by rational-istic and institutional theorizing. In line with the historical analysis of Norbert Elias on *The Civilizing Process* (1994), the dominant position interprets erratic emotions as needing control by calm reason and rationality. Within an institutional perspective, many approaches emphasized that the stabilization of expectations regarding the future by institutionalization would cause positive feelings of security, while their destabilization would cause feelings of uncertainty, anxiety, and fear (e.g. Giddens 1991). This perspective resonate in the discourse on risk and uncertainty. On the one hand, emotions have been addressed in opposition to the superior rationality attributed to science and experts, and were ascribed to lay-people's decision-making and risk-judgments. On the other hand, Beck argues that processes of individualization, which would liberate individuals from traditional class milieus, produce new risks and feelings of uncertainty. Recently, emotions have been acknowledged as a factor which is more independent of institutional and structural framing (Lupton 1999a: 148–72; Lupton & Tulloch 2002): in particular, in theorizing on voluntary risk taking and edge-work (Lyng 2005c).

Systems theory conceptualizes emotions in a similar way to traditional perspectives. Focusing on the processual logics of functional systems, emotions are positioned beyond the social. In his book on *ecological communication* Luhmann addresses negative emotions as anxieties and fears which might disturb the processual logics of functional systems (1989: 128).[10] Since anxieties cannot be managed through rationality – they are not accessible by rational considerations which might increase rather than reduce anxieties (1989: 129) – they would block necessary decisions and developments. Further traces of the institutional perspec-tive on emotions can be found in *Social Systems* (1995, 270), where Luhmann interprets destabilization of institutions negatively. He goes so far as to state that a modern society which is characterized by a faster rate of change would be "endangered by emotions," because it has to rely on the subject and its erratic emotional states.

Douglas's *cultural symbolic* perspective is very similar to this idea of equating positive emotions with stable institutions and order, and negative emotions with unstable institutions and disorder. Douglas interprets emotions within a framework of social order secured by established institutions which regulate social life as well as defending social groups against threats from outside. Dangers are transformed into threats to communities and trigger strong emotions such as anger, hate, anxiety, or fear. Otherness is interpreted as a threat to a social group or a self because it questions social rules and regulations. Douglas argued in her early anthropological work that otherness is used in rituals to strengthen the established boundaries of a group and as a source of power (1966: 159–85). But otherness sometimes causes excitement, and can become a means of changing boundaries as well.

The *governmentality* perspective focuses on the positive aspects of emotions as being part of the governance of people's self-conduct. Governmental strategies use people's enthusiasm and desires by opening up opportunities for self-improvement. The right decisions are morally supported and, therefore, emotionally rewarded when taken (e.g. following medical advice on how best to behave as pregnant women in order to support babies' health). Thus, emotions tend to appear conceptually as corresponding with the norms constructed by governmentality. This implies at the same time that people experience deviations from society's moral commitments as rather negative.

While Beck follows the classical perspective on emotions in many respects, he differs in one. The *risk society perspective* interprets negative emotions not exclusively as unreasonable, bringing forward faiths and ideologies, and excluding scientific arguments. Instead, Beck emphasizes that anxieties can be a vehicle for reasonable and necessary social changes and more societal self-reflexivity. Fear and anxiety caused by the socioculturally mediated reality of dangers and the experiences of bad risk management can become a resource for political power[11] or even a new political subject.

Under the influence of postmodern thinking, *cultural turn* theorizing has changed the focus from stability, order, and identity to disorder, social change, multiple and shifting identities, and how differently emotions are attached. Emotions are theorized more independently in the classical approaches where emotions were seen in opposition to or synchronized with institutions. Instead, for example, Lash pointed out that "risk cultures, ... presume not a determinate ordering, but a reflexive or indeterminate disordering. Risk cultures lie in non-institutional and anti-institutional sociations. Their media are not procedural norms but substantive values. ... Risk cultures ... are based less in cognitive than in aesthetic reflexivity" (Lash 2000: 47). "Reflexive (aesthetic) judgements are estimations that are based on 'feelings' of pleasure and displeasure but also on feelings of shock, overwhelmedness, fear, loathing as well as joy ... Reflexive judgements – which are estimations based in feelings – take place not through the understanding, but through the imagination and more immediately through sensation" (Lash 2000: 53).

In *edgework* the question of the link between emotions and risk is at the center of theorizing. Risk taking itself is seen as a source of positive emotions (Lyng 1990, 2005c; see also Lupton 1999a: 148–72). This contrasts with the widely disseminated focus on concerns and anxieties regarding risk in other approaches. Rather, influenced by the *cultural turn* and a pragmatist approach to social phenomena, edgework refers to the individual's subjective experiences, the embodied excitement described by people who take high risks voluntarily (Lyng 1990, 2005c). Lyng does not spare any pains to show the unique character of the edgework experience which transcends the mundane socially structured experiences of everyday life. As an embodied experience, edgework cuts off ties to cognitive rationality, self-reflection, and thereby to the social sphere as a whole. Lyng reattaches edgework to social conditions by arguing that edgework's seductive character is a result of ongoing modernization. In modernity the real self would become distorted by the social: an over-socializing "me" would increasingly control the "I" (Mead), or the working conditions would become alienated (Marx), or general rationalization would disenchant the world (Weber). By cutting off such social restrictions, edgework returns the experience of a "real" self to and is therefore even more tempting the individual. Lyng complements the *liberation thesis* of edgework by taking up a contradictory explanation, which states that managing high risks and uncertainties is exactly what the risk society demands from its citizens (Simon 2005). Referring to Foucault's concept of the *limit experience*, Lyng argues that citizens of late modern societies increasingly desire the options which are provided by the uncertainties of late modernity and use edgework as a means of reflexively shaping their self (Lyng 2005c and in chapter 5 of this book). Thus, edgework is again a source of positive emotions, but as a result of the additional social rewards.

Table 7.2 Comparison of Risk Approaches on Five Dimensions

	Values	Knowledge	Rationality	Power	Emotion
Cultural approaches	Risks are threats for the value system of social groups and social identities	Specific socioculturally mediated forms of knowledge/knowledge production	Sociocultural rationales of risk management	Socio-cultural forms of power	Dichotomy of rationality and emotions; but emotions as a resource for social change as well
Risk society	Individualized culture and self-culture; survival and ecological values	Limits of knowledge and control as the fragmentation of knowledge production produce risks Loss of class knowledge and other traditional knowledge produces uncertainities	Calculative scientific- or expert-rationality meets its limit and is challenged by social and subjective rationalities	New power of "subpolitics," ad-hoc coalitions between the formal political organization and the nonpolitical. Political consumers and other new organized actors populate the public arena of subpolitics	Negative emotions as a resource for political resistance. Emotions enforce a new political subject, "the coalition of anxiety"

Systems theory	Culture as the realm of possible meanings communication can refer to	Only the scientific functional system describes risk as a problem of "true knowledge"	"Risk" is the core concept of modern, functionally differentiated societies to describe themselves. Since an overall integrating social rationality is lost, risk conflicts increase	Power/non-power as the code of the political system	Dichotomy of rationality and emotions. Unsteady emotions endanger modern society
Governmentality	Culture as background against which societies are governed	Socially available risk-knowledge structures individuals' behavior	Instrumental rationality and social rationalities are connected within governmental practice	Power is understood as "discursive power," which structures individuals' sense making and behavior. Risk is a specific rationale to govern societies connected to (Neo-) Liberalism.	Governmental strategies use people's desires for self-improvement
Edgework	Duality of socio-cultural context and subject. Culture contradicts or meets individuals' desires	Embodied, practical knowledge; ability to manage risks even beyond learnable skills	Situated, subjective, and embodied rationale which has its origins beyond the social	Power to resist (or to master) social demands by direct embodied experiences of a "real self"	The motivation for high risk taking is its emotional attraction, which can be heightened by specific social contexts of living

Promises, Pitfalls, and Perspectives of Risk Theorizing

The approaches outlined above represent mainstream theories on risk. While each perspective focuses on a specific argument, they are at the same time less concerned about other aspects. We might even say that it is a prerequisite of establishing a specific argument to move other aspects to the background. Thus, Krimsky and Golding's insight from *Social Theories of Risk* (1992) still remains; we have a range of approaches and perspectives rather than an all-embracing theory. It is even questionable whether such a theory would be helpful. We might be better off with a range of competing approaches which allow consideration of the sometimes contradictory aspects of risk phenomena, and support ongoing discussion. The *cultural turn* delivers a practical guide as to how we can manage such a diversity of theories. The central idea is to use a range of different approaches to describe, understand, or explain social phenomena. The observable similarities and differences then produce a "crystal" of perspectives which would lead to further insights (Denzin & Lincoln 2003).

Such eclecticism is not against theorizing or the usefulness of a problem-oriented theory. Theories are needed in order to confront reality with hypotheses or to direct research. At the same time, empirical data (or at least everyday knowledge) are necessary to develop hypotheses to integrate them into a larger picture. Theorizing is an ongoing task which has to remain open to aspects which are not yet acknowledged sufficiently. Going back to empirical research with the available set of theories is always a prelude to encouraging further theorizing.

For some phenomena, specific theories are more suitable than others, because theories are developed in a specific sociohistorical context, they refer to theoretical traditions, and they tend to focus on a specific kind and range of phenomena. The risk society theory and the cultural theory have become famous for their attempts to understand the occurrence of new social (environmental) movements, governmentality explains how modern societies are governed, and systems theory asks why rational strategies to manage societies regularly fail. Finally, edgework aims to explain increasing high-risk-taking activities. These theoretical perspectives are accompanied by specific ways of asking for problems and solutions. Additionally, the theorists who use and develop a theory significantly decide how a theory is applied. Douglas's usage of the cultural approach might be an expression of her conservative political position (Lupton 1999a; Lash 2000) and thereby explains her "improper" use of the grid/group scheme. At the same time, her emphasis on the superiority of forms of organization which are able to manage higher social complexity derives from her (functionalist) theoretical framework. Beck might be criticized for his theorizing, which would overgeneralize his personal embeddedness in German culture and Munich experiences (Dingwall 1999; Scott 2000: 34). This background might help one to understand his emphasis on the positive effects of individualization and the notion of a more self-reflexive society driven by active politicized citizens. It might also be possible to interpret his way of theorizing as an expression of critical Marxist socialization, focusing on social conflicts and searching for the historical rupture ("revolution").

However, such considerations are only of interest in so far as they open avenues for a better understanding of social processes and theoretical decisions. They must be observed regarding their effects on our own theorizing, whether they prevent further considerations or lead to more sophisticated theoretical developments.

The approaches' perspectives of critique

Theoretical approaches open and close specific forms of critique. The distinction between real and perceived risks is important because it is a strong semantic probably available in every society (Krohn & Krücken 1993: 12). Realist critique uses "real facts" to expose beliefs and ideologies as unreasonable, and is often successful regarding new technological developments and inventions. Positivist positions justify themselves because "they work." In this perspective, all the different interpretations and ideologies of the world can be confronted with an assumed reality of expected harms, losses, or injuries which are hardly discussable. The objectivity of the facts silences doubt. In a constructivist perspective, critique aims to show that even scientific expert knowledge is socially constructed. There is no direct access to the world in principle. It is always mediated by the social. Therefore critique addresses realist assumptions regarding the character of the world and the "hidden" power structures, interests, and values. It is emphasized that a world which is fundamentally produced by the human being can always be different. This supports claims for the legitimacy of any critique. Both positions contribute important perspectives to the risk discourse. However, strategies which draw exclusively on one perspective would be problematic. A realist approach is too narrow because it underestimates the possibility of failure of scientific knowledge and neglects the value decisions regularly implied in objective risk-knowledge. The constructivist perspective becomes weak when it denies that there are facts which have real impacts, even though we do not know about them or interpret them differently.

Theoretical responses to this situation attempt to combine both perspectives by a reflexive or weak constructivism or a critical realism (see Beck 1999; Tulloch in chapter 6 of this book), while practical responses acknowledge the limits of scientific knowledge. They lead to the insight that we can only test new technologies in real-life conditions of *society as laboratory* (Gross & Krohn 2005). Since the possibility of failure is acknowledged, more sensible applications seem necessary. Therefore the precautionary principle (Morris 2000) can be seen as a way to protect society against the hasty introduction of technical innovations (Japp 1996; 2000a). The reverse critique follows Beck's warning that the transformation of science opens the door to all kinds of irrational fears and concerns. In this perspective, the weakening of scientific rationality must be turned back and only scientific criteria should be allowed in the precautionary approach (e.g. Pieterman 2001; Burgess 2004).

However, not only the epistemological status but also the general logic of theorizing structures our critique.

Cultural theorizing emphasizes that we cannot detach the reality of risks from cultural values. For example, Douglas's grid/group theorizing is about the threats to the identity of a group or the identity of its members, which depend on sociocultural prejudices rather than objective risks. Cultural theorizing therefore questions all claims of objective risks which neglect cultural values. A second line of critique goes along with the functionalist perspective. Even though different cultures are functionally equivalent (or interchangeable), Douglas and Wildavsky (1982) favor solutions which are able to cope with higher complexity. Those solutions guarantee continuous advancement by the development of higher internal complexity and the striving for the newest and best developments as delivered by market culture. These are the typical modern ideas of continuous scientific and economic progress that we find, for example, in Parsons' work (Parsons 1980).

Cultural turn literature contributes critique of the normative implications of grand theorizing in favor of more descriptive research strategies ("thick descriptions"). Moreover, subjective constructions of risk, and hence the embodied experiences, are emphasized by some contributions in critique on pure language-based approaches. Finally, cultural turn literature addresses the often neglected researcher's impact on research and results in order to promote more self-reflexive research. This includes personal preferences as well as the unequal power relations between researcher and his or her object. The cultural turn promotes the "empowerment" of the object of research.

Systems theory interprets risk against the background of the functional differentiation of society. It sees risk conflicts as problems of the different logics of autonomous but structurally coupled systems and gives solutions as to how they can be reconciled. Critique is directed at the lack of insight into the autonomous character of such systems. In this perspective, the search for real consensus is not only very unlikely but also not even desirable. Good solutions have to respect the autonomous character of partial interests and system logics. For instance, we cannot expect private firms not to work in line with the maximization of profits. But they are highly sensitive regarding financial issues. Hence normative or moral questions are considered as soon as they have a financial impact.

Governmentality focuses on the intertwining of institutional direct and indirect governance which frames the individual's self-conduct. The approach pays attention to the institutional construction of social realities and their historical genealogy. Since social realities are understood as produced by men, they could always be different. This implies a fundamental legitimacy of critique on the social, particularly regarding whether social conduct provides a desirable life for individuals. Furthermore, the ability to influence social developments and their immanent complexity is the basis for the fundamental critique of governmentality literature on all attempts to formulate hypotheses about general historical developments. Such hypotheses regarding the necessity of historical developments would cover involved interests or normative roots as well as the contingency of historical developments.

The *risk society* focuses on risk problems which are real as well as socially constructed. Risk society's critique aims at the social production of (non-)knowledge: It questions the lack of reintegration of fragmented knowledge which is necessary to avoid harms and dangers. An acknowledgment of the fallibility of human knowledge implies evading unnecessary risks which could irretrievably narrow future options. Furthermore, the risk society argues for the public to contribute to risk decisions to broaden the legitimacy of far-reaching decisions in areas which normally lie outside democratically legitimized decision making.

In the classical perspective of *edgework* as liberation, the critique focuses on the alienation of the self by the social (regulations, norms, rules, etc.) and the disenchantment of the world. The solution is to give more space within the social to develop a desirable self and a re-enchanted social world. Against this, in the over-fulfillment thesis of social demands, the question is rather how more people could be encouraged to become engaged into honing their techniques of self-development and uncertainty management in order to enable people to take their chances in an increasingly uncertain social world.

The approaches' systematic weaknesses

Even though all approaches provide us with specific forms of critique, they are accompanied by a range of weaknesses.

Focusing on new risks and social change, Beck's theorizing on the *risk society* neglects the continuities in class-specific (or old) allocation of risks and how they influence or mix with new risks. This weakness is supported by the assumption of an inescapable sociohistorical change toward a risk society which implies that the old inequalities are losing their power to structure social discourse and political impact, while there is strong empirical evidence of persistent and increasing inequalities in many European countries. Therefore many researchers repeatedly claim that more detailed analyses are needed to do justice to continuing inequalities (e.g. Elliott 2002; Mythen 2005).

The focus on the politicizing effect of new risks underestimates the variety of other possibilities for responding to risk and how they are rooted in underlying sociocultural diversity. Social class capital (Bourdieu 1986) or social milieus (Vester 2005) still structure people's responses, independent of alleged individualization processes and risk logics. Beck refers only to a general self-culture, but ignores its systematic embeddedness in sociocultural milieus and socially structured allocation of material and immaterial resources. Related to this aspect, Beck's concept of the subject remains rather abstract. He assumes that one has to understand him/herself as the "planning office of their own life" to avoid becoming disadvantaged. But Beck does not develop a systematic account of the sociostructural and sociocultural conditions of becoming a capable social actor.

Furthermore, the rise of subpolitics brings forward the question of legitimacy. Is politics driven by the logic of media coverage socially more legitimate or rather an expression of unequal power to influence and dominate the media, or an expression of a public driven by unreasonable fears?

If we measure the risk society against Beck's claim to be developing a theory which grasps the most central social changes since World War II, we might acknowledge that he in many respects meets the changing self-description of societies such as Germany. But does the risk society not lose sight of central structural patterns of social reproduction, when social inequalities regarding, for example, life expectancy, health and illness, and educational attainment are neglected? Does the risk society not become part of the processes which make social inequalities invisible? One might ask where the critical contribution of such a theory is, which no longer centrally addresses social inequalities.

The *governmentality* literature focuses on the strategies that governmental or other institutional actors use for managing populations by risk and how they contribute to societal discourse. Even though in empirical research other strategies than risk are acknowledged to manage uncertainties such non-probabilistic techniques are not yet fully integrated in theorizing.

Mainly following the perspective of institutional practices, the bottom-up perspective of how the governed populations sometimes successfully resist and even change governmental practices is little acknowledged. Instead, there is the tendency to see governmentality in terms of the (successful) application of programs and there failure as a lack of quality. Moreover, the governmentality approach does not sufficiently explain other phenomena as the immanent and constitutive contradictions within governmental practices which could be understood, in terms of systems theory, as a result of the self-referential activities of autonomous social subsystems. For example, that a sign for the success of a program can be its failure (e.g. the failure of prisons to prevent crime or to better the inmates). Consequently, some authors criticize that there is little in the governmentality literature about built-in contradictions of governmental practices as a prerequisite for their existence or success (Weir 1996: 383–8; Lemke 2000: 41–3).

Similar to the risk society, this approach has not developed an account of a cultural notion of the subject different from the rational or prudent subject understood as a prerequisite for liberal governance. "Foucault himself and those taking up his perspectives on the regulation of subjects via the discourses of governmentality may be criticized for devoting too much attention to ... discourses and strategies and not enough to how people actually respond to them as part of their everyday lives" (Lupton 1999a: 102).[12]

Finally, in a rather historical reconstructive perspective, governmentality can explain the past, but its lack of imaginative power regarding possible futures might be criticized from the risk society's point of view. Attempts such as the linear extension of the observed implementation of risk technologies into the future (Castel 1991) are rather questionable. Such an assumption neglects all the other reasonable and inevitable strategies to manage uncertainty where probabilistic calculation meets its limit (see O'Malley 2004).

Systems theory focuses on the structural logics of social systems. In so doing, aspects which are normally attributed to a subject are neglected, or, like emotions, are even seen as disturbing social processes. In this sense there is no consideration of embodied emotions as a positive resource for the communication processes of functional systems[13] or of emotions as a positive source for social critique (compare Beck 1992b).

Moreover, like the other approaches, cultural theorists might criticize Luhmann for not developing an elaborated concept of culture. Doing extensive historical analysis of changes in sociocultural semantics, Luhmann conceptualized culture not systematically but as a general resource for sense making. However, one might consider the built-in pessimism of changing social systems purposefully a conservative attitude favoring evolution and defending already developed institutions and social structures. The relative abstract level of analysis and the claim for a non-normative theory may conceal implicit normative considerations as in *Ecological Communication* (Luhmann 1989) the critique of the ecological movement as just denying what is and not providing political alternatives.

Douglas and Wildavsky's *cultural theorizing* has been criticized for its bias to the center (hierarchy and market), which neglects the possibility of positive influences by social movements (sect-like or egalitarian culture) for societal self-reflection and change. With the focus on culture there is no way of understanding social movements as a reasonable response to new types of (social) risk. In the cultural perspective we can no longer formulate a critique on the basis of the reality of dangers, uncertainty, or non-knowledge. Such critique can always be discredited as a specific culturally and normatively driven perspective of an issue which could be interpreted in other ways as well.

Moreover, the approach does not sufficiently theorize how blurred rules could support the constitution of social groups or societies and how they can help to respond flexibly to societal changes. Since it is developed in the perspective of *order theory* (Bonss 1995: 12ff.; Bauman 1991), disorder is generally interpreted negatively as transgression or risk.

The *cultural turn* complements theoretically developed approaches on risk rather than offering an independent perspective. When it becomes dominant as an exclusive focus on culture, the influence of other aspects as norms and institutions or sociostructural factors is neglected. Instead, there is a tendency to focus on the transgression of the symbolic production of meaning. Risk is then understood as danger to everyday sense making and symbols. The tendency of cultural turn literature to focus on thick descriptions of the everyday might be a hindrance to developing more complex theoretical arguments. A regular critique addressed to grand theorizing, which emphasizes that things are more complicated when we look at single cases, contributes little to knowledge (Tulloch & Lupton 2003).

Furthermore, even so-called *descriptions* rely on at least everyday knowledge or assumptions which must be considered in research. Therefore the concept of combining different theoretical approaches in a multi-theory approach (Denzin & Lincoln 2003) can shed light on the contributions of different perspectives for understanding risk. However, such multiple perspective studies are still very rare. Some compare at least risk society and governmentality approaches (Ericson & Haggerty 1997; Mythen & Walklate 2005).

Lyng (in chapter 5 of this book) finishes his considerations on *edgework* with the open question of whether the thesis of *enchantment* or of *over-fulfillment* will conclusively explain edgework activities. He thereby refers to a central issue in his theorizing. Even though starting with the immediate experience of edgework, the link to general theorizing of Marx or Beck lacks a cultural level in between which would enable us to theorize in more detail on the diversity of edgework activities, their differences, and the motivations behind them, and whether and to what extent edgework is significantly influenced by gender (Ferrell 2005: 79; Lois 2005), ethnicity, and age.

The strong focus on the seductive character of edgework as an embodied experience and the direct link to general societal theorizing neglects the socio-cultural diversities and other factors in between. Referring to a realist understanding of high-risk activities fails to see that, in the subjective perspective of edgeworkers, these high risks might not exceed the risks of being killed in a road accident or dying of cancer. The subjective evaluation of competing risks in life may simply help to explain why for some people edgework is preferable to dying without having any fun in their life (Douglas & Calvez 1990: 461; Lupton & Tulloch 2002).

The self-presentation of edgeworkers is very much part of the modern norm of being an autonomous subject, discovering a real self or "being special." Edgework therefore obviously takes place within or in concord with modernity as much as beyond or against it. Such narrations might therefore be inappropriate as contrasts to modernity, but rather indicate the contradictory process of modernization itself.

Theorizing as process

Often (theoretical) controversies do not lead to final unequivocal solutions. For example, *realist* and *constructivist* ideas of reality are rather reconciled in an accepted coexistence of "this as well as that." It is rather typical that such distinctions indicate ongoing controversies such as: scientific knowledge versus local knowledge, scientifically proven knowledge versus collective and biographical (tacit, intuitive, embodied) knowledge, facts versus values, cognitive versus emotional rationality, making decisions versus bearing decisions of others, self versus otherness, cognition versus body, certainty versus uncertainty, populations versus individuals, and so on. They significantly structure our understanding of risk problems; consequently, risk theorizing is precisely about which distinctions are made, how they are legitimized, and what is excluded thereby and why. Frequently, theoretical changes take place because such distinctions cease to be addressed rather than because they are resolved. There is often no final solution but a process: theorizing.

The aim of this book has been to encourage theorizing by showing how different approaches to risk developed and how they guide our understanding of the world. Theories help us to see some things by simultaneously concealing others. Therefore the book suggests a rather eclectic use of theories and concepts to get a grip on empirical phenomena, but also values theories as a resource to develop far-reaching questions.

It invites further theorizing on risk by supporting a critical and self-critical approach.

Perspectives for further research

Currently the following themes are fulcrums of debate and avenues for further research:

- *Non-rational forms of knowledge*, such as local, situational, embodied, intuitive, or tacit knowledge are already debated in several contexts, for example in cultural theorizing (Lash 2000), high risk taking (Lyng 2005a), coping with the unforeseeable at the work place (Böhle et al. 2004), and responses to complex decision-making situations in organizations (Japp 1990).
- Diverse perspectives on *emotions* and the increasing research in other disciplines[14] call for a more sophisticated conceptualization in risk theorizing (Pixley 2004; Zinn 2004, 2006).
- Questions of cultural representation and immediate embodied experience of *suffering* (Wilkinson 2005) could draw on Bourdieu's work on cultural reproduction as well as biographical concepts of "trajectories of suffering" (Riemann & Schuetze 2005).
- The socio-cultural and embodied constitution of an able social actor and how individuals' responses to risk are structured by personal and milieu-specific experiences and socialization.
- Conditions of *trust* and *mistrust* have been brought to the foreground by the practical needs of decision-makers (Taylor-Gooby 2006).[15]
- The more general problem of *uncertainty* instead of risk might lead away from a narrowed perspective on the management of dangers to the examination of different forms of uncertainty management (Ericson & Doyle 2004b; O'Malley 2004; Zinn 2005).
- The discussion on methodological nationalism and transnational approaches might help to readjust risk research into global risk phenomena (Beck 2005, 2007).

Endnotes

1. For more detail about Douglas's years in Oxford and the influence of the British anthropologist Evans-Pritchard on her work, see Fardon (1999: 24–46).

2. They differ from other, especially historically earlier, societies describing themselves in terms of destiny and acts of divine providence.

3. See O'Malley in chapter 3 of this book.

4. In other applications, there is the question of how to cope with the aftermath of crossing the boundaries, as in "righteous slaughter" (Katz 1988) or in failing to rescue mountaineers (Lois 2005).

5. Because of the negative connotation of "sect," Douglas later supplanted the term by "enclave." Many proponents of this approach now use the term "egalitarian" (see Thompson et al. 1990; Adams 1995; Lupton 1999a).

6. It is contested in systems theory whether self-observation of social systems can lead to a form of "non-normative" rationality which could supplant a substantial or teleological rationality, and whether that would lead to better results (Japp in this book).

7. A second-order observer observes how others observe – in this case, possible losses.

8. This makes clear, for example, that a decision-maker's *risk* is the affected people's *danger*. The response to the decisions of others is fundamentally different from the response to one's own decisions independently of their outcomes.

9. This might have something to do with a politically conservative attitude (Lupton 1999a; Lash 2000) or the shared origins in functionalist thinking (compare "theoretical background") or just the traditional contradiction between rationality and emotions to which they refer.

10. Further attempts to elaborate the concept of emotions within systems theory are published in the journal *Soziale Systeme*, volume 10, issue 1.

11. Against such an interpretation, Giddens (1990: 134–7) exemplifies a range of other possibilities for responding to the risk society which do not lead to political resistance.

12. Lyng's discussion of Foucault's notion of the limit experience might be helpful but does not refute the critique.

13. But compare recent considerations in the journal *Soziale Systeme*, volume 10, issue 1, 2004.

14. For example, in psychology (Loewenstein et al. 2001) and the psychometric paradigm (Slovic et al. 1999).

15. While the problem is often framed as a problem of distrust of the public which would hinder the smooth implementation of political decisions, it might become accepted that a level of mistrust is a reasonable and necessary response to institutional activities which tend to become separated from public interests.

Glossary

Alienated labor: A form of work carried on under structural conditions that separate workers from the products and process of labor. (SL)

Code: According to systems theory, the binary distinction which orients the operations of a function system with the effect that communications belonging to the system can identify each other (e.g. truth/untruth for the system of science, and property/no property for the economic system). (KPJ/IK)

Communication: In systems theory, the basic social operation. Each communicative operation is seen as a unity of information, message, and understanding. In contrast to the term "action," which implies an attribution to one entity that is acting, "communication" therefore requires at least two entities involved. (KPJ/IK)

Contingency: In systems theory, a situation with a huge number of possible actions/selections, none of which is determined as the necessary one by an external authority. (KPJ/IK)

Critical realism: Term especially associated with the cultural analysis of Raymond Williams who (i) distinguishes the growth of naturalism and realism in the nineteenth century beyond earlier dramatic forms in emphasizing contemporaneity, secular causality, and social inclusiveness in human relationships, and (ii) notes an emerging difference between naturalism and realism in artistic forms. "Naturalism as a doctrine of character formed by environment could emerge ... as a passive form: people were stuck where they were ... A counter sense of realism, mainly within Marxism, insisted on the dynamic quality of all 'environments', and on the possibility of intervention to change them" (1978: 5). Critical realism arises from the combination of realist epistemology and this examination of the potential of both high and popular cultural forms to "resist," "intervene," and "change" both culture and society. As Giddens argues, "If we regard language as situated in social practices, and if we reject the distinction between consciousness and the unconscious ... we reach a different concept of the subject – as agent ... Meaning is not constructed by the play of signifiers, but by the intersection of the pro-duction of signifiers with objects and events in the world, focused and organized by the acting individual" (1984: 91). This combination of realism as epistemology, the causal relationship between "deep generative structures" and the surface of appearances of everyday social life, and the "change" agency of producers and audiences of cultural texts has been central to critical realist analysis of historical texts by McLennan (1981), art and literature by Wolffe (1981), radio and television soap opera by Allen (1985), and television drama by Tulloch (1990, 2006). (JT)

Cultural turn: The theoretical shift (embracing alternatively realism and conventionalism/constructivism) that marked many academic dis-ciplines in the 1970s and 1980s as they rejected both empiricism and "scientific" Marxism. The "science" behind empiricism and scientific Marxism was criticized for reducing knowledge, culture, and experi-ence to, in the one case, the "surface of appearances" and, in the other case, a reductive economics. Culture, seen as meaningful symbolic action constructed in everyday life, was understood as profoundly important in mediating both the facticity of nature (as viewed by posi-tivist empiricists) and the economic determination of society (as theo-rized by some "reductive" versions of Marxism). "Cultural turn" marked the extension and expansion of the concept of culture in its association with everyday life and lifestyles to fields of knowledge: cultural studies, cultural history, cultural geography, cultural psychology, and cultural evolution, which have been seen as part of a paradigmatic shift in the social sciences and humanities. In this paradigm, the construction of ideas and aesthetics – the realm of cultural production – was increas-ingly given primacy in understanding issues of social status, power, and resistance. Thus Lovell (1981) argued that while "as a realist Marx makes a causal link between experience/appearances and those objects and relations in the real social world which they are appearances of ...

Althusser places a wedge between the two by arguing that experience/ appearances are produced only as a result of 'ideological practice', which is in turn only determined by the social relations of production in the 'last instance'. Hindess and Hirst sever this slender connection altogether, so that the ideological practice which determines experience, including the individual's experience of his or her social identity, becomes a fully autonomous practice, limited only by its "conditions of existence," After the cultural turn, ideation (and issues of knowledge) as well as aesthetic practice (producing pleasure) were given more autonomous space in the growing analysis of everyday life, with the difference between critical realism and relativist conventionalism marked by the degree to which the "last instance" of economic power was examined at all. In critical realist analysis, economic relations of production "in the last instance" ensured a continuing hegemony of structural power; whereas in relativist conventionalism, power was seen as primarily discursive, lodged in hegemonic theories and language. As the cultural turn continues in its intellectual power – more recently critiquing the concept of culture itself as creating embedded distinctions between "different cultures," societies, and groups according to different everyday behaviors and beliefs, and preferring more mobile and impermanent terms such as "cultural hybridity" and "cultural flow" – so the debate between realism and conventionalism over issues of power and identity also continues. (JT)

Decision: In systems theory, a certain type of communication that is explicitly framed as contingent. Before the decision this contingency appears as a multitude of possible selections; after the decision, the contingency appears as the difference between the chosen alternative and all the others that would have been possible. Observers can disagree about whether or not a communication has the character of a decision. (KPJ/IK)

Detraditionalization: The erosion of traditional values and traditional contexts of action. (SL)

Disenchantment: Max Weber's term for the loss of meaning and spiritual inspiration that accompanies the rationalization process. (SL)

Edgework: High-risk activities undertaken voluntarily that involve a clearly observable threat to one's physical or mental well-being or one's sense of an ordered existence. (SL)

First-order observation: Mode of observation that identifies facts or objects as given. Every observation uses a distinction and marks (names) one side of this distinction. For example, something is observed as a danger. This implies that there is some other state from which danger is distinguished, typically safety. But in the moment of observation, the distinction on which it is based remains invisible; only the side of danger is marked. It needs a second-order distinction in order to recognize the distinction behind an "identified" entity or state. (KPJ/IK)

Flow: Mihaly Csikszentmihalyi's term for a state of focused attention or deep concentration on a limited set of stimuli, accompanied by a distorted sense of time, a feeling of personal transcendence, and merging of the individual with the objects at hand. (SL)

Function system: A social system focusing on only one societal function and operating with specialized communication, based on a binary code, in order to fulfill this function. Function systems include the political system, the economic system, and the legal system. (KPJ/IK)

Functional differentiation: The primary differentiation of modern society in a number of function systems. As all functions are in principle of equal importance for society, there is no privileged function system and consequently no top or center in a functionally differentiated society. (KPJ/IK)

Functional equivalent: A social element (e.g. rule, culture, or institution) which delivers the same function for the constitution of a system as another element and can therefore be used alternatively. (JZ)

Genealogy: A form of analysis that emphasizes the contingent nature of the present rather than its existence as the effect of some teleology or unfolding logic. By implication, genealogical analysis recognizes that prior developments provide conditions of existence for their successors, but do not determine their nature and effects. (PO)

Government: Those practices whereby life and conduct are shaped by various bodies in coordinated ways, following similar rationales, and with similar ways of identifying problems and ways of going about solving them. This deliberately decenters the state, focusing attention on the ways in which social ordering and individual conduct are effected by many agencies and subjects. (PO)

Governmental rationality: A more or less systematically organized and internally consistent set of categories, problematics, and formulae of how to govern "well." (PO)

Government(al) technology: An arrangement of practices, techniques, architectures, instruments, and so on, designed to achieve a specific effect within a problematic (q.v.). For example, "the market" emerges as a neoliberal technology which, by increasing competitiveness, is believed to increase efficiency and encourage individual and organizational enterprise and initiative. Because technologies reflect particular visions of problems for government, the nature and forms of technologies are likely to be closely linked to the nature of the governmental rationalities that deploy them. (PO)

Governmentality: An analytical approach that sets as a central focus the relationship between mentalities of government – or governmental rationalities (q.v.) – and the government technologies (q.v.) that are developed or adopted in order to govern in these terms. It is characterized by a focus on genealogical method (q.v.), and a resistance to explanation (especially in terms of interests or causation) and to grand theory. It is also characterized by an agnosticism, for analytical purposes, about what is "real," as an aid to understanding how governmental mentalities define "reality." It is also the name given to the specific framework of government that emerged from the seventeenth century onward in Europe. (PO)

Grid/group typology: Douglas and Wildavsky's grid/group analysis provides a model for analyzing both social structural power and subcultural values, especially in exploring the continuity and survival of social institutions in the face of resistance from social groups and cultures on the "outside boundaries" of society. Douglas and Wildavsky favor the continuity and resilience of institutions in the face of "boundary" values, which they characterize (whether found among religious or environmentalist groups) as having a global rather than local focus, a "regenerating" moral fervor, an obsession with conspiracies of evil, a fear of infiltration from outside, and a symbolic emphasis on science and technology. (JT)

Hyperreality: An experience of existential conditions which feels more real than the reality of everyday life. (SL)

"I":   In George Herbert Mead's theory, the spontaneous, free-willed dimension of the self. (SL)

Individualization, institutional individualism: A *contradictory* mode of societalization (Beck 1992b: 90, 127). The concept is positioned on the institutional level of objective life situations. It analytically combines three aspects. First is the *removal* from "historically prescribed social forms and commitments in the sense of traditional contexts of dominance and support" (ibid.) as established in social class milieus and the societal division of labor between men and women (1992b: 87). This goes along, secondly, with a *loss of stability.* In the disenchantment dimension, traditional securities regarding "practical knowledge, faith and guiding norms" would lose their value to orient individuals' activities (ibid.). Finally, people are *reintegrated* by new social commitments of secondary institutions such as the welfare state and markets (1992b: 131). Individualization produces precarious freedoms which are indicated by a new immediacy of the individual and society. It thus produces new risks, uncertainties, and chances, and might under specific sociocultural circumstances decrease or even increase social inequalities. (JZ)

Life-world: A term introduced by E. Husserl and central to the work of A. Schutz and T. Luckman. Most generally, it refers to the sociocultural contexts of everyday life. It is about the world we live in prior to more reflective re-presentation or analysis. (JZ)

Limit experience: In Michel Foucault's work, the process of breaching the boundaries separating the consciousness and unconsciousness, reason and unreason, pleasure and pain, and life and death, in order to reveal how distinctions between true and false are uncertain and contingent. (SL)

Manufactured uncertainty: A peculiar mélange of risk, more knowledge, more unawareness and reflexivity, and therefore new risks (Beck 1999: 112, 140). More and better knowledge produces new decision-making situations and thereby more risks to make wrong decisions. At the same time, measures to manage risks might produce new (unexpected) risks. For example, pre-natal diagnostics help to calculate the probability that the fetus will have serious illnesses. At the same time, these calculations are probabilities which do not tell us anything about the real condition of a specific child when it is born. Additionally, pre-natal checks on the health status of the child might be risky for its health or even terminate the pregnancy. (JZ)

"Me":   In George Herbert Mead's theory, the dimension of the self formed by the stable, internalized expectations of others in one's community. (SL)

Modernization, modernity: Distinctions between different historical phases neglect the contradictory and diverse processes of social change. Therefore it is regularly contested when exactly modernity or modernization started and significantly changed itself. The terms are rather analytical tools. Often the seventeenth and eighteenth centuries are seen as a time when ongoing processes, such as secularization, rationalization, individualization, industrialization, and functional differentiation, intensified. In theorizing on reflexive modernization these processes form a so-called *first modernity*, *simple modernity*, or *classical industrial modernity*, which is distinguished from a *second modernity* or *reflexive modernity*. The latter radically question the institutions of first modernity while basic principles remain. For example, the idea of scientific enlightenment remains while, as a result of its success, science becomes relativized by social critique and self-critique. (JZ)

Organized irresponsibility: The institutional mechanisms in modernity which prevent organizations or individual actors being held responsible for harms. For example, *threshold values*, the *polluter-pays principle*, and the insistence on evidence proven beyond doubt leads to the acceptance of pollutions, dangers, and risks where nobody can be made responsible for the negative outcomes. The *global market* is one form of organized irresponsibility (Beck 1999: 6f.). (JZ)

Oversocialization: A process in which the social world has become so reified that it has become completely opaque to individual understanding and action. (SL)

Precarious freedoms: Individualization or institutional individualism produce precarious freedoms. They are a result of liberation from traditional boundaries, which (allegedly) opens up space for individually shaping one's fate, but goes along with precarious social positioning. A person is even more in danger of failing because he or she is dependent on circumstances which elude his or her control. (JZ)

Problematic: In the governmentality approach, a way of regarding that which is to be governed as a specific type of problem, by implication requiring a certain kind of solution. For example, neoliberalism works with a problematic of welfare dependency. This regards various political and social problems as effects of the welfare state eroding personal enterprise and independence. In turn this sets up such "solutions" as winding back access to welfare, encouraging "active citizens," and stimulating competition. (PO)

Quasi-subject: Beck uses the concept of the "quasi-subject" occasionally with respect to Latour's concept of the quasi-object, but he outlines the concept on more detail in terms of the change of subjectivity in reflexive modernization (Beck et al. 2003: 21–8): The quasi-subject is the result as well as the producer of its networks, situation, location, and form. We can apply this notion to risks as well. Similarly, risks produce social reality and are produced by social reality at the same time. (JZ)

Rationalization: In Max Weber's theory, regularities and patterns of action within civilizations, institutions, organizations, strata, classes, and groups that reflect the dominance of universally applied rules, laws, and regulations. (SL)

Realism: This has been compared usefully as epistemology with empiricism and conventionalism (constructivism) by Lovell (1981). "Empiricist ontology posits a real world which is independent of consciousness and theory, and which is accessible through sense-experience (p. 10) … The limit position which all conventionalisms more or less approach is one in which the world is in effect constructed in and by theory. Given that there is no rational procedure for choosing between theories, relativism is the inevitable result. Epistemological relativism does not necessarily entail a denial that there is a real material world. But if our only access to it is via a succession of theories which describe it in mutually exclusive terms, then the concept of an independent reality ceases to have any force or function (p. 15) … Modern epistemological realism accepts much of the conventionalist critique of empiricism. In particular it concedes that knowledge is socially constructed and that language, even the language of experience, is theory-impregnated. Yet it retains the empiricist insistence that the real world cannot be reduced to language or to theory, but is independent of both, and yet knowable ... The task of knowledge is to produce knowledge of that real independent world, and not simply elegant and internally consistent constructions which endlessly refer inwards to themselves (p. 17) ... The realist Rom Harre (1972: 187) has accounted for the power of science to provide adequate explanations of phenomena in its development of theories which have what he terms "ontological depth." Theories develop models of real structures and processes which lie at a 'deeper' level of reality than the phenomena they are used to explain. The theory explains the phenomenon because the phenomenon and the 'deep structures' are causally connected" (p. 18). (JT)

Reflexivity, reflexive, reflection: In the context of reflexive modernization, *reflexivity* means "self-confrontation with the consequences of risk society which cannot (adequately) be addressed and overcome in the system of industrial society" (Beck 1999: 73) or, more precisely, the application of the principles of modernity to its own institutions. On the institutional as well as individual level, *reflexive* refers to the reflex-like response to social conditions without enough time, resources, and knowledge of a future which is, in principle, uncertain (1992b: 88). This has to be distinguished from the notion of *reflection* as a growing self-awareness. (JZ)

Relations of definition: Similar to Marx's *relation of production*, the *relations of definition* refer to "the specific rules, institutions and capacities that structure the identification and assessment of risk in a specific cultural context. They are the legal, epistemological and cultural power matrix in which risk politics is conducted" (Beck 1999: 149). (JZ)

Risk (cultural perspective): The transgression of symbolic boundaries. These boundaries might be socioculturally or individually constructed. Whether they are linked to "real" risks or not depends on the respective approach. (JZ)

Risk (edgework): A clearly observable threat to one's physical or mental well-being or to one's sense of an ordered existence. (JZ)

Risk (governmentality): In governmentality terms, risk appears as a specific governmental technology. Broadly speaking, risk uses probabilistic techniques to predict outcomes. Consequently, nothing is, in its given nature, a risk: the status of risk is bestowed on it as an effect of its being subjected to risk analysis. As a result of such categorization, most risks are subject to some form of preventative intervention. However, there is no hard-and-fast rule on this in the governmentality literature. Risk may also be used to refer to all efforts to govern in terms of a calculated future, including those understood in terms of "uncertainty" (PO).

Risk (risk society): The notion of risk in Beck's theorizing combines the immateriality of mediated and contested definitions of risk with its materiality manufactured by experts and industries world-wide (Beck 1999: 4). A risk refers to an uncertain future and is therefore at least partly hypothetical. Furthermore, Beck sometimes refers to risk calculation as the modern strategy to control the future rationally. From the risk society's perspective these forms of statistical-probabilistic calculation are eroded and demand new reasonable strategies to manage uncertainties and ignorance. (JZ)

Risk/danger distinction (systems theory): Risk is a possible future loss or damage that is attributed to a decision. Danger is a possible future loss or damage that is attributed to an external cause: that is, to other decision-makers or the natural environment. (KPJ/IK)

Risk society: A term coined by Ulrich Beck (1992b) to refer to a new epoch in which risk consciousness becomes the dominant way of thinking about, and responding to, immediate and potential problems. In risk society, many existing solidarities, such as class and gender, are reconstituted in terms of their members' experience of shared risks. Risk society is regarded by many who use the term as an effect of the pathological development of science and technology to the point where their harmful potentialities outweigh their benefits. (PO)

Second-order observation: Mode of observation that observes which distinction another observation uses. It reveals that every observation depends on the distinction used for it. This undermines all assumptions about an objectively given reality. (KPJ/IK)

Self-culture (politics): Self-culture is characterized by (1) "staging the self in processes of aesthetic lifestyle creation" and (2) the "internalized, practicing consciousness of freedom." It is rarely about certain goals and forms of commitment but the everyday idea of practice and confronts thereby formalized regulations in the test of practice. (3) It directs activities and engagement for issues which seem individually important, instead of responding to externally given issues prescribed by and decided within hierarchical organization (Beck & Beck-Gernsheim 2002: 43). Self-culture politics is not identical to emancipation. It might also appear together with xenophobia, violence, and all manner of panic movements. (JZ)

Stratificatory differentiation: The premodern form of primary societal differentiation. It is based on a hierarchy of social strata, on top of which there are social positions with religious and moral authority (monarchs, priests), providing a general, binding frame for all societal actions. (KPJ/IK)

Subpolitics: An area of public discourse and conflict where formerly nonpolitical or political issues are discussed and influenced beyond the formalized democratic institutions significantly influenced by media coverage, NGOs, and citizen groups. (JZ)

Uncertainty: In much governmentality work, and the "risk society" literature, uncertainty normally refers to situations in which risk cannot be deployed, and where reliance is placed on other, "subjective" techniques of estimating the future. However, this distinction is not rigidly adhered to, and in some governmentality accounts, uncertainty is used to refer both to uncertainty in the narrower sense, and to risk. (PO)

Zombie-categories are "living dead" categories such as *class* which no longer refer to a class consciousness but have become a socially meaningless category produced by the arbitrary definitions of researchers. (JZ)

References

Achternbusch, H. (1986) *Du hast keine Chance, aber nutze Sie. 3. Die Atlantik-schwimmer, Schriften 1973–79.* Suhrkamp, Frankfurt am Main.

Adams, J. (1995) *Risk.* UCL Press, London and Bristol, PA.

Abolafia, M. Y. (1996) Hyper-rational gaming. *Journal of Contemporary Ethnography* 25(2), 226–50.

Alaszewski, A. (2006) Diaries as a source of social suffering: a critical commentary. *Health, Risk and Society* 8(1), 43–58.

Alexander, J. C. (1996a) Critical reflections on "reflexive modernization." *Theory, Culture and Society* 14, 133–8.

Alexander, J. C. (1996b) Social science and salvation: risk society as mythical discourse. *Zeitschrift für Soziologie* 25, 251–62.

Allen, R. (1985) *Speaking of Soap Opera.* University of North Carolina, Chapel Hill, NC.

Ang, I. (1996) *Living Room Wars: Rethinking Media Audiences for a Postmodern World.* Routledge, London.

Baker, T. & Simon, J. (2002) *Embracing Risk: The Changing Culture of Insurance and Responsibility.* University of Chicago Press, Chicago.

Barry, A., Osborne, T. & Rose, N. (1993) Liberalism, neo-liberalism and governmentality: an introduction. *Economy and Society* 22, 265–6.

Barry, A., Osborne, T. & Rose, N. (1996) *Foucault and Political Reason.* UCL Press, London.

Bauman, Z. (1991) *Modernity and Ambivalence.* Cornell University Press, Ithaca, New York.

Beck, U (1986) *Risikogesellschaft: auf dem Weg in eine andere Moderne.* Suhrkamp, Frankfurt am Main.

Beck, U. (1992a) From industrial society to risk society: questions of survival, social structure and ecological environment. *Theory, Culture & Society* 9, 97–123.

Beck, U. (1992b) *Risk Society: Towards a New Modernity.* Sage: London and Newbury Park, CA.

Beck, U. (1994) The reinvention of politics: towards a theory of reflexive modernization. In: Beck, U., Giddens, A. & Lash, S., *Reflexive Modernization: Politics, Tradition and Aesthetics in the Modern Social Order.* Polity, Cambridge, pp. 1–55.

Beck, U. (1995a) *Ecological Enlightenment: Essays on the Politics of the Risk Society.* Humanities Press, Atlantic Highlands, NJ.

Beck, U. (1995b) *Ecological Politics in an Age of Risk.* Polity, Cambridge.

Beck, U. (1996) World risk society as cosmopolitan society? Ecological questions in a framework of manufactured uncertainties. *Theory, Culture & Society* 14(4), 1–32.

Beck, U. (1997) *The Reinvention of Politics.* Polity, Cambridge.

Beck, U. (1998) Politics of risk society. In: Franklin, J. (ed.), *The Politics of Risk Society.* Polity, Cambridge, pp. 9–22.

Beck, U. (1999) *World Risk Society.* Polity, Malden, MA.

Beck, U. (2000a) *The Brave New World of Work.* Polity, Cambridge.

Beck, U. (2000b) Risk society revisited: theory, politics and research programmes. In: Adam, B., Beck, U. & Van Loon, J. (eds.), *The Risk Society and Beyond: Critical Issues for Social Theory.* Sage, London, pp. 211–29.

Beck, U. (2000c) *What is Globalization?* Polity, Cambridge.

Beck, U. (2002) *The Silence of Words and Political Dynamics in the World Risk Society.* Available at: http://logosonline.home.igc.org/beck.htm.

Beck, U. (2005a) *Power in the Global Age.* Polity, Cambridge.

Beck, U. (2005b) How not to become a museum piece. *British Journal of Sociology* 56, 335–43.

Beck, U. (2006) *Cosmopolitan Vision.* Polity, Cambridge.

Beck, U. (2007) *Weltrisikogesellschaft: Auf der Suche nach der verlorenen Sicherheit.* Suhrkamp, Frankfurt am Main.

Beck, U. & Beck-Gernsheim, E. (1995) *The Normal Chaos of Love.* Polity, Cambridge.

Beck, U. & Beck-Gernsheim, E. (2002) *Individualization: Institutionalized Individualism and its Social and Political Consequences.* Sage, London and Thousand Oaks, CA.

Beck, U. & Lau, C. (2005) Second modernity as a research agenda: theoretical and empirical explorations in the "meta-change" of modern society. *British Journal of Sociology* 56(4), 525–57.

Beck, U., Bonss, W. & Lau, C. (2001) Theorie reflexiver Modernisierung – Fragestellungen, Hypothesen, Forschungsprogramme. In: Beck, U. & Bonss, W. (eds.), *Die Modernisierung der Moderne.* Suhrkamp, Frankfurt am Main., pp. 11–59.

Beck, U., Bonss, W. & Lau, C. (2003) The theory of reflexive modernization: problematic, hypotheses and research programme. *Theory, Culture &
Society* 20(2), 1–33.

Beck, U., Bonss, W. & Lau, C. (2004) Entgrenzung erzwingt Entscheidung:
Was ist neu an der Theorie reflexiver Modernisierung? In: Beck, U. & Lau, C.
(eds.), *Entgrenzung und Entscheidung*. Suhrkamp, Frankfurt am Main,
pp. 13–62.

Beck, U., Giddens, A. & Lash, S. (1994) *Reflexive Modernization: Politics,
Tradition and Aesthetics in the Modern Social Order*. Stanford University
Press, Stanford, CA.

Beck-Gernsheim, E. (1983) Vom "Dasein für andere" zum Anspruch auf
ein Stück "eigenes Leben." Individualisierungsprozesse im weiblichen
Lebenszusammenhang. *Soziale Welt* 34(3), 307–40.

Bellah, R. N. (1986) *Habits of the Heart*. Harper and Row, New York.

Berger, P. & Luckmann, T. (1967) *The Social Construction of Reality*. Anchor,
Garden City, NY.

Bernstein, P. L. (1996) *Against the Gods: The Remarkable Story of Risk*. John
Wiley & Sons, Inc., New York.

Beveridge, W. (1942) *Social Insurance and Allied Services* (Cmd. 6404). Her
Majesty's Stationery Office, London.

Böhle, F., Pfeiffer, S. & Sevsay-Tegethoff, N. (2004) *Die Bewältigung des
Unplanbaren*. VS Verlage Für Sozialwissenschaften, Wiesbaden.

Boholm, A. (1998) Visual images and risk messages: commemorating
Chernobyl. *Risk Decision and Policy* 3, 125–43.

Boholm, A. (2002) The cultural nature of risk: can there be an anthropology
of uncertainty? *Ethnos: Journal of Anthropology* 68(2), 1–21.

Bonnell, V. E. & Hunt, L. A. (1999) *Beyond the Cultural Turn*. University of
California Press, Berkeley, CA.

Bonss, W. (1995) *Vom Risiko: Unsicherheit und Ungewissheit in der Moderne*.
Hamburger Edition, Hamburg.

Bora, A. (1999) *Differenzierung und Inklusion. Partizipative Öffentlichkeit
im Rechtssystem moderner Gesellschaften*. Nomos, Baden-Baden.

Bougen, P. (2003) Catastrophe risk. *Economy and Society* 32, 253–74.

Bourdieu, P. (1986) The forms of capital. In: Richardson, J. (ed.), *Handbook
of Theory and Research for the Sociology of Education*. Greenwood Press,
New York, pp. 241–58.

Bourdieu, P. et al. (1999) *The Weight of the World: Social Suffering in
Contemporary Society*. Polity, Cambridge.

Boyne, R. (2003) *Risk*. Open University Press, Buckingham and Philadelphia.

Bradbury, J. A. (1989) The policy implications of differing concepts of risk.
Science, Technology, & Human Values 14(4), 380–99.

Bruce, St. (2000) *Fundamentalism*. Blackwell, Malden, MA.

Brunsson, N. (1985) *The Irrational Organization*. John Wiley & Sons, Chichester, MA.

Burchell, G. (1993) Liberal government and techniques of the self. *Economy and Society* 22, 267–82.

Burchell, G., Gordon, C. & Miller, P. (1991) *The Foucault Effect: Studies in Governmentality*. University of Chicago Press, Chicago.

Burgess, A. (2004) *Cellular Phones, Public Fears, and a Culture of Precaution*. Cambridge University Press, New York.

Campbell, C. (1989) *The Romantic Ethic and the Spirit of Modern Consumerism*. Blackwell, Oxford.

Castel, R. (1991) From dangerousness to risk. In: Burchell, G., Gordon, C. & Miller, P. (eds.), *The Foucault Effect: Studies in Governmentality*. Harvester Wheatsheaf, London, pp. 281–98.

Castells, M. (1989) *The Informational City*. Blackwell, Oxford.

Clark, G. (1999) *Betting on Lives: The Culture of Life Insurance in England 1695–1775*. Manchester University Press, Manchester.

Csikszentmihalyi, M. (1985) Reflections on enjoyment. *Perspectives in Biology and Medicine* 28(4), 489–97.

Culpitt, I. (1999) *Social Policy and Risk*. Sage, London.

Dean, M. (1995) Governing the unemployed self in an active society. *Economy and Society* 24, 559–83.

Dean, M. (1997) Sociology after society. In: Owen, D. (ed.), *Sociology After Postmodernism*. Sage, London, 205–28.

Dean, M. (1999a) *Governmentality: Power and Rule in Modern Society*. Sage, London.

Dean, M. (1999b) Risk, calculable and incalculable. In: Lupton, D. (ed.), *Risk and Sociocultural Theory*. Cambridge University Press, Cambridge, pp. 67–84.

Deckers, J. (2005) Are scientists right and non-scientists wrong? Reflections on discussions of GM. *Journal of Agricultural and Environmental Ethics* 18(5), 451–78.

Defert, D. (1991) Popular life and insurance technology. In: Burchell, G., Gordon, C. & Miller, P. (eds.), *The Foucault Effect: Studies in Governmentality*. Harvester Press, London, pp. 211–34.

Denzin, N. & Lincoln, S. (1998) *Collecting and Interpreting Qualitative Materials*. Sage, Thousand Oaks, CA.

Denzin, N. K. & Lincoln, Y. S. (2003, 2nd edn) *Collecting and Interpreting Qualitative Materials*. Sage, Thousand Oaks, CA., and London.

Dingwall, R. (1999) "Risk society": the cult of theory and the millennium? *Social Policy & Administration* 33, 474–91.

Donzelot, J. (1979) The poverty of political culture. *Ideology and Consciousness* 5, 71–86.

Donzelot, J. (1980) *The Policing of Families.* Hutchinson, London.

Donzelot, J. (1988) The promotion of the social. *Economy and Society* 17(3), 395–427.

Doran, N. (1994) Risky business: codifying embodied experience in the Manchester Unity of Oddfellows. *Journal of Historical Sociology* 7, 131–54.

Douglas, M. (1963) *The Lele of the Kasai.* Oxford University Press, London.

Douglas, M. (1966) *Purity and Danger: An Analysis of Concepts of Pollution and Taboo.* Praeger, New York.

Douglas, M. (1985) *Risk Acceptability According to the Social Sciences.* Routledge & Paul Kegan, London.

Douglas, M. (1986) *How Institutions Think.* Syracuse University Press, Syracuse, NY.

Douglas, M. (1990) Risk as a forensic resource. *Daedalus* 119(4), 1–16.

Douglas, M. (1992) *Risk and Blame: Essays in Cultural Theory.* Routledge, London and New York.

Dauglas, M. & Calvez, M. (1990) The self as risk taker: A cultural theory of contagion in relation to AIDS. *Sociological Review*, 38, 445–464.

Douglas, M. & Wildavsky, A. B. (1982). *Risk and Culture: an Essay on the Selection of Technical and Environmental Dangers.* University of California Press, Berkeley.

Duff, C. (1999) *Stepping through the Eye of Power: Foucault, Limits and the Construction of Masculinity.* Available at: www.qut.edu.au/edu/cpol/foucault/duff.html.

Eichener, V., Heinze, R. G. & Voelzkow, H. (1991) Von staatlicher Technikfolgenabschätzung zu gesellschaftlicher Techniksteuerung. *Aus Politik und Zeitgeschichte*, B 43/91, pp. 3–14.

Elias, N. (1994) *The Civilizing Process.* Blackwell, Oxford and Cambridge, MA.

Elliott, A. (2002) Beck's sociology of risk: a critical assessment. *Sociology* 36, 293–315.

Enzensberger, H. M. (1994) *Civil Wars: From LA to Bosnia.* New Press, New York.

Ericson, R. (1994) The division of expert knowledge in policing and security. *British Journal of Sociology* 45, 149–75.

Ericson, R. V. & Doyle, A. (2003) *Risk and Morality.* University of Toronto Press, Toronto.

Ericson, R. & Doyle, A. (2004a) Catastrophe risk, insurance and terrorism. *Economy and Society* 33, 135–73.

Ericson, R. & Doyle, A. (2004b) *Uncertain Business: Risk, Insurance and the Limits of Knowledge.* University of Toronto Press, Toronto.

Ericson, R. & Haggerty, K. (1997) *Policing the Risk Society*, University of Toronto Press, Toronto.

Ericson, R., Doyle, A. & Barry, D. (2003) *Insurance as Governance.* University of Toronto Press, Toronto.

Ewald, F. (1986) *L'Etat providence*. B. Grasset, Paris.

Ewald, F. (1991) Insurance and risks. In: Burchell, G., Gordon, C. & Miller, P. (eds.), *The Foucault Effect: Studies in Governmentality*. Harvester Wheatsheaf, London, pp. 197–210.

Ewald, F. (1993) *Der Vorsorgestaat*. Suhrkamp, Frankfurt a. M.

Ewald, F. (2002) The return of Descartes's malicious demon: an outline of a philosphy of precaution. In: Baker, T. & Simon, J. (eds.), *Embracing Risk: The Changing Culture of Insurance and Responsibility*. University of Chicago Press, Chicago, pp. 273–301.

Farberow, N. L. (1980) Indirect self-destructive behavior: classification and characteristics. In: Farberow, N. L. (ed.), *The Many Faces of Suicide*. McGraw-Hill, New York, pp. 15–27.

Fardon, R. (1999) *Mary Douglas*. Routledge, London and New York.

Feeley, M. & Simon, J. (1992) The new penology: notes on the emerging strategy of corrections and its implications. *Criminology* 30, 449–74.

Feeley, M. & Simon, J. (1994) Actuarial justice: the emerging new criminal law. In: Nelken, D. (ed.), *The Futures of Criminology*. Sage, New York, pp. 173–201.

Ferreira, C., Boholm, A. & Lofstedt, R. (2001) From vision to catastrophe: a risk event in search of images. In: Flynn, J., Slovic, P. & Kunreuther, H. (eds.), *Risk, Media and Stigma: Understanding Public Challenges to Modern Science and Technology*. Earthscan, London.

Ferrell, J. (1993) *Crimes of Style: Urban Graffiti and the Politics of Criminality*. Northeastern University Press, Boston.

Ferrel, J. (2005). The only possible adventure: Edgework and anarchy. In: Lyng, S. (ed.), *Edgework. The Sociology of Risk-Taking*. Routledge, London and New York, pp. 75–88.

Fischhoff, B., Slovic, P. & Lichtenstein, S. (1983) The public vs. the "the experts." In: Covello, V. T., Flamm W. G., Rodericks J. V. & Tardiff R. G. (eds.), *The Analysis of Actual vs. Perceived Risks*. Plenum, New York, pp. 235–49.

Foucault, M. (1976) *The History of Sexuality*. Vol. 1: *An Introduction*, Pantheon, New York.

Foucault, M. (1978) Governmentality. *Ideology and Consciousness* 6, 5–12.

Foucault, M. (1980) *Power/Knowledge: Collected Interviews and Other Essays 1971–1977*. Harvester Press, Brighton.

Foucault, M. (1982) The subject and power. *Critical Inquiry* 8, 777–95.

Foucault, M. (1984a) *The History of Sexuality* Vol. 2: *The Uses of Pleasure*. Pantheon, New York.

Foucault, M. (1984b) *The History of Sexuality* Vol. 3: *The Care of the Self*. Pantheon, New York.

Foucault, M. (1991a) Governmentality. In: Burchell, G., Gordon, C. & Miller, P. (eds.), *The Foucault Effect: Studies in Governmentality*. Harvester Wheatsheaf, London, pp. 87–104.

Foucault, M. (1991b) *How an "Experience-Book" is Born. Remarks on Marx: Conversations with Duccio Trombadori.* Semiotext(e), New York, p. 33.

Fowlkes, M. R. & Miller, P. Y. (1987) Chemicals and community at Love Canal. In: Johnson, B. B. & Covello, V. T. (eds.) *The Social and Cultural Construction of Risk: Essays on Risk Selection and Perception.* Reidel, Dordrecht et al., pp. 55–78.

Fox, N. (1998) "Risks," "hazards" and life choices: reflections on health at work. *Sociology* 32, 665–87.

Fox, N. (1999) Postmodern reflections on "risk," "hazards" and life choices. In: Lupton, D. (ed.), *Risk and Sociocultural Theory.* Cambridge University Press, Cambridge, pp. 12–33.

Frankel, B. (1997) Confronting neoliberal regimes: the post-Marxist embrace of populism and realpolitik. *New Left Review* 226, 57–92.

Freiberg, A. (2000) Guerillas in our midst? Judicial responses to governing the dangerous. In: Brown, M. & Pratt, J. (eds.), *Dangerous Offenders: Punishment and Social Order.* Routledge, London, pp. 51–70.

Fuchs, P. (1992) *Die Erreichbarkeit der Gesellschaft. Zur Konstruktion und Imagination gesellschaftlicher Einheit.* Suhrkamp, Frankfurt am Main.

Furedi, F. (1997) *Culture of Fear: Risk-Taking and the Morality of Low Expectation.* Cassell, London and Washington.

Furedi, F. (2002) *The Culture of Fear.* Continuum, London and New York.

Garland, D. (2003) The rise of risk. In: Ericson, R.V. & Doyle, A. (eds.), *Risk and Morality.* University of Toronto Press, Toronto, pp. 48–86.

Giddens, A. (1984) *The Constitution of Society.* Polity, Cambridge.

Giddens, A. (1990) *The Consequences of Modernity.* Stanford University Press, Stanford, CA.

Giddens, A. (1991) *Modernity and Self-Identity: Self and Society in the Late Modern Age.* Polity, Cambridge.

Giddens, A. (1994a) *Beyond Left and Right: The Future of Radical Politics.* Stanford University Press, Stanford, CA.

Giddens, A. (1994b) Living in a post-traditional society. In: Beck, U., Giddens, A. & Lash, Scott (eds.), *Reflexive Modernization: Politics, Tradition, and Aesthetics in the Modern Social Order.* Stanford University Press, Stanford, CA., pp. 56–109.

Giddens, A. (1998) Risk society: the context of British politics. In: Franklin, J. (ed.), *The Politics of Risk Society.* Polity, Cambridge.

Giddens, A. (1999). *The Third Way: the Renewal of Social Democracy.* Polity, Malden, MA.

Giddens, A. (2000) *The Third Way and its Critics.* Polity, Cambridge.

Giegel, H.-J. (ed.) (1992) *Kommunikation und Konsens in modernen Gesellschaften.* Suhrkamp, Frankfurt am Main.

Gigerenzer, G. (2006) Out of the frying pan into the fire: behavioral reactions to terrorist attacks. *Risk Analysis,* 26(2), 347–51.

Goffman, E. (1967) Where the action is. In: Goffman, E. (ed.), *Interaction Ritual: essays on face-to-face behavior.* Doubleday, Garden City, NY, pp. 149–270.

Gough, I. (1984) *The Political Economy of the Welfare State.* Macmillan, London.

Grimm, J. & Grimm, W. (1854) *Deutsches Wörterbuch.* Hirzel, Leipzig.

Gross, M. & Krohn, W. (2005) Society as experiment: sociological foundations for a self-experimental society. *History of the Human Sciences* 18, 63–86.

Habermas, J. (1987) *The Philosophical Discourse of Modernity.* MIT Press, Cambridge, MA.

Habermas, J. (2001) *The Postnational Constellation: Political Essays.* MIT Press, Cambridge, MA.

Hackstaff, C. (1999) *Marriage in a Culture of Divorce.* Temple University Press, Philadelphia.

Hahn, A. (1989) Verständigung als Strategie. In: Haller, M., Hoffmann Nowotny, H.-J. & Zapf, W. (eds.), *Kultur und Gesellschaft. Verhandlungen des 24. Deutschen Soziologentags. Zürich 1988.* Campus, Frankfurt am Main, New York, pp. 346–59.

Hahn, A., Eirmbter, W. H. & Jacob, R. (1992) AIDS: Risiko oder Gefahr? *Soziale Welt*, 43(4), 400–21.

Halfmann, J. & Japp, K. P. (1993) Modern social movements as active risk observers: a systems-theoretical approach to collective action. *Social Science Information*, 32(3), 427–46.

Hannah-Moffat, K. (1999) Moral agent or actuarial subject: risk and Canadian women's imprisonment. *Theoretical Criminology*, 3, 71–95.

Hannah-Moffatt, K. (2001) *Punishment in Disguise.* University of Toronto Press, Toronto.

Hannah-Moffat, K. & O'Malley, P. (2007) *Gendered Risks.* Cavendish, London.

Hapke, U. & Japp, K. P. (2001) *Prävention und Umwelthaftung. Zur Soziologie einer Modernen Haftungsform.* Deutscher Universitäts-Verlag, Wiesbaden.

Haraway, D. (1991) *Simians, Cyborgs and Women: The Reinvention of Nature.* Free Association Books, London.

Harre, R. (1972) *Philosophies of Science: An Introductory Survey.* Oxford University Press, Oxford.

Harrison, J. R. & March, J. G. (1984) Decision making and postdecision surprises. *Administrative Science Quarterly*, 29, 26–42.

Hayward, K. (2005) *City Limits: Crime, Consumer Culture and the Urban Experience.* Cavendish, London.

Heimer, C. (1988) Social structure, psychology, and the estimation of risk. *Annual Review of Sociology*, 14, 491–519.

Hewitt, J. P. (1984) *Self and Society: a Symbolic Interactionist Social Psychology*. Allyn and Bacon, Boston.

Hilgartner, St. (1992) The social construction of risk objects: or, how to pry open networks of risk. In: Short, J. F. Jr & Clarke, L. (eds.), *Organizations, Uncertainties, and Risk*. Westview Press, Boulder, CO, pp. 39–53.

Hiller, P. (1993) *Der Zeitkonflikt in der Risikogesellschaft. Risiko und Zeitorientierung in rechtsförmigen Verwaltungsentscheidungen*. Duncker & Humblot, Berlin.

Hiller, P. (1997) Risikoregulierung durch Verhandlungssysteme. Das Beispiel der Regulierung ökologischer Altlasten in den neuen Bundesländern. In: Hiller, P. & Krücken, G. (eds.), *Risiko und Regulierung. Soziologische Beiträge zu Technikkontrolle und präventiver Umweltpolitik*. Suhrkamp, Frankfurt am Main.

Hoffman, B. (2003) The logic of suicide terrorism. *Atlantic Monthly*, 291(5), pp. 40–47.

Hollway, W. & Jefferson, T. (1997) The risk society in an age of anxiety: situating fear of crime. *British Journal of Sociology*, 48, 254–66.

Holyfield, L. (1997) Generating excitement: experienced emotion in commercial leisure. In: Erickson, R. J. & Cuthbertson-Johnson, B. (eds.), *Social Perspectives on Emotion*, Vol. 4. JAI Press, Greenwich, CT, pp. 257–82.

Holyfield, L. (1999) Manufacturing adventure: the buying and selling of emotions. *Journal of Contemporary Ethnography*, 28(1), 3–32.

Holyfield, L. & Jonas, L. (2003) From river god to research grunt: Identity, emotions, and the river guide. *Symbolic Interaction*, 26(2), 285–306.

Holzer, B. (2006) Political consumerism between individual choice and collective action: social movements, role mobilization and signaling. *International Journal of Consumer Studies*, 30(5), 405–15.

Holzer, B. & Sørensen, M. P. (2003) Rethinking subpolitics: beyond the "Iron Cage" of modern politics? *Theory, Culture & Society*, 20(2), 79–102.

Hood, C. & Rothstein, H. (2001) Risk regulation under pressure: problem solving or blame shifting? *Administration & Society*, 33(1), 21–53.

Horlick-Jones, T. (2000) Towards a new risk analysis? *Risk and Human Behaviour Newsletter*, 8, 7–13.

Janis, I. L. (1972) *Victims of Group Think*. Houghton Mifflin, Boston.

Japp, K.P. (1990) Das Risiko der Rationalität für technischökologische Systeme. In: Halfmann, J. & Japp, K. P. (eds.) *Riskante Entscheidurgen und Katastrophenpotentiale*. Westdeutscher Verlag, Opladen.

Japp, K. P. (1992) Selbstverstärkungseffekte riskanter Entscheidungen. Zum Verhältnis von Rationalität und Risiko. *Zeitschrift für Soziologie*, 21(1), 31–48.

Japp, K. P. (1996) *Soziologische Risikotheorie. Funktionale Differenzierung, Politisierung und Reflexion*. Juventa, Weinheim and München.

Japp, K. P. (1997) Die Idee ökologischer Prävention als moderner Mythos. Das Beispiel der Umweltgefährdungshaftung. *Kritische Vierteljahresschrift für Gesetzgebung und Rechtswissenschaft*, 80(1), 80–99.

Japp, K. P. (2000a) *Risiko.* Transcript Verlag, Bielefeld.

Japp, K. P. (2000b) Distinguishing non-knowledge. *Canadian Journal of Sociology*, 25(2), 225–38.

Japp, K. P. (2003a) Zur Selbstkonstruktion transnationaler Regime: Der Fall BSE. In: Bonacker, Th., Brodocz, A. & Noetzel, T. (eds.), *Die Ironie der Politik. Über die Konstruktion politischer Wirklichkeiten.* Campus, Frankfurt am Main., New York, pp. 232–49.

Japp, K. P. (2003b) Zur Soziologie des fundamentalistischen Terrorismus. In: *Soziale Systeme. Zeitschrift für soziologische Theorie*, 9(2), 54–87.

Japp, K. P. (2004) Kollektive Rationalität in sozialen Systemen. In: Stykow, P. & Beyer, J. (eds.), *Gesellschaft mit beschränkter Hoffnung. Reformfähigkeit und die Möglichkeit rationaler Politik.* VS, Wiesbaden.

Joas, H. (1996) *The Creativity of Action.* University of Chicago Press, Chicago.

Juergensmeyer, M. (2001) *Terror in the Mind of God: The Global Rise of Religious Violence.* University of California Press, London and Los Angeles.

Junge, M. (1996) Individualisierungsprozesse und der Wandel von Institutionen. Ein Beitrag zur Theorie reflexiver Modernisierung. *Kölner Zeitschrift für Soziologie und Sozialpsychologie*, 48, 728–47.

Kahneman, D. & Tversky, A. (1984) Choices, values, and frames. *American Psychologist*, 39(4), 341–50.

Kahneman, D., Slovic, P. & Tversky, A. (1982) (eds.) *Judgment under Uncertainty: Heuristics and Biases.* Cambridge University Press, Cambridge.

Kaldor, M. (1999) *New and Old Wars: Organized Violence in a Global Era.* Stanford University Press, Stanford, CA.

Kates, R. W. & Kasperson, J. X. (1983) *Comparative Risk Analysis of Technological Hazards* (a review). *Proceedings of the National Academy of Sciences USA*, 80, pp. 7027–38.

Katz, J. (1988) *The Seductions of Crime: Moral and Sensual Attractions in Doing Evil.* Basic Books, New York.

Kemshall, H. (1998) *Risk in Probation Practice.* Dartmouth Publishing, Aldershot.

Kemshall, H. (2002) *Risk, Social Policy and Welfare.* Open University Press, Buckingham.

Kemshall, H. & Maguire, M. (2001) Public protection, "partnership" and risk penality. *Punishment and Society*, 3, 237–54.

Klein, N. (2005) *The Rise of Disaster Capitalism.* Available at: http://www.thenation.com/doc.mhtml?20050502&s=klein.

Knight, F. (1921) *Risk, Uncertainty and Profit.* A. M. Kelley, New York.

Knights, D. & Verdubakis, T. (1993) Calculations of risk: towards an under-standing of insurance as a moral and political technology. *Accounting, Organizations and Society,* 18, 729–64.

Knorr Cetina, K. D. (2003) Transitions in post-social knowledge societies. In: Ben-Rafael, E. & Sternberg, Y. (eds.), *Identity, Culture and Globalization.* Brill, Leiden, Boston, and Köln.

Knorr Cetina, K. & Bruegger, U. (2000) The market as an object of attach-ment: exploring postsocial relations in financial markets. *Canadian Journal of Sociology,* 25(2), 141–68.

Kreitner, R. (2000) Speculations of contract, or how contract law stopped worrying and learned to love risk. *Columbia Law Review,* 100, 1096–127.

Krimsky, S. & Golding, D. (1992) *Social Theories of Risk.* Praeger, Westport, CT.

Krohn W. & Krücken, G. (1993) *Riskante Techonologien: Reflexion und Regulation.* Suhrkamp, Frankfurt am Main.

Krücken, G. (1997) *Risikotransformation. Die politische Regulierung technisch-ökologischer Gefahren in der Risikogesellschaft.* Westdeutscher Verlag, Opladen.

Ladeur, K.-H. (1999) Risikobewältigung durch Flexibilisierung und Prozeduralisierung des Rechts. Rechtliche Bindung von Ungewißheit oder Selbstverunsicherung des Rechts? In: Bora, A. (ed.), *Rechtliches Risikomanagement. Form, Funktion und Leistungsfähigkeit des Rechts in der Risikogesellschaft.* Duncker & Humblot, Berlin, pp. 41–63.

Lash, S. (2000) Risk culture. In: Adam, B., Beck, U., Van Loon, J. (eds.), *The Risk Society and Beyond: Critical Issues for Social Theory.* Sage, London, pp. 47–62.

Lash, S. (2003) Reflexivity as non-linearity. *Theory, Culture, and Society,* 20(2), 49–57.

Latour, B. (1993) *We Have Never Been Modern.* Harvard University Press, Cambridge, MA.

Latour, B. (2005) *Reassembling the Social: an introduction to actor-network-theory.* Oxford University Press, Oxford.

Leiss, W. (1995) Down and dirty: the use and abuse of public trust in risk communication. *Risk Analysis,* 15(6), 685–92.

Lemke, T. (2000) Neoliboralismus, Staat und Selbsttechnolgien. Ein Kritischer Überblick über die governmentality studies. *Politische Vierteljahresschrift,* 41, 31–47.

Loewenstein, G. F., Weber, E. U., Hsee, C. K. & Welch, N. (2001) Risks as feelings. *Psychological Bulletin,* 127, 267–86.

Lois, J. (2005) Gender and emotion management in the stages of edgework. In: Lyng, S. (ed.), *Edgework: The Sociology of Risk Taking.* Routledge, New York, pp. 117–152.

Lovell, T. (1981) *Pictures of Reality: Aesthetics, Politics and Pleasure.* British Film Institute, London.

Luhmann, N. (1982) *The Differentiation of Society*. Columbia University Press, New York.

Luhmann, N. (1989) *Ecological Communication*. Polity, Cambridge.

Luhmann, N. (1993) *Risk: A Sociological Theory*. A. de Gruyter, New York.

Luhmann, N. (1995) *Social Systems*. Stanford University Press, Stanford, CA.

Luhmann, N. (1997) *Die Gesellschaft der Gesellschaft*. Surhkamp, Frankfurt am Main.

Lupton, D. (1999a) *Risk*. Routledge, London and New York.

Lupton, D. (ed.) (1999b) *Risk and Sociocultural Theory*. Cambridge University Press, Cambridge.

Lupton, D. & Tulloch, J. (2002) "Life would be pretty dull without risk": voluntary risk-taking and its pleasures. *Health, Risk and Society*, 4(2), 113–24.

Lyng, S. (1990) Edgework: a social psychological analysis of voluntary risk taking. *American Journal of Sociology*, 95, 851–86.

Lyng, S. (1993) Disfunctional risk taking: criminal behavior as edgework. In: Bell, N. & Bell, R. (eds.), *Adolescent Risk Taking*. Sage, London, pp. 107–30.

Lyng, S. (2004) Crime, edgework, and corporeal transaction. *Theoretical Criminology*, 8(3), 359–75.

Lyng, S. (ed.) (2005a) *Edgework: The Sociology of Risk-Taking*. Routledge, New York and London.

Lyng, S. (2005b) Edgework and the risk-taking experience. In: Lyng, S. (ed.), *Edgework: The Sociology of Risk-Taking*. Routledge, New York and London, pp. 3–14.

Lyng, S. (2005c) Sociology at the edge: social theory and voluntary risk taking. In: Lyng, S. (ed.), *Edgework: The Sociology of Risk-Taking*. Routledge, New York and London, pp. 17–49.

Lyng, S. & Franks, D. D. (2002) *Sociology and the Real World*. Rowman and Littlefield, Boulder, CO.

Lyng, S. G. & Snow, D. A. (1986) Vocabularies of motive and high-risk behaviour: the case of skydiving. In: Lawler, E. J. (ed.), *Advances in Group Processes 3*. JAI, Greenwich, CT, pp. 157–79.

Lyotard, J. (1979) *La Condition postmoderne*. Minuit, Paris.

MacCrimmon, K. R. & Wehrung, D. R. (1988) *Risk Taking: The Management of Uncertainty*. Free Press, New York and London.

March, J. G. & Olsen, J. P. (1976) *Ambiguity and Choice in Organizations*. Universitetsvorlaget, Bergen.

March, J. G. & Olsen, J. P. (1989) *Rediscovering Institutions: The Organizational Basis of Politics*. Free Press, New York and London.

March, J. G. & Olsen, J. P. (1995) *Democratic Governance*. Free Press, New York.

March, J. G. & Shapira, Z. (1987) Managerial perspectives on risk and risk taking. *Management Science*, 33, 1404–18.

Marshall, B. K., Picou, J. S. & Schlichtmann, J. R. (2004) Technological disasters, litigation stress, and the use of alternative dispute resolution mechanisms. *Law and Policy*, 26(2), 289–307.

Marx, K. & Engels, F. (1976 [1932]). *The German Ideology*. Progress, Moscow.

McLennan, G. (1981) *Marxism and the Methodologies of History*. Verso, London.

Mead, G. H. (1950[1934]) *Mind, Self, and Society: From the Standpoint of a Social Behaviorist*. University of Chicago Press, Chicago.

Merleau-Ponty, M. (1962) *Phenomenology of Perception*. Routledge and Kegan, London.

Miller, E. M. (1991) Assessing the risk of inattention to class, race/ethnicity, and gender: comment on Lyng. *American Journal of Sociology*, 96(6), 1530–4.

Miller, J. (1993) *The Passion of Michel Foucault*. Simon and Schuster, New York.

Miller, M. (1992) Rationaler Dissens. Zur gesellschaftlichen Funktion sozialer Konflikte. In: Giegel, H.-J. (ed.), *Kommunikation und Konsens in modernen Gesellschaften*. Suhrkamp, Frankfurt am Main.

Miller, P. & Rose, N. (1990) Governing economic life. *Economy and Society*, 19, 1–31.

Miller, W. J. (2005) Adolescents on the edge: the sensual side of delinquency. In: Lyng, S. (ed.), *Edgework: The Sociology of Risk-Taking*. Routledge, New York, pp. 153–71.

Milovanovic, D. (2005) Edgework: a subjective and structural model of negotiating boundaries. In: Lyng, S. (ed.), *Edgework: The Sociology of Risk Taking*. Routledge, New York, pp. 51–72.

Mitchell, R. G. (1983) *Mountain Experience: The Psychology and Sociology of Adventure*. University of Chicago Press, Chicago.

Morris, J. (2000) *Rethinking Risk and the Precautionary Principle*. Butterworth-Heinemann, Oxford.

Münch, R. (1996) *Risikopolitik*. Suhrkamp, Frankfurt am Main.

Murray, J. A. H. (1933) *The Oxford English Dictionary: Being a Corrected Re-issue of a New English Dictionary on Historical Priciples*. Clarendon Press, Oxford.

Mythen, G. (2004) *Ulrich Beck*, Pluto, London.

Mythen, G. (2005) Employment, individualization and insecurity: rethinking the risk society perspective. *The Sociological Review*, 53(1), 129–49.

Mythen, G. & Walklate, S. (2005) Criminology and terrorism: which thesis? Risk society or governmentality? *British Journal of Criminology*, 46(3), 379–98.

Nassehi, A. (1993) *Die Zeit der Gesellschaft. Auf dem Weg zu einer soziologischen Theorie der Zeit.* Westdeutscher Verlag, Opladen.

Novas, C. & Rose, N. (2000) Genetic risk and the birth of the somatic individual. *Economy and Society*, 29, 485–513.

O'Connor, J. (1984) *Accumulation Crisis.* Blackwell, New York.

O'Malley, P. (1992) Risk, power and crime prevention. *Economy and Society*, 21, 252–75.

O'Malley, P. (1996) Risk and responsibility. In: Barry, A., Osborne, T. & Rose, N. (eds.), *Foucault and Political Reason: Liberalism, Neo-Liberalism and Rationalities of Government.* University College of London Press, London, pp. 189–208.

O'Malley, P. (2003) Moral uncertainties: contract law and distinctions between speculation, gambling and insurance. In: Ericson, R. (ed.), *Risk and Morality.* University of Toronto Press, Toronto.

O'Malley, P. (2004) *Risk, Uncertainty and Government.* Glasshouse, London.

O'Malley, P. & Mugford, S. (1994) Crime, excitement, and modernity. In: Barak, G. (ed.), *Varieties of Criminology.* Praeger, Westport, CT, pp. 189–211.

O'Malley, P., Weir, L. & Shearing, C. (1997) Governmentality, criticism, politics. *Economy and Society*, 26, 501–17.

Offe, C. (1985) *Disorganized Capitalism: Contemporary Transformations of Work and Politics.* MIT Press, Cambridge, MA.

Ollman, B. (1971) *Alienation: Marx's Conception of Man in Capitalist Society.* Cambridge University Press, Cambridge.

Osborne, T. (1996) Security and vitality: drains, liberalism and power in the nineteenth century. In: Barry, A., Osborne, T. & Rose, N. (eds.), *Foucault and Political Reason.* Chicago University Press, Chicago, pp. 99–122.

Otway, H. (1992) Public wisdom, expert fallibility: toward a contextual theory of risk. In: Krimsky, S. & Golding, D. (eds.), *Social Theories of Risk.* Praeger, Westport, CT, and London, pp. 215–28.

Otway, H. & Wynne, B. (1989) Risk Communication: paradigm and paradox. *Risk Analysis*, 9, 141–5.

Parsons, T. (1980) Health, uncertainty and the action structure. In: Fiddle, S. (ed.), *Uncertainty. Behavioural and Social Dimenions.* Praeger, New York.

Pasquino, P. (1978) Theatricum politicum: the genealogy of capital: police and the state of prosperity. *Ideology and Consciousness*, 4, 41–54.

Pasquino, P. (1980) Criminology: the birth of a special savoir. *Ideology and Consciousness*, 7, 17–32.

Pawson, R. & Tilley, N. (1994) What works in evaluation research? *British Journal of Criminology*, 34(3), 291–301.

Perrow, C. (1984) *Normal Accidents: Living with High-Risk Technologies.* Princeton University Press, Princeton, NJ.

Peters, T. (1987) *Thriving on Chaos: Handbook for a Management Revolution.* Knopf, New York.

Pidgeon, N., Hood, C., Jones, D., Turner, B. & Gibson, R. (1992) Risk perception. In: The Royal Society (ed.) *Risk: Analysis, Perception and Management.* Report of a Royal Society Study Group. London, pp. 89–134.

Pidgeon, N. F., Kasperson, R. E. & Slovic, P. (2003) *The Social Amplification of Risk.* Cambridge University Press, Cambridge and, New York.

Pieterman, R. (2001) Culture in the risk society: an essay on the rise of a precautionary culture. *Zeitschrift für Rechtssoziologie,* 22(2), 145–68.

Pixley, J. (2004) *Emotion in Finance: Distrust and Uncertainty in Global Markets.* Cambridge University Press, Cambridge and New York.

Polanyi, M. (1958) *Personal Knowledge: Towards a Post-Critical Philosophy.* Routledge and Kegan, London.

Polanyi, M. (1967) *The Tacit Dimension: The Terry Lectures Delivered at Yale University in 1962.* Routledge and Kegan Paul, London.

Poole, M. & Wyver, J. (1984) *Powerplays: Trevor Griffiths in Television.* British Film Institute, London.

Power, M. (1997) From risk society to audit society. *Soziale Systeme,* 3(1), 3–21.

Power, M. (2004) *The Risk Management of Everything.* DEMOS, London.

Pratt, J. (1998) *Governing the Dangerous.* Federation Press, Sydney.

Procacci, G. (1978) Social economy and the government of poverty. *Ideology and Consciousness,* 4, 55–72.

Procacci, G. (1998) Poor citizens: social citizenship and the crisis of the welfare state. In: Hänninen, S. (ed.), *The Displacement of Social Policies* (Vol. 4). University of Jväskylä, SoPhi, Jväskylä, Finland, pp. 7–30.

Rapp, R. (1995) Risky business: genetic counselling in a shifting world. In: Rapp, R. & Schneider, S. (eds.), *Articulating Human Histories.* University of California Press, Berkeley.

Reber, A. (1995) *Implicit Learning and Tacit Knowledge: An Essay on the Cognitive Unconscious.* Oxford University Press, New York.

Reddy, S. (1996) Claims to expert knowledge and the subversion of democracy: the triumph of risk over Uncertainty. *Economy and Society,* 25, 222–54.

Renn, O. (1992) Concepts of risk: a classification. In: Krimsky, S. & Golding, D. (eds.), *Social Theories of Risk.* Praeger: Westport, CT, and London, pp. 53–79.

Riemann, G. & Schütze, F. (2005) 'Trajectory' as a basic theoretical concept for suffering and disorderly social processes. In: Miller, R. L. (ed.), *Biographical Research Methods,* Sage, London.

Ritzer, G. (1999) *Enchanting a Disenchanted World.* Pine Forge Press, Thousand Oakes, CA.

Ritzer, G. (2000) *Sociological Theory.* McGraw-Hill, New York.

Rohrmann, B. & Renn, O. (2000) Risk perception research: An introduction. In: Renn, O. & Rohrmann, B. (eds.), *Cross-Cultural Risk Preception: A survey of empirical studies*. Kluwer, Derdrecht, London and Boston, pp. 11–53.

Rose, N. (1996a) Governing "advanced" liberal democracies. In: Barry, A., Osborne, T. & Rose, N. (eds.), *Foucault and Political Reason: Liberalism, Neo-Liberalism and Rationalities of Government*. UCL Press, London, pp. 37–64.

Rose, N. (1996b) The death of the "social"? Refiguring the territory of government. *Economy and Society*, 25, 327–56.

Rose, N. (1998) Governing risky individuals: the role of psychiatry in new regimes of control. *Psychiatry, Psychology and Law*, 5, 177–95.

Rose, N. (1999) *The Powers of Freedom*. Cambridge University Press, Cambridge.

Rose, N. (2003) The neurochemical self and its anomalies. In: Ericson, R. & Doyle, A. (eds.), *Risk and Morality*. University of Toronto Press, Toronto, pp. 407–37.

Rothstein, H., Huber, M. & Gaskell, G. (2006) A theory of risk colonization: the spiralling regulatory logics of societal and institutional risk. *Economy and Society*, 35(1), 91–112.

Ruhl, L. (1999) Liberal governance and prenatal care: risk and regulation in pregnancy. *Economy and Society*, 28, 91–117.

Schlesinger, P., Dobash, R. E., Dobash, R. P. & Weaver, C. (1992) *Women Viewing Violence*. British Film Institute, London.

Schmidt, J. F. K. (1997) Politische Risikoregulierung als Risikoerzeugung? Zur Bedeutung von Gefährdungshaftung und Versicherung im Rahmen gesellschaftlicher Risikobearbeitung. In: Hiller, P. & Krücken, G. (eds.), *Risiko und Regulierung. Soziologische Beiträge zu Technikkontrolle und präventiver Umweltpolitik*. Suhrkamp, Frankfurt am Main., pp. 279–308.

Scott, A. (2000) Risk society or angst soociety? In: Adam, B., Beck, U. & Van Loon, J. (eds.), *The Risk Society and Beyond Critical Issues for Social Theory*. Sage, London, Thousand oaks, and New Delhi, pp. 33–43.

Sennett, R. (1977) *The Fall of Public Man*. Knopf, New York.

Shackle, G. L. S. (1976) Time and choice: Keynes Lecture in Economics from *Proceedings of the British Academy*, vol. LXII. Oxford University Press, Oxford, pp. 3–23.

Shalin, D. N. (1992) Critical theory and the pragmatist challenge. *American Journal of Sociology*, 98(2), 237–79.

Short, J. F. (1984) The social fabric at risk: toward the social transformation of risk analysis. *American Sociological Review*, 49, 711–25.

Simon, J. (1987) The emergence of a risk society: insurance, law, and the state. *Socialist Review*, 95, 61–89.

Simon, J. (2002) Taking risks: Extreme sports and the embrance of risk in advanced liberal societies. In: Baker, T. & Simon, J. (eds.), *Embracing Risk: The Changing Culture of Insurance and Responsibility*. University of Chicago Press, Chicago, IL.

Simon, J. (2005) Edgework and insurance in risk societies: some notes on Victorian lawyers and mountaineers. In: Lyng, S. (ed.), *Edgework: The Sociology of Risk-Taking*. Routledge, New York, pp. 203–26.

Simpson, J. A. & Weiner, E. S. C. (1989) *The Oxford English Dictionary*. Clarendon Press, Oxford.

Slovic, P. (1992) Perception of risk: reflections on the psychometric paradigm. In: Krimsky, S. & Golding, D. (eds.), *Social Theories of Risk*. Praeger, Westport, CT, and London.

Slovic, P. (1999) Trust, emotion, sex, politics, and science: surveying the risk-assessment battlefield. *Risk Analysis*, 19(4), 689–701.

Slovic, P. (2000) *The Perception of Risk*. Earthscan, London.

Slovic, P., Fischhoff, B. & Lichtenstein, S. (1977a) Cognitive processes and societal risk taking. In: Jungermann, H. & de Zeeuw, G. (eds.), *Decision Making and Change in Human Affairs*. Riedel, Dordrecht, pp. 7–36.

Slovic, P., Fischhoff, B. & Lichtenstein, S. (1977b) Behavioral decision theory. *Annual Review of Psychology*, 28, 1–28.

Smith, C. W. (2005) Financial edgework: trading in market currents. In: Lyng, S. (ed.), *Edgework: The Sociology of Risk-Taking*. Routledge, New York, pp. 187–200.

Starr, C. (1969) Social benefits versus technological risk. *Science*, 165, 1232–8.

Strydom, P. (2002) *Risk, Environment and Society: Ongoing Debates, Current Issues and Future Prospects*. Open University Press, Buckingham.

Sunstein, C. R. (2002) *Risk and Reason: Safety, Law, and the Environment*. Cambridge University Press, Cambridge.

Taylor, I. (1995) Private homes and public others: an analysis of talk about crime in suburban South Manchester in the mid-1990s. *British Journal of Criminology*, 35(2), 263–85.

Taylor-Gooby, P. (2006) Social divisions of trust: Scepticisms and democracy in the GM nation? Debate. *Journal of Risk Research*, 9, 75–95.

Taylor-Gooby, P. & Zinn, J. O. (2006) Current directions in risk research: new developments in psychology and sociology. *Risk Analysis*, 26(2), 397–411.

Teubner, G. & Willke, H. (1984) Kontext und Autonomie: Gesellschaftliche Selbststeuerung durch reflexives Recht. *Zeitschrift für Rechtssoziologie*, 6(1), 4–35.

Thompson, E. P. (1963) *The Making of the English Working Class*. Gollancz, London.

Thompson, H. S. (1966) *Hell's Angels: A Strange and Terrible Saga*. Ballantine, New York.

Thompson, H. S. (1971) *Fear and Loathing in Las Vegas: A Savage Journey to the Heart of the American Dream*. Warner, New York.

Thompson, M., Ellis, R. & Wildavsky, A. B. (1990) *Cultural Theory*. Westview Press, Boulder, CO.

Tibi, B. (1998) *The Challenge of Fundamentalism: Political Islam and the New World Disorder*. University of California Press, Berkeley.

Tudor, A. (1995) Culture, mass communication and cultural agency. *Theory, Culture & Society*, 12, 81–107.

Tulloch, J. (1990) *Television Drama: Agency, Audience and Myth*. Routledge, London.

Tulloch, J. (2006) *One Day in July: Experiencing 7/7*. Little Brown, London.

Tulloch, J. & Lupton, D. (2003) *Risk and Everyday Life*. Sage, London.

Tulloch, J. (2005) *Shakespeare and Chekhov in Production and Reception: Theatrical Events and Their Audiences*. University of Iowa, Iowa City.

Tversky, A. & Kahneman, D. (1987) Rational choice and the framing of decisions. In: Hogarth, R. & Reder, M. (eds.), *Rational Choice: The Contrast between Economics and Psychology*. University of Chicago Press, Chicago, pp. 67–84.

Van Loon, J. (2002) *Risk and Technological Culture: Towards a Sociology of Virulence*. Routledge, London.

Vaughan, D. (1996) *The Challenger Launch Decision: Risky Technology, Culture, and Deviance at NASA*. University of Chicago Press, Chicago and London.

Vester, M. (2005) Class and culture in Germany. In: Devine, F., Savage, D. M., Scott, J. & Crompton, R. (eds.) *Rethinking Class: Culture, Identities & Lifestyle*. Palgrave Macmillan, Basingstoke and New York, pp. 69–94.

Vollmer, H. (1996) Akzeptanzbeschaffung: Verfahren und Verhandlungen. *Zeitschrift für Soziologie*, 25(2), 147–64.

Wacquant, L. J. D. (1995) The pugilistic point of view: how boxers think and feel about their trade. *Theory and Society*, 24, 489–535.

Waldmann, P. (1998) *Terrorismus. Provokation der Macht*. Gerling, München.

Waldmann, P. (2003) Opfer als Täter. *Frankfurter Allgemeine Zeitung*, 6.8.2003, p. 9.

Walkerdine, V. (1985) Video replay: families, film and fantasy. In: Burgin, V., Donald, J., & Kaplan, C. (eds.), *Formations of Fantasy*. Routledge, London.

Walklate, S. (1997) Risk and criminal victimization: a modernist dilemma? *British Journal of Criminology*, 37(1), 35–46.

Warfield, R. (1999) Considering an exercise of self and justice in the later Foucault. *Carleton University Student Journal of Philosophy*, 18(1), http://www.carleton.ca/philosophy/cusjp/v18/n1/warfield.html.

Weber, M. (1948) Science as a vocation. In: Gerth, H. M. C. W. (ed.), *Weber, Max: essays in sociology*. Routledge & Kegan Paul, London, pp. 129–56.

Weber, M. (1958) *The Protestant Ethic and the Spirit of Capitalism*. Trans. T. Parsons. Charles Scribner's Sons, New York.

Weingart, P. (1984) Anything goes – rien ne va plus. *Kursbuch*, 78, 61–75.

Weir, L. (1996) Recent developments in the government of pregnancy. *Economy & Society*, 25, 372–92.

Wildavsky, A. (1988) *Searching for Safety*. Transaction Books, New Brunswick and London.

Wilkinson, I. (2005). *Suffering: A Sociological Introduction*. Polity, Cambridge.

Wilkinson, I. (2006) Health, risk and "social suffering." *Health, Risk & Society*, 8(1), 1–8.

Williams, R. (1978) Realism, naturalism and their alternatives. *Cine-Tracts*, 1(3), (Fall 1977–Winter 1978), pp. 1–6.

Willke, H. (1992) *Ironie des Staates*. Suhrkamp, Frankfurt am Main.

Wolfe, T. (1979) *The Right Stuff. Farrar, Straus, and Giroux*. Farrar Straus, New York.

Wolffe, J. (1981) *The Social Production of Art*. Macmillan, London.

Wynne, B. (1975) The rhetoric of consensus politics: A Critique of Technology Assessment. *Research Policy*, 4, 1–51.

Wynne, B. (1982a) *Rationality and Ritual: the Windscale Inquiry and Nuclear Decisions in Britain*. British Society for the History of Science, Chalfont St Giles.

Wynne, B. (1982b) Institutional mythologies and dual societies in the management of risk. In: Kunreuther, H. C. & Ley, E. V. (eds.), *The Risk Analysis Controversy: An Institutional Perspective*. Springer-Verlag, Berlin, Heidelberg, and New York, pp. 127–43.

Wynne, B. (1987) *Risk Management and Hazardous Waste: Implementation and the Dialectics of Credibility*. Springer-Verlag, Berlin, New York.

Wynne, B. (1989) Frameworks of rationality in risk management: towards the testing of naive sociology. In: Brown, J. (ed.), *Environmental Threats: Perception, Analysis and Management*. Belhaven Press, London and New York, pp. 33–47.

Wynne, B. (1992) Risk and social learning: reification to engagement. In: Krimsky, S. & Golding, D. (eds.), *Social Theories of Risk*. Praeger, New York.

Wynne, B. (1996) May the sheep safely graze? A reflexive view of the expert-lay knowledge divide. In: Lash, S., Szerszynski, B. & Wynne, B. (eds.), *Risk, Environment & Modernity*. Sage, London, Thousand Oaks, CA, and New Delhi, pp. 44–83.

Wynne, B. (2002) Risk and environment as legitimatroy discourses of technology: reflexivity inside out? *Current Sociology*, 50(3), 459–77.

Young, J. (2003) Merton with energy, Katz with structure. *Theoretical Criminology*, 7(3), 389–414.

Zelizer, V. A. R. (1983) *Morals and Markets: The Development of Life Insurance in the United States.* Transaction Books, New Brunswick.

Zey, M. (ed.) (1992) *Decision Making: Alternatives to Rational Choice Models.* Sage, Newbury Park, CA.

Zinn, J. (2002) Conceptional considerations and an empirical approach to research on processes of individualization. *Forum: Qualitative Social Research*, 3(1).

Zinn, J. O. (2004) *Literature Review: Sociology and Risk* (SCARR, WP 1). University of Kent, Canterbury.

Zinn, J. O. (2005) The biographical approach – a better way to understand behaviour in health and illness? *Health, Risk & Society*, 7, 1–9.

Zinn, J. O. & Taylor-Gooby, P. (2006a) Risk as an interdisciplinary research area. In: Taylor-Gooby, P. & Zinn, J. O. (eds.), *Risk in Social Science.* Oxford University Press, Oxford, pp. 20–53.

Zinn, J. O. & Taylor-Gooby, P. (2006b) The challenge of (managing) new risks. In: Taylor-Gooby, P. & Zinn, J. O. (eds.), *Risk in Social Science.* Oxford University Press, Oxford, pp. 54–75.

Zwick, D. (2005) Where the action is: internet stock trading as edgework. *Journal of Computer-Mediated Communication*, 11(1).

Index